Annuity Markets

Annuity Markets

Edmund Cannon and Ian Tonks

UNIVERSITY PRESS

OXFORD

UNIVERSITY PRESS

Great Clarendon Street, Oxford OX2 6DP

Oxford University Press is a department of the University of Oxford.
It furthers the University's objective of excellence in research, scholarship,
and education by publishing worldwide in

Oxford New York

Auckland Cape Town Dar es Salaam Hong Kong Karachi
Kuala Lumpur Madrid Melbourne Mexico City Nairobi
New Delhi Shanghai Taipei Toronto

With offices in

Argentina Austria Brazil Chile Czech Republic France Greece
Guatemala Hungary Italy Japan Poland Portugal Singapore
South Korea Switzerland Thailand Turkey Ukraine Vietnam

Oxford is a registered trade mark of Oxford University Press
in the UK and in certain other countries

Published in the United States
by Oxford University Press Inc., New York

© Edmund Cannon and Ian Tonks 2008

British Library Cataloguing in Publication Data
Data available
Library of Congress Cataloging in Publication Data
Data available

Typeset by SPI Publisher Services, Pondicherry, India
Printed in Great Britain
on acid-free paper by
Biddles Ltd., King's Lynn, Norfolk

ISBN 978–0–19–921699–4

1 3 5 7 9 10 8 6 4 2

To Alison and Penny

Preface

This book provides a broad overview of annuity markets. Annuities have been analysed by a variety of disciplines and we believe that our synthesis of results from actuarial science, demography, economics, finance, and insurance will enable both academics and practitioners to understand the range of issues and potential solutions in this growing industry.

Governments around the world are shifting their pension policies away from pay-as-you-go systems towards individual savings schemes, which need to be converted into a pension at retirement. Annuity markets provide this function. The book starts by outlining the context of public policy towards pensions policy. It then explains the different types of annuities available, and data available on these products. We examine how annuities are priced and describe actuarial methods of mortality measurement and reserving. We describe the history of annuities, and the experience of annuity markets in a number of countries other than the UK. The book then outlines the theory behind annuities, and explains how annuities insure consumers against longevity risks. We go on to describe how annuity markets function: how they work, and whether they are efficient, leading on to a discussion of the annuity puzzle. We examine the supply of annuities in terms of the providers, the regulatory framework, and assets available to back the annuity liabilities. The book concludes by discussing recent developments in annuity markets.

This book is aimed at several audiences. We hope that academics, researchers, and practitioners will find this a useful resource both as a survey of research to date and also a convenient introduction to areas where they may not have full expertise. Although some of the material in this area is highly complicated, we have attempted to provide intuitive explanations using simple models which can easily be generalized. Where readers wish to pursue more advanced analysis we provide pointers to relevant research papers. This book could also serve as a text for an advanced undergraduate or masters level unit on annuities or pensions: it is conveniently structured around 11 chapters which would fit neatly into a single semester.

It is commonly observed that one can wait a long time for a bus and then several arrive all at once. Something rather like that has happened with annuities, since our book arrives very shortly after three others: Rocha and Thorburn's *Developing Annuity Markets* in 2006, MacKenzie's *Annuity Markets and Pension Reform* in 2006, and Sheshinski's *The Economic Theory of Annuities* in 2008. Rocha and Thorburn describe the experience of annuities in Chile; Mackenzie's book is a policy-oriented description of annuity markets within the wider context of pension reform; and Sheshinki provides a rigorous theoretical analysis of the economics of annuities. Our book is more general than these other books, as well as being aimed at different audiences, and will probably end up being more of a complement than a substitute.

The book arose out of a number of research projects on annuities. Originally our interest in the subject stemmed from an ESRC grant in 2001 on 'Optimal Consumption Patterns of the Retired with Non-Income Risks: Implications for an Ageing Population' Ref: L138251031, which was part of the ESRC Programme on Understanding the Evolving Macroeconomy. Additional funding was provided by the Centre for Market and Public Organisation at the University of Bristol during 2002/03. We have benefited from a number of presentations and discussion with participants in the EU Research Training Network on 'Financing Retirement in Europe: Public Sector Reform and Financial Market Development', and the UBS/FMG Pensions Programme at the London School of Economics. We were subsequently commissioned to write a paper for the Department of Work and Pensions on a 'Survey of Annuity Pricing' in 2004 and to write a paper on the 'Money's Worth of Compulsory Purchase Annuities' in 2007. Our book draws heavily on this research.

We thank a number of people who have contributed to our understanding of annuity markets, those who have helped in our research, and colleagues who have read through and commented on various drafts of the manuscript. These include Peter Andrews, Miki Arimori, Jane Beverley, David Blake, Tom Boardman, Billy Burrows, Monika Butler, Duncan Cannon, Andrew Cullen-Jones, David DeMeza, Kevin Dowd, Rebecca Driver, Becca Fell, Sean Finucane, Elsa Fornero, Catherine Gale,

Tatiana Goussarova, Cherif Guermat, Brian Harrison, George Hawkins, Alexa Hime, Bob Howard, Joachim Inkmann, Gavin Jones, Todd Kaplan, Sally Lane, Tim Leunig, Paula Lopes, Martin Lunnon, Margaret Maciver, Helen McCarthy, Sarah Meagher, Christopher O'Brien, Mike Orszag, John Piggott, David Raymont, Clement Van-de-Coevering, Mike Wadsworth, Eduardo Walker, David Webb, Simon Whitehead, and Garry Young. Of course these people do not necessarily share the views expressed in this book, and we alone are responsible for any errors.

Contents

List of Figures   xiv
List of Tables   xviii

1. Introduction and the context of annuity markets   1
   1.1. Context of annuities within pensions policy   2
   1.2. Structure of the book   16
2. Description of annuity markets   19
   2.1. Types of annuities   19
   2.2. Data on annuity rates   27
       2.2.1. Purchased life annuities (voluntary)   28
       2.2.2. Compulsory purchase annuities market   35
3. A short history of annuities   43
   3.1. Annuities from Classical Times up to the Middle Ages   43
   3.2. Annuities in the period of developing financial
       markets   46
   3.3. Annuities and UK pension provision since 1945   53
   3.4. Recent developments in UK financial markets   64
4. Modelling life expectancy   70
   4.1. Definitions, concepts, and actuarial notation   70
   4.2. Mortality data in the UK   76
   4.3. Patterns of mortality   82
   4.4. Projecting mortality in the future   86
5. Annuity markets around the world   95
   5.1. Australia   98
   5.2. Chile   100
   5.3. Germany   106
   5.4. Italy   107
   5.5. Singapore   109
   5.6. Sweden   111

5.7. Switzerland	112
5.8. United States of America	115
6. Money's worth calculations	117
6.1. Evidence on money's worth of UK annuities	118
6.2. Evidence on money's worth in the UK's compulsory annuities market	122
6.3. Evidence on international money's worth	131
7. Annuity demand theory	140
7.1. A simple model of annuity demand	141
7.2. Annuitization and purchasing annuities	148
7.3. Expected-utility maximization	150
7.4. Risk aversion and the form of risk	157
7.5. Exotic utility functions	161
7.6. Solving expected utility models	165
7.7. Numerical simulations	170
8. Reasons for the annuity puzzle	180
8.1. Social welfare payments and pre-annuitized wealth	181
8.2. Investing in alternative assets or deferring annuitization	184
8.3. The pattern of expenditure in retirement	189
8.4. Theory of adverse selection in annuity markets	192
8.4.1. The Eckstein–Eichenbaum–Peled approach	193
8.4.2. The adverse selection models of Abel and Walliser	196
8.5. Behavioural factors	200
8.5.1. Cumulative prospect theory and loss aversion	201
8.5.2. Framing effects	204
8.5.3. Poor financial education	206
9. Evidence on the workings of annuity markets	210
9.1. Evidence on selection effects	210
9.2. Evidence on the demand for annuities	219
10. Supply of annuities	226
10.1. Market shares of annuity business in the UK	228
10.2. Regulation of annuity providers	234
10.2.1. EU regulations and Solvency 2	234
10.2.2. UK annuity regulation	235
10.3. Managing interest rate risk and bond markets	241

10.4. Managing longevity risk   246
       10.4.1. Longevity bonds   248
       10.4.2. Reinsurance and securitization   249
       10.4.3. Example of mortality securitization   252
       10.4.4. Mortality swaps   256
11. Conclusions   259

Glossary   266
Bibliography   268
Index   282

List of Figures

1.1. The three tiers or pillars of pension policy   3

1.2. Pension fund assets in selected OECD countries, 2005
(percentage of GDP)   6

1.3. Pension fund assets in selected non-OECD countries, 2005
(percentage of GDP)   7

1.4. Time profile of old-age dependency ratios   10

1.5. Life expectancy at birth in England and Wales 1953–2003   11

1.6. Uncertainty associated with US projected social security benefits
expenditure (percentage of GDP)   12

1.7. Growth in UK annuity sales 1994–2006   16

2.1. Immediate (voluntary) annuity rates by age and gender   28

2.2. Immediate (voluntary) annuity rates for men aged 65   29

2.3. Immediate (voluntary) annuity rates for men aged 65, minimum
and maximum annuity rates quoted 1980–98   33

2.4. Evidence on non-linear pricing: CPA rates, men, 65, December
2007. Relationship between annuity rate and purchase price for
small purchase prices   34

2.5. Evidence on non-linear pricing: CPA rates, men, 65, December
2007. Relationship between annuity rate and purchase price for
large purchase prices   34

2.6. Annuity rates for men in the compulsory annuity market   37

2.7. Annuity rates for women in the compulsory annuity market   38

2.8. Number of annuity quotes in Moneyfacts   39

2.9. Comparison of annuity rates in CPA market with bond yields   40

3.1. Participation in private pension schemes 2002–03, millions   59

3.2. Distribution of number of pension annuities sold by size of fund,
2001–06   63

4.1. Illustration of survival probabilities   72

4.2. Illustration of the rectangularization hypothesis 73

4.3. Period and cohort life tables 80

4.4. Revisions to life expectancy in the UK 89

4.5. Mortality fan charts 90

4.6. Survival fan charts 91

5.1. Importance of life insurance across countries: life insurance premiums as a percentage of GDP by country 96

5.2. A/E metrics for 65-year-old males in selected OECD countries 97

5.3. Pension and insurance assets in Chile (percentage of GDP), 1990–2003 101

5.4. Insurance premia in Chile: Total, life, and annuities (percentage of GDP), 1990–2003 102

5.5. Stock of pensions by product type in Chile 103

5.6. Number of life insurers, annuity providers and pension providers in Chile, 1988–2003 104

5.7. Market concentration indices of annuity and pension providers in Chile 104

5.8. Annuity rates and government bond yields in Chile 105

5.9. Growth in Swiss annuity market 114

6.1. Money's worth for voluntary annuities, male, lives, aged 65 121

6.2. *Ex post* money's worth for voluntary annuities, male, lives, aged 65 122

6.3. Money's worth for compulsory annuities, male, 65, level, using 'Lives' mortality over different mortality tables 124

6.4. Overall money's worth for compulsory annuities, male, 65, level, using combined 'Lives' and combined 'Amounts' mortality 127

6.5. Money's worth for compulsory annuities, male, level, different ages, using 'Lives' Mortality 127

6.6. Money's worth for compulsory annuities, female, 65, level, using 'Lives' mortality 128

6.7. Money's worth for compulsory annuities, male, 65, real, using 'Lives' mortality 128

6.8. Money's worth of annuities in Chile 1999–2005 134

6.9. Money's worth of annuities in Switzerland 2000–05 135

6.10. Money's worth of compulsory annuities ('Lives') and claims ratios for motor, domestic, and commercial property insurance 138

7.1. Annuitization in a two-period model with conventional annuities and bonds 142

7.2. Annuitization in a two-period model with conventional and deferred annuities—a perfect annuity market   145

7.3. Annuitization in a two-period model—finding a solution using utility maximization   146

7.4. Deriving annuity equivalent wealth   147

7.5. Annuitization with risk neutrality   159

7.6. Present subjective values of future expected utilities under different forms of subjective discounting   162

7.7. Optimal consumption plans without perfect annuities   171

7.8. Optimal consumption plans with perfect annuities   171

7.9. Planned consumption paths without annuities and Epstein–Zin preferences taken from Kocherlakota (1996)   176

7.10. Optimal consumption paths without annuities contrasting various Epstein–Zin preferences with TAS-GD preferences   177

8.1. Annuitizing when there is a pre-existing pension of S 183

8.2. The budget constraint with a high degree of pre-annuitization and imperfect annuity markets   184

8.3. A perfect information separating equilibrium   193

8.4. An adverse selection separating equilibrium   194

8.5. Non-existence of a pooling equilibrium   196

8.6. Potential annuity contracts in the Abel–Walliser model   197

8.7. Pooling equilibrium and adverse selection in Abel's model   198

8.8. Adverse selection and welfare payments   199

8.9. Contrasting risk aversion and loss aversion   202

8.10. Different presentations of annuity options   206

9.1. Cumulative survival probabilities for 65-year-old male cohort 2000   212

9.2. Cumulative survival probabilities for 65-year-old male cohort in 2000   213

9.3. Distribution of US male population versus annuitant age at death conditional on survival to age 65   213

10.1. Female mortality after age 60, England and Wales, 1902 and 2002   227

10.2. Distribution of CPA annuity sales in 2005 across parent companies   230

10.3. Six firm concentration ratio 1985–2005 in CPA market (based on individual company FSA returns)   231

10.4. Distribution of CPA gross annuity payments in 2005 across parent companies   232

10.5. The FSA's twin peaks approach to life insurance regulation   237

10.6. Relationship between definitions of capital requirements   238

10.7. Approaches to calculating capital resources   240

10.8. Type of debt instrument held by insurance companies   242

10.9. Life-insurers: Fixed interest approved securities: Bond durations   243

10.10. Spreads between monthly bond yields of different maturities 1979–2007   244

10.11. Spread between long-term and short-term UK daily government bond yields 1980–2007   244

10.12. Summary data on volumes of long bonds and mortgages   245

10.13. Relationship between annuitant and annuity provider   247

10.14. Relationship between annuity provider and alternative risk management choices   250

10.15. Illustration of the securitization of mortality risk   253

10.16. Reinsurance cash flows payments as a function of S_t 254

10.17. Annuity provider's outgoing net cash flows payments as a function of S_t 254

10.18. Mortality bond coupon payments as a function of S_t 255

10.19. Mortality swap payment arrangements   256

List of Tables

1.1. Private pension funding in selected countries 2001–05 5

1.2. Assets under management for eight countries 1999 (€ billion) 8

1.3. Ageing-related public spending pressures (per cent of GDP) 11

1.4. EU countries' gross public pension expenditure as a share of GDP:
Comparison of the 2005 projections with the 2001 projections 13

1.5. Scenarios for the size of the annuity market (estimated annual
flows: £ billion) 15

2.1. Examples of pension annuity prices 21

2.2. Comparison of monthly annuity rates for level and escalating annuities 24

2.3. Male aged 65, voluntary single level annuities 30

2.4. Time series properties on voluntary annuity and consol rates 1957–2002 31

2.5. Time series properties on compulsory annuity and 10-year bond
rates 1994–2007 40

3.1. Roman annuity rates 44

3.2. Growth in number and value of purchased life annuities, pension
annuities, and outstanding personal pension schemes 1954–2005:
Annual averages over successive five-year periods 55

3.3. Pension annuity sales by size of fund 62

4.1. CMI studies of UK pensioner mortality 78

4.2. CMI estimates of numbers of annuitants and death rates for
various categories of annuity types 81

4.3. Summary of UK Life Tables 88

4.4. Annuity rates with uncertain mortality 92

5.1. Size of life insurance industry in selected countries (annual gross
life premiums as percentage of GDP) 96

5.2. Size of the Australian annuity market 99

5.3. Data on Australian life insurance industry 100

5.4. Private annuities and public pensions in Germany 107

5.5. Annuity contract features in Singapore by CPF-approved insurers   110

5.6. Assets and liabilities in the Swedish NDC   112

5.7. Size of Swiss annuity market   114

5.8. Size of US annuity market: Annuity premiums received   115

6.1. *Ex ante* money's worth of UK annuities, male, lives, aged 65   120

6.2. Money's worth for compulsory annuities, male, 65, level   124

6.3. Money's worth for compulsory annuities, male, level, various ages   125

6.4. Money's worth for compulsory annuities, female, 65, level, lives   126

6.5. Money's worth for compulsory annuities, male, 65, real, lives   126

6.6. International evidence on money's worth of annuities in 1999   132

6.7. Money's worth of US annuities in 1995   133

6.8. Money's worth of annuities in Australia in 1999   136

6.9. Money's worth of annuities in Singapore in 2000 for 55-year-olds   136

6.10. Money's worth of German annuities in 2002   137

7.1. Combinations of life annuities needed for three-period model   151

7.2. Annuity equivalent wealth   172

7.3. Conventional-annuity equivalent wealth   173

7.4. Expected unconsumed wealth   174

7.5. Optimal annuitization with habitual preferences   175

7.6. The value of annuities when agents have Epstein–Zin preferences   177

8.1. Summary of optimal annuitization decision models with stochastic returns   188

8.2. Comparison of demand for annuities under conventional model and prospect theory   203

9.1. Overview of the compulsory and voluntary annuities in the UK sold by the sample firm over the period 1981–98   220

10.1. Analysis of term holdings for Norwich Union   242

10.2. Assets for insurance business of Norwich Union, 2004   247

10.3. Largest reinsurers in the world in 2006   251

1

Introduction and the context of annuity markets

This book provides a survey on the economic theory of the supply and demand for life annuities and examines the factors that are likely to affect the evolution of annuity markets in the future. We concentrate on the life annuity market in the UK—the largest and most developed in the world—but will also make reference to other countries' annuities markets, where they exist, and our observations and analysis are relevant to any annuities market.

As countries grapple with the demographics of ageing populations, it is predicted that the demand for annuity products will increase. This is because pension reforms are often associated with setting up individual-based funded non-state schemes, and because of the identified shift of workers in occupational schemes between defined benefit (DB) and defined contribution (DC) pension schemes. Any funded DC scheme requires instruments to convert the accumulated capital into a retirement income stream. This is what an annuity accomplishes. The supply situation is more complicated because most annuity products are based on bonds, and the state of the government bond market is determined to a large extent by a government's policies on the size and management of its national debt.

First, a definition: a life annuity converts a stock of wealth at retirement into a flow of income that is payable to the beneficiary (called an annuitant) until death. An annuitant pays a premium to a life insurance company which then undertakes to pay an agreed income to the annuitant, usually on a monthly basis. Because the life annuity is paid until the annuitant dies, it insures him or her against longevity risk, or in other words, it insures him or her against running out of savings to support consumption expenditure in old age.

Annuities are nearly always purchased as part of a pension. In the standard life-cycle model, during the early part of their life, individuals make labour supply decisions and consume and save to maximize permanent lifetime income and they may also wish to save in a pension scheme for tax-efficiency reasons. This period of savings is referred to as the accumulation phase of a pension scheme. From retirement onwards individuals cease working and consume by running down their savings. This period is called the decumulation phase of a pension scheme and with individual pensions and defined contribution occupational pensions this involves converting the value of the pension fund into an income stream: the annuitization decision.

1.1. Context of annuities within pensions policy

The provision of private annuities and the size of the annuity market in a particular country depend on the structure of retirement provision in that country. James and Vittas (2000) observe that developed countries with large state-pension provision typically have small annuity markets (Germany, France, Japan, Italy), whereas countries in which the value of the state pension is small, have more developed annuity markets (USA, UK, Chile, Switzerland, Singapore). On the other hand, developing and underdeveloped countries with low state-pension provision also have poorly developed annuity markets (India, China). To understand the structure of annuity markets in any country, it is necessary to set the development of the annuity market in the context of the pension system within that country. We will therefore start by examining the general approach of public policy towards pensions, and go on to examine pension structure within a selected group of countries, and how that pension structure relates to the development of annuity markets in the same country.

Most developed countries have adopted a public policy towards pensions, typically taking the form of some compulsory savings or taxation, subsidies, and the provision of state retirement income payable until death. The World Bank (1994) classifies three tiers or pillars of pension provision in operation (Figure 1.1).[1]

The first pillar is classified as a mandatory state scheme, and is normally unfunded and pays a flat-rate subsistence pension. With an unfunded or pay-as-you-go (PAYG) scheme there is no underlying fund of assets, so that current workers pay the pensions of the retired, and this type of scheme

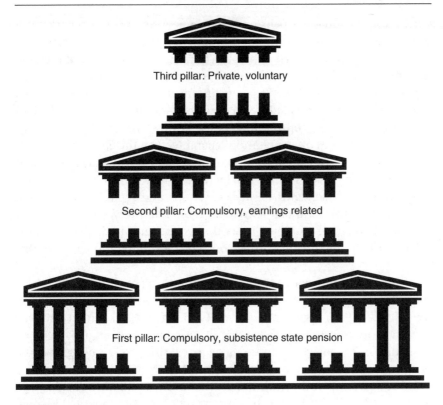

Third pillar: Private, voluntary

Second pillar: Compulsory, earnings related

First pillar: Compulsory, subsistence state pension

Figure 1.1. The three tiers or pillars of pension policy

represents an inter-generational transfer between the working population and the retired population. The first pillar focuses on redistribution, and ensures there is a safety net below which the elderly cannot fall in terms of pension provision. The size of this safety net will vary across countries, and will typically be tied in with other social security protection.

The second pillar is mandatory and is related to earnings over the employee's life, such that the pension is actuarially fair. As we explain below, the pension may be funded or unfunded and may pay either a defined contribution or a defined benefit pension. As distinct from the first pillar, which serves to provide a minimum income, the second pillar aims to maintain the income level between work and retirement, and provides earnings-related benefits paid for by earnings-related contributions.

The third pillar represents all forms of voluntary private pension provision, of which there are two basic types: group (including occupational)

3

schemes and individual pension schemes. Group pension schemes are usually funded and require contributions throughout the employee's working life. In a funded scheme, contributions from an individual (and/or an employer) are paid into a fund which accumulates over time, and the pensioner is allowed to draw on this fund in retirement. Occupational schemes are provided by an employer and may pay on a defined benefit or a defined contribution basis. Defined benefit (DB), such as final salary, schemes offer a pension, guaranteed by the employer, usually defined in terms of some proportion of final year earnings, and are related to the number of years of employment. Defined contribution (DC) (or money purchase) schemes are always funded and typically convert the value of the pension fund at retirement into an annuity. Under a defined benefit scheme, the employer bears the risk of fund underperformance. In contrast, in a defined contribution scheme, the pensioner bears this risk.

In addition, a defined contribution plan also exposes the pensioner to the risk of converting the fund into an annuity at a particular point in time. Bodie (1990) suggests that as well as longevity risk and investment risk there are a further three sources of retirement income risk faced by individuals: (a) replacement rate inadequacy, since their savings may be insufficient to maintain an adequate standard of living in retirement; (b) social security risk, if the government changes the retirement benefit system; and (c) inflation risk, if the purchasing power of a nominal income is eroded by rising prices. Rocha and Thorburn (2006) also discuss credit risk of the annuity supplier, and Lopes and Michelides (2005) examine the implications of credit risks of annuity suppliers.

All funded pension schemes, whether group- or individual-based, need to be accessed at retirement by the newly retiring pensioner. There are three ways of accessing retirement funds: (a) as a lump sum, whereby the accumulated funds are simply withdrawn by the pensioner, without any restriction on their usage; (b) phased withdrawals, where there are limits on the amounts of the funds that the pensioner can access; and (c) annuitization, where the accumulated pension funds are converted into an income stream for all (life annuity) or part of (temporary or term or partial annuity) the remainder of the pensioner's life. An important distinction between an annuity and a phased withdrawal is that the former provides insurance against exhausting one's savings, whereas the latter offers no longevity insurance.

In a defined benefit group scheme, the annuitization may take place implicitly within the pension fund; in a defined contribution scheme, the

Table 1.1. Private pension funding in selected countries 2001–05

	Total investments of pension funds					
	In % of GDP					US$ million
	2001	2002	2003	2004	2005	2005
OECD Countries						
Australia	57.7	58.1	54.4	51.4	58.0	409,372
Canada	53.3	47.8	52.1	48.9	50.4	569,216
Denmark	27.2	25.5	27.4	29.8	33.6	87,032
France	3.9	6.6	7.0	6.0	5.8	123,660
Germany	3.4	3.5	3.6	3.8	3.9	107,856
Italy	2.3	2.3	2.4	2.6	2.8	49,520
Japan	13.9	14.1	15.3	15.2	18.8	864,707
Korea		1.5	1.6	1.7	1.9	14,652
Netherlands	102.6	85.5	101.3	108.7	124.9	779,843
Spain	5.8	5.7	6.2	9.0	9.1	112,207
Sweden	8.2	7.6	7.7	12.4	14.5	51,716
Switzerland	104.4	96.7	103.6	108.5	117.4	428,634
UK	72.5	68.9	65.1	68.8	70.1	1,541,100
USA	96.2	84.1	96.2	99.6	98.9	12,348,250
Total OECD	86.7	75.5	84.8	87.3	87.6	17,914,971
Non-OECD Countries						
Brazil		9.3	12			64,444*
Bulgaria	0.5	1.0		2.1	2.8	776
Colombia				10.4	15.3	15,167
Estonia	2.0	14.7		1.9	3.2	449
Indonesia	2.3	2.5	0.1			278*
Israel			29.0			30,381*
Slovenia	0.1	0.4		1.7	2.4	879
South Africa				33.9		57,337*
Thailand	7.5	8.8		5.0		8,984

* Denotes 2003 data.

Source: OECD global pension statistics.

annuitization takes place explicitly through a contract with an annuity provider.

Comparing funded pension schemes across countries, we find that only a small number of countries have sizeable funded pension schemes. Table 1.1 shows the stock of pension assets for major developed countries 2001–05. The USA, UK, and Netherlands have large amounts of pension fund assets relative to GDP in their economies, reflecting the importance of funded schemes in these countries.[2] In contrast, major economies such as Japan, France, and Germany have a relatively small percentage of pension fund assets, reflecting the fact that these economies' pension schemes are predominantly unfunded pay-as-you-go systems.

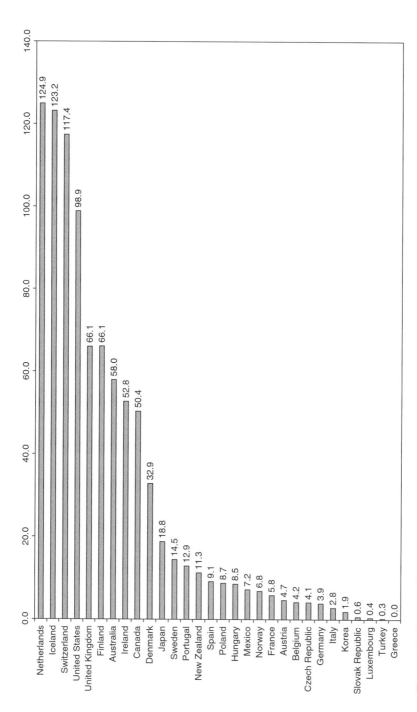

Figure 1.2. Pension fund assets in selected OECD countries, 2005 (percentage of GDP)

Source: OECD Global Pension Statistics.

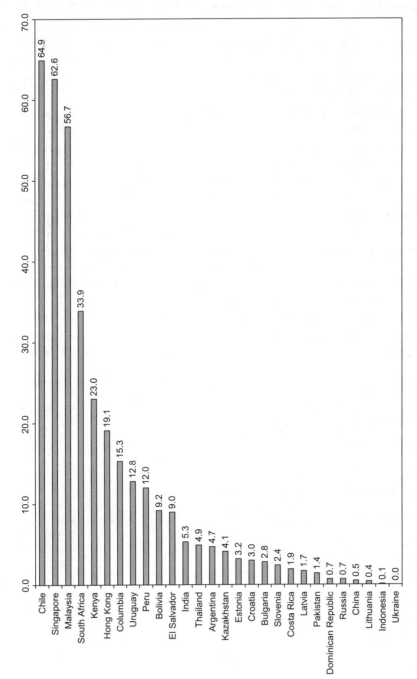

Figure 1.3. Pension fund assets in selected non-OECD countries, 2005 (percentage of GDP)

Source: OECD Global Pension Statistics.

Figures 1.2 and 1.3 show the rankings of OECD and non-OECD countries by the size of pension fund assets relative to GDP. The Netherlands, Iceland, Switzerland, and the USA stand out amongst the OECD countries as having very high ratios, and importance, of pension assets to GDP. For non-OECD countries, Chile, Singapore, and Malaysia have large amounts of pension fund assets.

Pension fund management is only one part of the very large global investment management industry, which represents the management of investment portfolios by professional fund managers.[3] Such delegated portfolio management also includes unit trusts (mutual funds), investment trusts (closed-end funds), and investment policies (life insurance, endowment policies). Franks, Mayer, and da Silva (2003) report that the estimated extent of global assets under external management during 1999 was of the order of €33 trillion. Table 1.2 shows the assets under management in seven European countries and in the USA. Franks, Mayer, and da Silva (2003) explain that in all of these countries the amount of assets managed has increased substantially throughout the 1990s. In the UK, USA, France, Germany, and the Netherlands, over the period 1994–99 the amount of assets managed more than doubled; net assets of Spanish Institutional investors trebled over the same period; and assets under management in Italy in 1999 were six times greater than in 1994. Davis and Steil (2001) produce similar estimates, and suggest that the recent increase is part of a longer trend of institutionalization of the savings markets around the world. In 1970, the total financial claims of the financial sector was 4 per cent of GDP for the G7 countries. By 1998, this figure had almost doubled to 7.91 per cent.

Table 1.2. Assets under management for eight countries 1999 (€ billion)

Country	Pension funds	Insurance companies	Mutual funds
France	66	830	705
Germany	129	673	515
Ireland	47	32	150
Italy	65	169	412
Netherlands	397	220	83
Spain	32	62	219
UK	1,270	1,266	345
Total Euro-7	2,006	3,252	2,429
USA	7,225	2,403	6,388

Source: Franks, Mayer, and da Silva (2003).

Table 1.2 shows that pension assets are a significant part of the global investment management industry: pension funds, mutual funds, and insurance funds account for roughly equal shares of total assets, though both mutual funds and insurance funds will include some pension savings. Pension funds are relatively important in the UK and in the USA, and we can see from Table 1.2 that in the USA mutual funds are also important institutional investors.

As Table 1.2 also shows, although France and Germany do not have large funded pension schemes, they have relatively large insurance and mutual fund sectors. It is important to recognize that individuals in different countries may be making their own provisions for their retirement through other savings vehicles. UCITS (Undertaking for Collective Investment in Transferable Securities) are important savings vehicles in France and Germany (Franks, Mayer, and da Silva 2003). The UK's Pension Commission (2004) also discusses the use of housing wealth as a source of retirement income.

However, the populations of these countries are ageing. Figure 1.4 shows how the old-age dependency ratio has changed over the last fifty-five years, and how it is projected to change over the next forty-five years. The old-age dependency ratio (the ratio of persons in a country over the age of 65 to the number of persons between 15 and 64 years of age) is predicted to change from around 12 per cent in 1950 to over 40 per cent by 2050 in most developed countries. Developing countries will experience a significant increase as well.

Figure 1.5 shows the rising life expectancy for both men and women in the UK over the fifty-year period to 2003. Men's life expectancy has increased from 67 years to 76 years, and women's by 8 years to 81 in 2003. These changing demographics have implications for public spending. Table 1.3 shows projections for the percentage of GDP spending on age-related public expenditure up to the year 2006, in a report produced for the G10 group of countries by Visco (2005). This table demonstrates that these developed economies will be spending around 20 per cent of GDP on age-related public spending by the year 2060. Clearly there are differences between countries: the USA is projected to spend only 13.2 per cent, and at the other extreme France is likely to spend 23.9 per cent of GDP.

It is worth emphasizing that these numbers are forecasts with large standard errors. Visco (2005) emphasizes that policies on age-related spending may change, and he illustrates this with reference to a chart on the

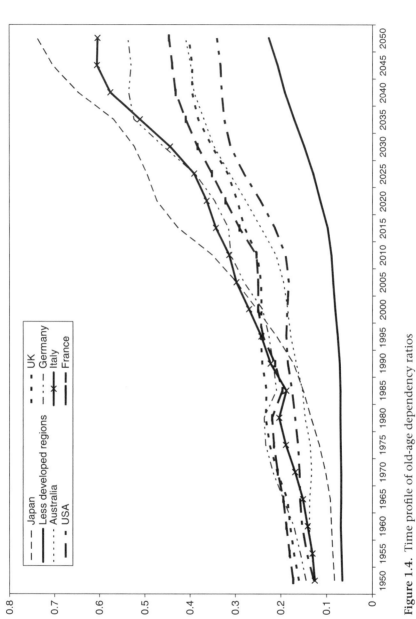

Figure 1.4. Time profile of old-age dependency ratios

Source: United Nations Population Division: *World Population Prospects: the 2006 Revision.*

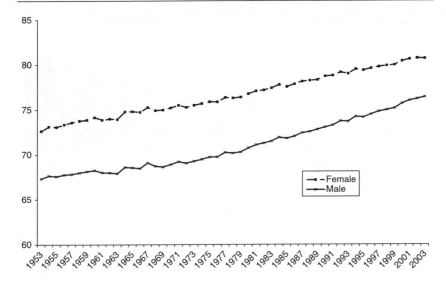

Figure 1.5. Life expectancy at birth in England and Wales 1953–2003

Source: Human Mortality Database. University of California, Berkeley (USA), and Max Planck Institute for Demographic Research (Germany). Available at www.mortality.org or www.humanmortality.de.

uncertainty of long-term forecasts produced by the US Congressional Budget Office. This is reproduced in Figure 1.6. The uncertainty associated with these projections represented by the shaded area around the expected outlays widens through time, and means that the projections could lie anywhere between 4 per cent and 9 per cent of GDP.

Table 1.3. Ageing-related public spending pressures (per cent of GDP)

	Old-age pension outlays		Health and long-term care spending	
	Circa 2000	Circa 2050	Circa 2000	Circa 2050
Belgium	9.0	13.0	6.3	10.6
Canada	4.7	6.4	6.3	10.5
France	12.1	14.5	6.9	9.4
Germany	11.8	13.8	5.7	8.8
Italy	14.2	14.4	5.5	7.6
Japan	7.9	8.5	5.8	8.2
Netherlands	5.2	8.3	7.2	12.0
Sweden	9.2	10.8	8.1	11.3
Switzerland	7.2	10.8	5.8	10.3
UK	5.0	5.6	7.9	11.0
USA	4.4	6.2	2.6	7.0

Source: Visco (2005).

11

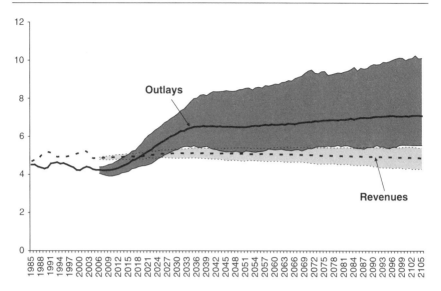

Figure 1.6. Uncertainty associated with US projected social security benefits expenditure (percentage of GDP)

Note: The dark lines indicate CBO's projections of expected outcomes, and the shaded areas show ranges of uncertainty around each projection.

Source: US Congressional Budget Office (2006).

Similarly, two reports produced by the EU Economics Directorate on each EU country's projected public expenditure on pensions as a percentage of that country's GDP are summarized in Table 1.4. It can be seen that the 2001 projections forecast that across the fifteen countries that were members of the EU in 2001, by 2050, allowing for demographic changes, 13.3 per cent of GDP would be spent on public pension spending. This represents an increase of 2.9 per cent of GDP allocated to public sector pensions over the figures in 2005.

However, when the projections were repeated in 2005, the projected increase had fallen by 0.4 per cent of GDP across all fifteen of the previous EU countries. Although this change is not large, there were substantial variations across countries. For example, Germany's projected expenditure on pensions had fallen by 3.8 per cent, and Portugal's had increased by 7.6 per cent. This table illustrates that the projections of the impending 'pensions crisis' can change dramatically over time, partly because of changes in demographic projections, which are highly

Table 1.4. EU countries gross public pension expenditure as a share of GDP: Comparison of the 2005 projections with the 2001 projections

Country	2001 projections			2005 projections			Δ2005 projections−2001 projections
	2005	2050	Δ2005/50	2004	2050	Δ2004/50	
Austria	14.5	17	2.5	13.4	12.2	−1.2	−4.8
Belgium	9.5	13.3	3.8	10.4	15.5	5.1	2.2
Denmark	11.3	13.3	2	9.5	12.8	3.3	−0.5
Finland	10.9	15.9	5	10.7	13.7	3.1	−2.2
France	12.2	15.8	3.6	12.8	14.8	2	−1
Germany	11.4	16.9	5.5	11.4	13.1	1.7	−3.8
Ireland	4.5	9	4.5	4.7	11.1	6.4	2.1
Italy	13.8	14.1	0.3	14.2	14.7	0.4	0.6
Luxembourg	7.4	9.3	1.9	10	17.4	7.4	8.1
Netherlands	8.3	13.6	5.3	7.7	11.2	3.5	−2.4
Portugal	10.9	13.2	2.3	11.1	20.8	9.7	7.6
Spain	8.8	17.3	8.5	8.6	15.7	7.1	−1.6
Sweden	9.2	10.7	1.5	10.6	11.2	0.6	0.5
UK	5.3	4.4	−0.9	6.6	8.6	2	4.2
EU15	*10.4*	*13.3*	*2.9*	*10.6*	*12.9*	*2.3*	*−0.4*
Cyprus				6.9	19.8	12.9	
Czech Republic				8.5	14	5.6	
Estonia				6.7	4.2	−2.5	
Greece				12.2	24.8	12.4	
Hungary				10.4	17.1	6.7	
Latvia				6.8	5.6	−1.2	
Lithuania				6.7	8.6	1.8	
Malta				7.4	7	−0.4	
Poland				13.9	8	−5.9	
Slovak Republic				7.2	9	1.8	
Slovenia				11	18.3	7.3	

Sources: Economic Policy Committee (2001) and Economic Policy Committee and the European Commission (DG ECFIN) (2006).

variable, and also because of political responses to the identification of the 'crisis': as the extent of the problem is identified, politicians enact or enforce changes to solve the impending problem.

The changing demographic profiles of these countries, with the ratio of pensioners-to-workers increasing, put pressure on PAYG schemes and public spending in general, since a dwindling number of working-age persons have to fund the expenditures and health needs of an increasing number of pensioners. Most countries are in the process of exploring changes to their pension policies, with one set of solutions putting more emphasis on funded pension schemes. In terms of pension policies, these solutions have typically involved combinations of reduction in benefits, restricting early retirement provisions, extending the statutory retirement age, increases in contributions, and switching to private sector provision.

The Economic Policy Committee and the European Commission (DG ECFIN) (2006) notes that countries have responded in different ways to the ageing population problem and the sustainability of public pensions. One group of countries, including Sweden and a number of new Member States such as Estonia, Latvia, Poland, and to a lesser extent Lithuania, Hungary, and Slovakia, have switched a part of their social security pension schemes into privately funded schemes. Another group of countries, including Germany, Greece, Spain, Italy, Austria, and Finland, have introduced or extended the provision of private voluntary pension schemes. Other countries have resisted the move to private pensions, and have opted to keep the standard earnings-related pay-as-you-go pension model, but have reduced the promised benefits (notably, early retirement options). This group of countries includes France, Belgium, the Czech Republic, and Slovenia.

Any country that switches all or part of its pension system to a funded private pension provision is going to be faced with a decision on how to convert the accumulated capital in the pension fund into a retirement income stream. That country's pension policy will need to identify which of the three retirement income streams (lump sum, phased withdrawal, or annuitization) or combination of these policies it intends to adopt. In the UK, the Pensions Commission (2004, 2005, 2006), set up in December 2002 by the government, reported on the adequacy of private pension savings in the UK. The commission noted the trend for pensions in the UK to be provided through defined contribution schemes, and observed that a consequence of this shift, away from unfunded pay-as-you-go and funded defined benefit schemes, is that there will be an increased demand for life annuities.

The Pensions Commission (2006) proposed the introduction of a national pension savings scheme for the UK, and these recommendations are being implemented in the proposed 'Personal Accounts' outlined in Department of Work and Pensions (2006). This new pension scheme is based around individual defined contribution schemes, and these will also need to be annuitized at retirement. Anticipating the increased demand for annuities in respect of its proposals, the Pensions Commission (2005) examined whether there is sufficient capacity in the annuity market to provide for the projected demand.

The amount of new annuity business currently sold by insurance companies in the UK's compulsory purchase annuity market in 2005 was

Table 1.5. Scenarios for the size of the annuity market (estimated annual flows: £ billion)

	2002	2012		
		Low	Medium	High
Individual annuities	7.2	16.6	18.1	19.7
Drawdown	2.3	5.3	5.8	6.3
Bulk buyout	1.4	1.5	35.4	128.1

Source: Pension Commission (2005).

£8.6 billion.[4] Watson-Wyatt (2003) and Wadsworth (2005) examine a number of scenarios for the growth of annuity demand over the ten-year period 2002–12, reproduced in Table 1.5, taken from Figure 5.16 in Pensions Commission (2005). According to the Pension Commission's Second Report and reiterated in HM Treasury (2006), the main driver in these estimates is the maturity of individual and company-defined benefit schemes. As increasing numbers of personal pension schemes mature, this will result in an increased demand for pension annuities. Table 1.5 shows that the demand for annuities could increase from about £7 billion in 2002 to between £16 and £20 billion by 2012. But these numbers could increase dramatically if existing defined benefit schemes are closed and replaced by bulk buyouts of annuities. Then depending on the extent of this switch, the demand for annuities in the UK could increase by up to £128 billion.

Figure 1.7 shows the growth in UK annuities and income drawdown over the period 1994–2006. In the UK, there is both a compulsory (Compulsory Purchase Annuity, CPA) market and a voluntary (Purchased Life Annuity, PLA) market. The UK government requires that anyone who has saved in a tax-privileged private pension must annuitize 75 per cent of their pension wealth. By 2006, the compulsory (CPA) market had grown to £9.58 billion worth of annuity premiums. In contrast in 2004, the voluntary (PLA) market only amounted to £56.4 million worth of sales, and the diagram shows that the PLA market has shrunk as the CPA market has grown, probably reflecting some substitution between compulsory and voluntary annuities. The bulk annuity market has been volatile, but as the global stock market has recovered since 2003, there has not been the predicted surge in transfers from defined benefit schemes to bulk buyouts as suggested in the Pension Commission Reports. Income drawdown continues to represent a significant alternative to annuitization.

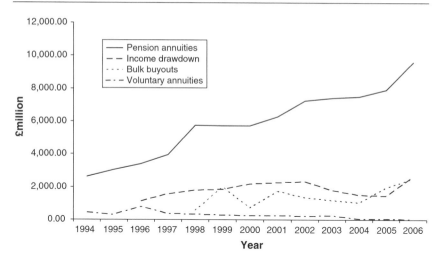

Figure 1.7. Growth in UK annuity sales 1994–2006

The Pensions Commission (2005) also suggests that if the proposed national pension savings scheme successfully targets that group of the population that is currently not provided for, they estimate that in the steady state this will represent an annual demand for annuities of £13 billion by the year 2040 at current earnings levels. This demand represents an additional increase on the numbers in Table 1.5 and Figure 1.6.

All of this evidence suggests that the demand for annuities in the UK will continue to rise substantially in the coming years, and therefore examining the functioning of the annuities market is relevant and timely for public policy, though the Pensions Commission notes that any capacity problems in the annuities market could be eased by allowing a relaxation of income drawdown rules, or by facilitating later retirement.

1.2. Structure of the book

Having set the scene for the increasing importance of annuities markets, we now proceed to describe the structure of this book. In Chapter 2, we outline the different types of annuity products that are available, and provide illustrative examples documenting annuity prices quoted by annuity providers, and the movement in annuity prices over time. Annuity products have been in existence since Roman times, and in Chapter 3 we document the historical development of annuity markets, and discuss the role of annuities in the UK's pension system. The actuarial profession has developed to enable insurance companies to value life insurance products on a scientific basis, and in Chapter 4 we consider the methods used by actuaries to price annuities, and describe the measurement of life expectancy.

In Chapter 5, we examine the structure and prevalence of annuity markets in a number of selected countries around the world, providing an international context for annuity markets. What is the evidence on whether annuities are fairly priced? In Chapter 6, we explain the money's worth calculation of annuities, and present evidence on the money's worth in the UK and in other countries. While there is strong evidence to suggest that annuities are probably priced slightly higher than would be suggested by actuarial considerations, estimated markups (sometimes called loadings) do not seem excessive compared with the cost of other financial services. There is little evidence to suggest that annuities are overpriced due to monopoly power.

Yaari (1965) demonstrates that a risk-averse individual who is concerned about longevity risk (uncertain length of life) will always purchase actuarially-fair annuity contracts, enabling the individual to smooth consumption in every period of retirement. We explain Yaari's annuitization result in Chapter 7, but note that this depends upon a variety of considerations and does not square with the evidence that actual annuity markets are small (Friedman and Warshawsky 1988, 1990; Mitchell et al. 1999). We model the demand for annuities in an expected utility framework, and demonstrate the value of annuities under various specifications of preferences.

There are a variety of reasons why it may be rational to avoid full annuitization and we discuss these in Chapter 8, although it is important to stress that the apparent dislike of annuitizing may be due to lack of comprehension or to psychological reasons that are not strictly rational (i.e., they are irrational in the sense that they do not maximize income in the best possible way). In Chapter 9, we report on the evidence of how annuities function. We discuss the evidence on selection effects, and the factors that determine whether people purchase annuities.

Private sector annuities are typically supplied by life insurance companies who match their annuity liabilities with bonds or similar assets. The reason for this is that annuities pay a constant stream of income and, absent mortality considerations, an annuity product is very similar to a bond product. Given the current types of bonds purchased, life insurers can be seen as producers who take bonds as an input and produce annuities as an output. This raises two issues, which we discuss in Chapter 10.

First, a significant determinant of annuity rates is the economy-wide interest rate, in particular the bond market. Since rates of return on bonds are currently low, it follows that annuity rates are also low. Of course, low bond yields are the result of a variety of factors, including overall government borrowing, monetary policy, international rates of return, and the low inflation environment since the mid-1990s. So it is possible—at least in principle—that the government could influence annuity rates through either monetary or fiscal policy. In practice, however, these policy instruments are used to meet other objectives and monetary policy is undertaken by central banks. Secondly, life insurers are assuming overall cohort mortality risk when they issue annuities, since they bear the cost of overall increases in life expectancy. It is currently very difficult to hedge this risk, due to a paucity of matching assets and a thin reinsurance market.

In Chapter 11, we provide our conclusions on annuity pricing. While annuity products continue to be an important component of a number of pensions systems, there are a number of public policy questions relating to both the supply and the demand side of annuities.

Notes

1. More recently, the World Bank has suggested two more pillars: a basic income and minimum health care (Holzmann and Hinz 2005).
2. Palacios and Pallares-Miralles (2000) identify these countries and Australia, South Africa, Switzerland, and Iceland as being countries with significant private pension fund assets. A combination of generous tax allowances on pension contributions (Dilnot and Johnson 1993) and a liberal regulatory regime for pension investments (Davis 1995) probably explain the dominance of funded pensions in these countries.
3. Investment management is also referred to as fund management, asset management, portfolio management, and money management (Tonks 2006).
4. Source: Calculations from FSA Insurance Returns, form 47 from Synthesis Database.

2

Description of annuity markets

In this chapter we outline the different types of annuity product that are available, and provide illustrative examples of annuity prices quoted by annuity providers, and the movement in annuity prices over time.

2.1. Types of annuities

The original meaning of 'annuity' was an asset that paid an annual income and there was no necessary connection to payments being tied to an individual or group of individuals being alive. An asset with life contingent payments was called a life annuity to distinguish it from a term-certain annuity. A term-certain annuity is a stream of payments made for a maximum number of years, independent of survival: if the individual dies before the term of such an annuity then payments are made to the individual's estate. These annuities are conceptually similar to conventional bonds, although the pattern of payments is different (since the principle is repaid gradually throughout the term of the annuity rather than refunded as a single lump upon the bond maturing). In modern usage, the word 'annuity' is increasingly used to mean a life annuity and the rest of our discussion will be confined to life annuities.

We start by distinguishing between three generic types of single-life annuity—conventional, temporary, and deferred—before going on to provide a more detailed discussion of annuity product types.[1] We will examine different sorts of conventional annuity and illustrate the differences with examples of the sums of money involved.

(Conventional Life) Annuity. This is an institutional arrangement that agrees to pay an individual an income each period until death in return for a lump sum (or premium) paid in advance, typically to an insurance company. This annuity allows the individual to insure against the risk of long life, because although an individual is unsure of his or her own length of life, insurance companies are willing to bear this risk as they offset different individuals' longevity risks.

Temporary Annuity. A temporary annuity is a stream of payments paid while the annuitant is alive, but with a maximum number of payments: payment ceases either on the death of the annuitant or when the maximum is reached, whichever happens first.

Deferred Annuity. A deferred annuity is a stream of payments beginning at some point in the future, made conditional on the annuitant being alive. In this case it is possible that no payments will ever be made.

In the UK there are two different annuity markets: a voluntary market and a compulsory market. The voluntary purchased life annuity market (PLA) is open to any individual, and annuity payments are treated as part income (which is taxed) and part capital repayment (which is not taxed). The compulsory-purchase annuity market (CPA) is open only to individuals who have accumulated their wealth in a tax-exempt DC pension plan and these annuity payments are taxed as income when received.

Single Level Annuities pay out exactly the same amount to an individual (the annuitant) every month until the annuitant dies.[2] For example in Table 2.1, the insurance company AXA is offering to pay a monthly pension of £557 per month to a 65-year-old man, in exchange for a initial payment (the premium) of £100,000. As women are expected to live longer than men, a woman of 65 would only get £518 per month from AXA.[3] Since there are 12 monthly payments in a year, the annual income generated from these AXA annuities is £6,684 and £6,216, respectively. This means that the annuity rates are 6.68 and 6.22 per cent, higher than the interest rate on a typical conventional savings account of less than 5 per cent. This differential arises because the savings account would preserve the capital, whereas the annuity runs down the capital. The difference between the annuity rate and the conventional interest rates is often referred to as 'mortality drag'.

Guaranteed Annuities pay out the annuity payment each month, for at least the length of the guarantee period, even if the annuitant dies before the end of the guarantee period; in which case the guaranteed annuity payments are made into the annuitant's estate. Guarantee periods are typically either 5 years or 10 years: the 10-year limit is the maximum allowed in the compulsory market, by Her Majesty's Revenue and Customs (HMRC, the UK's tax authority). Continuing our example of

Table 2.1. Examples of pension annuity prices

Provider	Monthly income—Level	Monthly income—3%	Monthly income—RPI
Male—60 years, single, no guarantees			
AEGON Scottish Equitable	552	386	n/a
AXA	499	344	299
B&CE Insurance Ltd	538	n/a	n/a
Canada Life Ltd	554	390	332
Friends Provident	523	366	n/a
Legal & General	549	380	336
Norwich Union	549	379	320
Prudential	528	362	328
Reliance Mutual	542	370	n/a
Scottish Widows	507	348	307
Standard Life	537	375	323
Male—65 years, single, no guarantees			
AEGON Scottish Equitable	616	451	n/a
AXA	557	403	358
B&CE Insurance Ltd	616	n/a	n/a
Canada Life Ltd	615	454	395
Friends Provident	606	445	n/a
Legal & General	606	442	397
Norwich Union	610	441	381
Prudential	602	436	400
Reliance Mutual	590	420	n/a
Scottish Widows	575	413	366
Standard Life	597	437	384
Male—70 years, single, no guarantees			
AEGON Scottish Equitable	708	544	n/a
AXA	639	486	440
B&CE Insurance Ltd	731	n/a	n/a
Canada Life Ltd	700	541	482
Friends Provident	717	550	n/a
Legal & General	687	526	482
Norwich Union	704	535	468
Prudential	686	523	495
Reliance Mutual	656	488	n/a
Scottish Widows	657	499	450
Standard Life	683	525	470
Female—60 years, single, no guarantees			
AEGON Scottish Equitable	526	357	n/a
AXA	472	314	270
B&CE Insurance Ltd	484	n/a	n/a
Canada Life Ltd	526	362	304
Friends Provident	469	317	n/a
Legal & General	521	351	307
Norwich Union	520	350	278
Prudential	516	352	315
Reliance Mutual	523	348	n/a
Scottish Widows	469	311	273
Standard Life	498	333	282

(cont.)

Table 2.1. (*Continued*)

Provider	Monthly income—Level	Monthly income—3%	Monthly income—RPI
Female—65 years, single, no guarantees			
AEGON Scottish Equitable	576	409	n/a
AXA	518	362	317
B&CE Insurance Ltd	537	n/a	n/a
Canada Life Ltd	578	416	358
Friends Provident	538	383	n/a
Legal & General	570	404	360
Norwich Union	572	403	333
Prudential	577	414	369
Reliance Mutual	559	388	n/a
Scottish Widows	524	368	326
Standard Life	550	388	335
Female—70 years, single, no guarantees			
AEGON Scottish Equitable	646	481	n/a
AXA	582	427	381
B&CE Insurance Ltd	613	n/a	n/a
Canada Life Ltd	650	491	433
Friends Provident	633	474	n/a
Legal & General	637	475	431
Norwich Union	647	476	406
Prudential	654	493	446
Reliance Mutual	614	444	n/a
Scottish Widows	604	442	398
Standard Life	624	463	409
Male—65 years, joint, no guarantees; spouse 65 years full annuity payment on death of male			
AEGON Scottish Equitable	523	363	n/a
AXA	471	321	278
B&CE Insurance Ltd	492	n/a	n/a
Canada Life Ltd	526	368	313
Friends Provident	450	306	n/a
Legal & General	524	360	318
Norwich Union	501	353	292
Prudential	504	347	316
Reliance Mutual	508	342	n/a
Scottish Widows	474	322	280
Standard Life	503	347	298
Male—65 years, single, 5-year guarantee			
AEGON Scottish Equitable	612	449	n/a
AXA	555	402	357
B&CE Insurance Ltd	611	n/a	n/a
Canada Life Ltd	613	452	394
Friends Provident	597	439	n/a
Legal & General	604	440	396
Norwich Union	606	438	379
Prudential	598	434	398
Reliance Mutual	587	418	n/a
Scottish Widows	568	410	364
Standard Life	594	435	382

(*cont.*)

Table 2.1. (*Continued*)

Provider	Available to	Monthly income—Level	Monthly income—3%	Monthly income—RPI
Male—65 years, single, no guarantees, smoker				
Just Retirement Ltd	Smokers only	663	507	449
Reliance Mutual	Smokers only	745	581	n/a
Tomorrow	Smokers only	712	549	467

Note: All examples are quotes at 15 December 2007 for a premium of £100,000.

Source for all tables: These data are a selection provided on the FSA website—Comparative Tables, © Financial Services Authority available at www.fsa.gov.uk/tables.

a 65-year-old man buying an annuity from AXA, we can contrast the monthly payments that he would receive of £557 for an annuity without a guarantee and £555 for an annuity with a five-year guarantee period. The monthly payment is slightly less for the guarantee period to take account of the fact that the first five years' payments will definitely be paid: however, since the probability of a 65-year-old man dying before the age of 70 is quite small, there is only a small premium in forgoing these payments in the event of death. The advantage of an annuity with the guarantee period is that the annuitant can be sure that there will be some payments made back from the life insurer and thus hedges against the possibility of receiving no payments in the event of a very early death. However, this advantage does not translate into a direct increase in the annuitant's welfare through higher retirement income and spending, since the benefit is felt by the annuitant's estate. This means that the benefits from a guaranteed annuity cannot easily be accommodated in an economic model of the type presented in Chapter 7.[4] The disadvantage is a lower income throughout retirement, although from the numbers in Table 2.1 it can be seen that the magnitude of this is small.

Value-Protected Annuities provide an alternative mechanism for receiving a return of capital in the event of the early death of the annuitant. If the cumulated sum of annuity payments at death is less than the initial premium, then the difference is returned to the estate of the deceased.

Inflation-linked Annuities will increase the annual payments by the rate of inflation to give the pensioner protection against erosion in the value of the annuity payments' purchasing power. In practice, the annuity payments will be based upon an official price index. In the UK this has traditionally been the Retail Price Index, although the government

Table 2.2. Comparison of monthly annuity rates for level and escalating annuities

Payment at beginning of year	1	3	5	7	9	11	13	15	17	19
Level annuity	557	557	557	557	557	557	557	557	557	557
Escalating 3%	403	428	454	481	511	542	575	610	647	686

Note: This table illustrates the difference between level and escalating annuities for AXA's quotes from Table 2.1, for a 65-year-old male, single, no guarantees.

now prefers an alternative measure called the Consumer Price Index. For example in November 2007 the RPI showed an increase of 4.4 per cent, while the CPI increased by 2.1 per cent, illustrating that price indices differ depending on goods in the index basket.[5] An ideal inflation-protected annuity would link the annuity payments to the basket of goods consumed by elderly people. So in practice an RPI-linked annuity is only an imperfect hedge against inflation for an annuitant. **Escalating Annuities** will increase the monthly payments by say 3 or 5 per cent to give the pensioner some protection against inflation, and to allow for possible increased income needs as the annuitant ages. In consequence the initial payments on inflation-linked and escalating annuities are lower than with level annuities. Continuing with the example of the AXA annuities, for a 65-year-old man, the monthly payments are compared in Table 2.2.

Comparing the level and escalating annuity products, the advantage of a level annuity is that it maximizes the initial income stream, especially if it has no guarantee. From the AXA example, an annuitant would have to live for 12 years before the annual income from the escalating annuity were higher than that from a level annuity and considerably more than 12 years before the money received overall were higher.[6] From the evidence of the term structure of interest rates, inflation rates are expected to be a little less than 3 per cent, so, in terms of money received, very similar arithmetic applies to inflation-protected annuities (although these do have the additional benefit of insuring against inflation risk).

Joint-Life or **Last-Survivor Annuities** pay an agreed annuity payment to an annuitant and the annuitant's partner while both are alive. Following the death of the annuitant the contract will pay either the same amount or an agreed reduced amount each month until the partner dies. Joint annuities always pay out smaller amounts than on single-life annuities because the expected number of annuity payments is higher.

Our discussion of the simple annuity theory in Chapter 7 is based on the maximization of an individual's utility. In the context of a household, it is more appropriate to consider maximization of household utility, which depends upon the utility of both partners. A joint-life annuity would smooth retirement income and consumption more effectively for the whole household and in the absence of other considerations would often be superior to a single-life annuity.

A second form of annuity based on two lives is a **Reversionary Annuity**. This form of annuity starts payment when the first-named individual dies and ceases payment when a second-named individual dies. Historically this would typically be arranged so that annuity payments started on the death of the husband and would pay an income to his wife until her death, thereby ensuring an income for the spouse with lower earning potential.

Investment-linked Annuities involve the fund backing the annuity to be invested in an equity product, and the annuitant will receive a random annuity payment which is related to the performance of the equity market. Investment-linked annuities are also a hedge against inflation, and can either be with-profits or unit-linked. With-profits' annuities mean that the pension fund is invested in a with-profits fund of an insurance company, so that annual bonuses are generated, which will allow the annuity payments to grow. The annuity payment from a 'unitized' annuity is directly related to the value of the underlying fund of investments.

Variable Annuities are a unit-linked investment product, with payments dependent on the performance of an underlying fund, but which includes flexible options and guarantees attached. Loh and Gosden (2007) provide cases to illustrate the flexibility of variable annuity products. For example, the annuity may pay a guaranteed income for a temporary period, at the end of which a level annuity with the remaining funds can be purchased. Alternatively, an annuitant may purchase a joint-life annuity to protect against longevity risk for a spouse, but following the death of a spouse, may wish to have the flexibility to revert to a single annuity. Variable annuities are very popular in the USA and Japan.

Some insurance companies offer annuities that pay a higher income if the annuitant has a health problem that is likely to reduce life expectancy. **Impaired-life Annuities** will pay an increased annuity payment if the annuitant has health problems certified by a doctor, such as cancer, chronic asthma, diabetes, heart attack, high blood pressure, kidney failure, multiple sclerosis or stroke. Ainslie (2000) provides an analysis of the annuity market for impaired lives. In 2005, the *Synthesis* database reports that of £8.5 billion sales of CPA annuities only £386 million (4.5 per cent) were impaired life. **Enhanced Annuities** pay a higher annuity payment if the annuitant is overweight or smokes regularly and these are self-certified. With both of these types of annuity the regular payment implicitly contains a higher proportion of capital repayment than for a normal annuity, although this distinction is not taken into account when tax is applied: to this extent these annuities receive slightly less favourable tax treatment. **Immediate Needs Annuities** are provided to elderly persons who need to be admitted to a nursing home. An immediate needs annuity offers enhanced rates, because like an impaired-life annuity, the annuitant has low life expectancy. The purchased annuity is paid gross to the nursing home, and is more tax efficient than an impaired-life annuity.

Phased-retirement or **Staggered-vesting**. Instead of converting the whole pension fund at one point in time, it is possible to schedule withdrawals over several years, buying a separate annuity at each successive withdrawal. This is achieved by splitting the fund into many separate segments. Each segment can now effectively be treated as a separate pension fund and taken as part tax-free lump sum and part annuity: segments can be converted at different times. Because of the current tax rules in the UK's CPA market, this annuitization process must be completed by age 75. We discuss the details of compulsory annuitization in Chapter 3, Section 3.3. Staggered-vesting allows individuals to convert only part of their pension fund into a pension if they decide that they do not need the full pension at one go. An example of when this may be useful is when an individual moves to part-time working before retiring completely.

Income Drawdown (**or Phased Withdrawal**) defers the purchase of an annuity, and instead generates an income by drawing from the fund itself. This facility allows pensioners to receive higher rates of return (since the fund can be invested in equity) and they could also benefit from increases in annuity rates if interest rates rose. Of course, these higher expected rates of return are offset by the riskiness of the returns compared to the certainty of an annuity. Because of the risk and also the administrative costs involved in setting up an Income Drawdown plan, the FSA recommends that this is only suitable for individuals with a pension fund of more than £100,000. HMRC sets maximum and minimum income that can be drawn down each year, and the amount withdrawn must be reviewed every three years to ensure that it will fall in the appropriate range. Following A-day, drawdown is referred to as unsecured income (pre-75 years of age) or alternatively secured income (drawdown post-75).

The **Bulk Annuities market** or bulk buyout market is where an annuity provider acquires a package of individual pension liabilities. Typically, in the event of the sponsor of a defined benefit occupational scheme becoming insolvent, the pension liabilities of the scheme would be passed on to a life insurer, who would receive a single premium in exchange for inheriting the pension liabilities. This market in the UK has been dominated by two insurance companies: Legal & General and Prudential. More recently, changes to accounting regulations, through FRS17 in the UK, and more generally International Accounting Standard (IAS) 19, require companies to recognize pension assets and liabilities recognized on their balance sheets.[7] This increased transparency, and its effect on share prices, has caused some companies to question their role in providing occupational pensions, and has led to the closure of a number of defined benefit schemes, with their pension liabilities being sold to a bulk annuity provider. According to Clark and Monk (2006), three-quarters of FTSE100 firms have closed their DB pensions to new members, and companies may use the bulk annuity markets to buy out their pension liabilities. Punter Southall (2006) notes that these opportunities have led to an influx of new entrants into the bulk buyout market, but as Figure 1.7 shows, the expansion to date of the bulk buyout market appears small, with sales around £2 billion per year, and this market has not yet reached the dramatic levels considered in Table 1.5.

2.2. Data on annuity rates

Warshawsky (1988) and Brown et al. (2001) document the movement in annuity prices in the USA. Cannon and Tonks (2004a) construct a consistent time series on UK annuity prices from 1957 to 2002 for the voluntary annuity market. Although the compulsory-purchase annuity market is both much larger and more interesting for government policy, it did not come to maturity until considerably later than 1957, and such a long run of data does not exist for the compulsory-purchase market. Finkelstein and Poterba (2002) compare the two markets in the year 2000. We know of no formal comparison over the earlier period of the 1980s and 1990s, but our informal analysis suggests that the variation of annuity rates in the two markets was similar.

2.2.1. *Purchased life annuities (voluntary)*

A detailed discussion of the voluntary market data can be found in Cannon and Tonks (2004*b*), and we summarize the most important points here. The data are primarily for level immediate voluntary annuities purchased for 1957–2002: data from 1973 onwards are for annuities with a five-year guarantee and earlier data have no guarantee. According to Stark (2002) over 70 per cent of purchased annuities are level annuities, so the series are reasonably representative: more importantly historical data are not available for any other types of annuity. The data were collected from a series of trade magazines such as *Pensions World* and *Money Management* for the later period and *The Policy* for the earlier period.

Figure 2.1 plots a series of five-year guaranteed annuity rates for men aged 60, 65, and 70, and for women aged 55, 60, and 65, over the period 1972–2007. It can be seen that annuity rates for men are consistently higher than for women of the same age; and that annuity rates are higher for both men and women as age increases. Age and sex are two personal

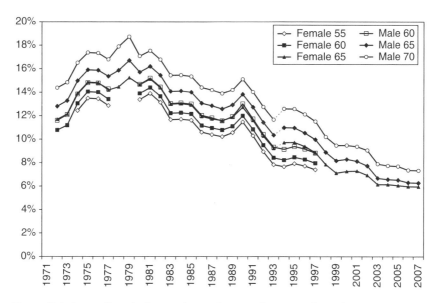

Figure 2.1. Immediate (voluntary) annuity rates by age and gender

Source: Female ages 55 and 60 and male age 60 and all other ages up to 1993 are taken from Cannon and Tonks (2004*b*). Female age 65 and male age 65 and 70 from 1994 onwards are taken from Moneyfacts and authors' own calculations. There is a small inconsistency between data in Cannon and Tonks (2004*b*) and the updated series, shown by the dotted lines between 1993 and 1994 for the relevant series.

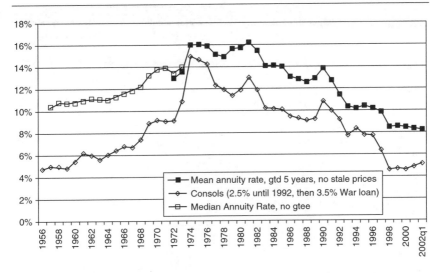

Figure 2.2. Immediate (voluntary) annuity rates for men aged 65

Source: Cannon and Tonks (2004*b*).

characteristics that annuity-providers condition on when quoting annuity prices, since life expectancy of women is higher than men, and of younger adults, of both sexes, is higher than older adults. The striking aspect of this graph is the extent to which the six series move together: we should expect this since the major cause of variation in annuity rates over a period as short as this is the variation in the entire term structure of interest rates—and clearly all annuity rates at any given point in time are based on the same term structure.[8]

Figure 2.2 illustrates the complete annual series for men aged 65 over a longer time period; and for comparison, the consol rate is also plotted as a representative long-term interest rate.[9] For 1972–2002 we plot the mean of the annuity series, but since there is some evidence that for 1957–73 the mean is biased down by stale prices, we plot the median for the earlier period. An updated series of voluntary UK annuity rates are given in Table 2.3.

Descriptive statistics are presented in Table 2.4 for the two sub-periods and also for the period as a whole (the annuity series for 1957–2002 created by splicing the series together). As can be seen from Figure 2.2, the series are highly correlated and the difference between them is falling over time. Both series appear to follow a unit root process and so we considered whether they are cointegrated. Roughly speaking, annuity

Table 2.3. Male aged 65, voluntary single level annuities

	No guarantee, median rate (%)	5-year guarantee, mean rate (%)	No guarantee, mean rate (%)
1957	10.41		
1958	10.78		
1959	10.72		
1960	10.75		
1961	10.92		
1962	11.13		
1963	11.08		
1964	11.00		
1965	11.26		
1966	11.56		
1967	11.81		
1968	12.17		
1969	13.22		
1970	13.74		
1971	13.89		
1972	13.39	12.80	
1973	13.99	13.27	
1974		14.98	
1975		15.91	
1976		15.87	
1977		15.36	
1978		15.86	
1979		16.70	
1980		15.71	
1981		16.20	
1982		15.45	
1983		14.07	
1984		14.11	
1985		14.00	
1986		13.06	
1987		12.85	
1988		12.58	
1989		12.92	
1990		13.82	
1991		12.73	
1992		11.43	
1993		10.35	
1994		10.18	10.99
1995		10.41	10.97
1996		10.18	10.54
1997		9.85	9.97
1998			8.90
1999			8.17
2000			8.29
2001			8.12
2002			7.73
2003			6.68
2004			6.57
2005			6.53
2006			6.31
2007			6.28

Source: Data in the first two columns is from Cannon and Tonks (2004*b*) taken respectively from *The Policy* and *Pensions World* (supplemented by *Money Management*). Data in the third column is collected by the authors from Moneyfacts.

Table 2.4. Time series properties on voluntary annuity and consol rates 1957–2002

	Annuity rate (%)	Consol rate (%)	Difference between annuity rate and consol rate (%)
Panel A: 1957–73			
Mean	11.87	6.96	4.91
St. Dev.	1.26	1.81	0.65
Correlation	0.97		
Panel B: 1972–2002			
Mean	12.67	9.54	3.13
St. Dev.	2.71	2.93	1.01
Correlation	0.94		
Panel C: 1957–2002 (spliced data)			
Mean	12.1	8.57	3.53
St. Dev.	2.39	2.90	0.96
Correlation	0.95		

Note: This table presents descriptive statistics on the time series of average annuity rates and consol rates over the period 1957–2002 and for the two sub-periods.

rates are the consol rate plus a premium based on life expectancy and although the last is trending down, probably with a unit root itself, it is sufficiently slow moving and low variance compared with interest rates that it is unlikely to affect the cointegration properties of the series on this relatively short time series. However, any rejection of a unit root in the difference between the two series would have to be very tentative: the conclusions of augmented Dickey–Fuller tests are sensitive to the precise form of the test, the number of lags in the analysis and the sample period chosen.

The consol rate (as well as shorter rates, not illustrated here) was roughly the same in both 1957 and 2002, making comparison of the beginning and end of the period straightforward. Although consol rates were the same, annuity rates were lower in 2002 than in 1957. Cannon and Tonks (2004*a*) show that all of this narrowing is due to increases in longevity: as life expectancy increases the gap between the annuity rate and the consol rate ('mortality drag') will narrow.[10]

In addition to the gradual trend of a narrowing gap between annuity and consol rates, there is also a temporary narrowing of the gap in the mid-1970s when all interest rates were high. The reason for this can be explained as follows: when interest rates are high the present value of future payments in the relatively distant future contribute very little to the total present value of an asset and most of the present value of the asset depends upon payments in the very near future. Since the probability of annuity payments in the near future is very high (in fact it is certain for the first five years of a guaranteed annuity), the expected present value of the annuity payments for the near future is almost the same as the expected present value of a consol. Of course, this reasoning relies upon annuities being priced fairly, but all of the evidence we shall present below suggests that this is approximately the case.

The series plotted so far are of simple average annuity rates for which we have quotes, with no attempts to weight these by importance of annuity provider. The spread between the best and worst annuity rate over this period is often about 2 per cent, but the worst rates may be stale (out-of-date) prices in our sources or prices being offered by firms that were not actually writing business. Evidence from the Continuous Mortality Investigation Bureau suggests that over this period there was considerable variety in mortality experiences of different life offices, and that this persisted over time (CMI 1993): it may be the case that some annuity rates were lower simply because annuitants were longer lived.[11] Such differences appear too large to be sustained in the twenty-first century because it is easy to obtain different annuity quotations (as has been seen above it is possible to get quotes for the compulsory-purchase market from the FSA). However, over the period for which the historical data were collected, prices of annuities were not easily available (e.g. they weren't published in the daily press, although they were reviewed twice in *Which?* magazine, in 1964 and 1970) and many life offices sold annuities on a regional basis through their own sales forces. So we do not view these spreads as evidence of market failure per se, although they are clearly consistent with market failure.[12] Figure 2.3 illustrates our estimated spreads from 1980 to 1998.

In theoretical work on annuities Abel (1986) and Walliser (2000) note that quantities of annuities purchased can be chosen by the purchaser, so that a large pension fund could be split into smaller annuity premiums, and indeed Stark (2002) reports that about one-third of annuitants purchase more than one annuity. This would suggest that life-assurance companies would be unable to offer lower annuity rates for larger purchase prices: they might wish to do so since larger purchase prices would be paid by richer individuals who would be healthier and have systematically higher life expectancy. For very small purchase prices life-assurance companies might wish to offer lower annuity rates because of the fixed cost of writing an annuity being larger relative to the premium. However, estimates of costs of writing an annuity do not suggest that this cost is high (in the range £25–£75), so this would not be prohibitive.[13]

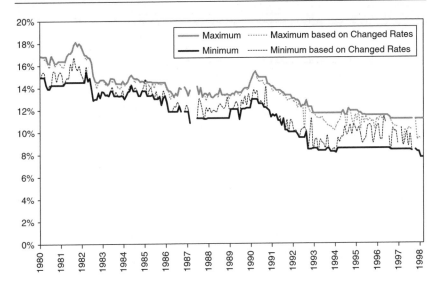

Figure 2.3. Immediate (voluntary) annuity rates for men aged 65, minimum and maximum annuity rates quoted 1980–98

Source: Cannon and Tonks (2004*b*).

Cannon and Tonks (2004*b*) find some historic evidence for non-linear pricing in the voluntary market for very low purchase prices and minimal non-linear pricing for larger purchase prices. Their figures are consistent with the formula in Finkelstein and Poterba (2004) for an anonymous life-assurance company over the period 1981–98: they report that if the annuity rate for a £10,000 purchase is X, then the annuity payment for a purchase of P is

$$\frac{PX + (P - 10{,}000)\,f}{10{,}000} \qquad (2.1)$$

where the policy fee $f = £18$ in 1998. The average annuity rate in 1998 was 8 per cent so suppose that this were the annuity rate offered for a purchase of £10,000. Then the annuity rate would range from 6.38 per cent for a purchase of £1,000 up to 8.12 per cent for a purchase of £30,000.

The most recent evidence on non-linear pricing for the compulsory-purchase market is slightly different. Figures 2.4 and 2.5 report annuity rates by purchase price for small and large purchases respectively in December 2007 (these figures are consistent with those shown in Table 2.1). For small purchases the annuity rate rises with purchase price in a way similar to that already reported, although it is noteworthy that

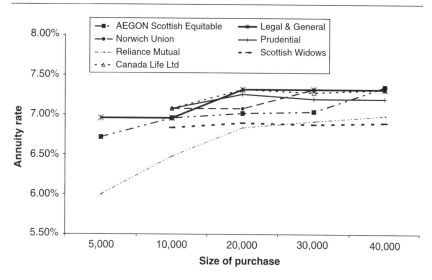

Figure 2.4. Evidence on non-linear pricing: CPA rates, men, 65, December 2007. Relationship between annuity rate and purchase price for small purchase prices

Source: FSA and authors' own calculations.

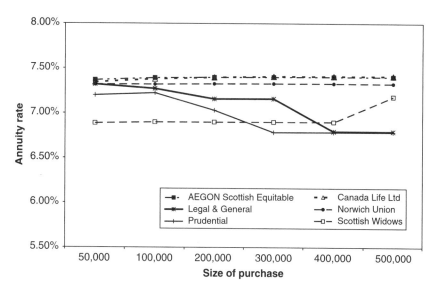

Figure 2.5. Evidence on non-linear pricing: CPA rates, men, 65, December 2007. Relationship between annuity rate and purchase price for large purchase prices

Source: FSA and authors' own calculation.

the largest overall provider, the Prudential, offers rates that are both competitive and relatively flat across all small purchase prices.[14]

For larger purchases the situation is quite different. Annuity rates appear independent of purchase price for most companies but Legal & General and Prudential offer much lower rates for larger purchases, suggesting a dislike for richer individuals who may be higher risk. It is impossible to determine how much richer individuals can overcome this by splitting their pension fund into several smaller funds: Stark's evidence (2002) is inconclusive since those individuals who do hold more than one annuity may do so for legal and tax reasons.[15] However, it is clear that not all companies are trying to avoid large purchase prices and AEGON Scottish Equitable's annuity rates would seem designed to deter smaller funds in favour of larger ones.

2.2.2. Compulsory purchase annuities market

Having discussed the voluntary annuities market, in this section we focus on nominal and real compulsory-purchase annuities, bought by individuals who have received tax breaks in accumulating pension funds, and who must annuitize a proportion of that fund and purchase annuities in the compulsory-purchase market where annuity rates are slightly better, possibly due to fewer selection effects as argued in Finkelstein and Poterba (2002).

We report data on quoted annuity rates provided by Moneyfacts over the period 1994–2007. These are taken from monthly quoted annuity rates that have been published in Moneyfacts from July 1994 to March 2007 by various annuity providers for both men and women of different ages.[16]

Moneyfacts provide annuity quotes for level annuities with no guarantee that pay a constant monthly income stream over the lifetime of the annuitant. We also have annuity quotes for level annuities with a five-year guarantee, meaning that in the event that the annuitant dies, the annuity income continues to be paid into the annuitant's estate for five years after the annuitant's death. Moneyfacts also publish RPI-linked annuities, which pay an annuity income that rises in line with the UK's Retail Price Index, and hence provides protection against inflation to the annuitant.

In Cannon and Tonks (2004b) and in the previous section, we discussed potential problems with inferring an average annuity rate from a cross-section of annuity quotes in the voluntary market. Because we drew our annuity prices from a wide range of sources we had to take care to avoid changes due to composition bias. There were also long periods of time when annuity prices of individual providers did not change and we were concerned that this might be due to the contemporary sources containing stale prices (in practice it was more likely to be due to the fact that interest rates were not changing very much). Neither of these problems are likely to affect our data-set on the compulsory market. We have a consistent source of data and any changes in the number of prices available are due to changes in the number of actual providers: in most cases we can identify changes in the number of prices with merger or acquisition of one provider by another. Although prices of individual providers rarely change on a monthly basis, changes are sufficiently frequent that there is no reason to believe that any prices are stale.

Figures 2.6 and 2.7 plot a series of annuity rates for men and women aged 65 and 75 over the period (75-year-olds' annuity rates were only quoted in Moneyfacts from August 1997 and RPI-linked annuities were only quoted from September 1998—in addition two months' data are missing). It can be seen that annuity prices move closely together, largely in line with interest rates.

As with the voluntary market annuity rates for men are consistently higher than for women of the same age; and annuity rates are higher for both men and women as age increases. Age and sex are two personal characteristics that annuity-providers condition on when quoting annuity prices, since life expectancy of women is higher than men, and of younger adults of both sexes is higher than older adults. The annuity rates on guaranteed annuities always lie below non-guaranteed annuities, and the rates on index-linked annuities lie below those on nominal annuities. Like the voluntary market the striking aspect of Figures 2.6 and 2.7 is the extent to which the series move together.

Figure 2.8 reveals that the number of main annuity providers during this period has fallen significantly: in 1994 Moneyfacts reports 23–5 quotes, but this falls to about 9 quotes by the end of the period. The FSA website also has reported about 9 or 10 annuity prices over the period 2005–07. It should be noted that some of the annuity providers only supply enhanced or similarly-restricted annuities, such as B&CE Insurance which supplies annuities to former construction workers. The number of annuities quoted for this part of the market has actually grown (some of these are provided by companies that also provide non-enhanced annuities). Figure 2.8 also shows that not all annuity providers quote for RPI-linked annuities in Moneyfacts.

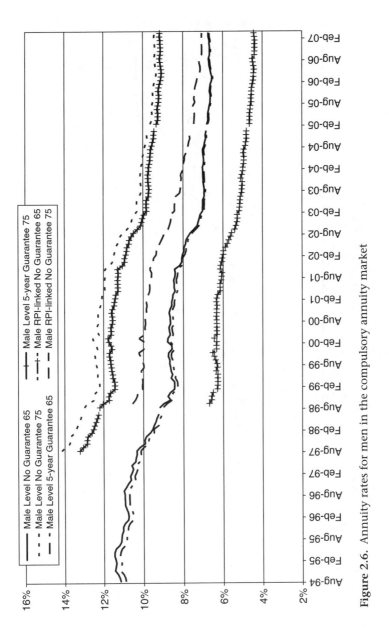

Figure 2.6. Annuity rates for men in the compulsory annuity market

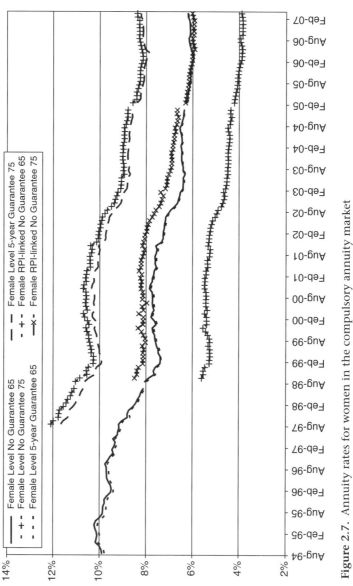

Figure 2.7. Annuity rates for women in the compulsory annuity market

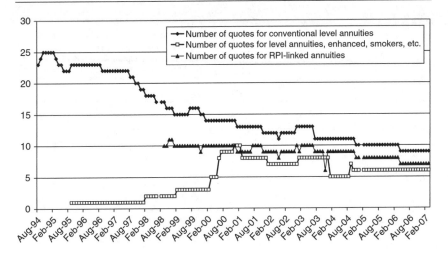

Figure 2.8. Number of annuity quotes in Moneyfacts

Although the number of annuity providers quoting annuity prices in the Moneyfacts database has fallen, insurance companies may still be willing to provide annuities if contacted directly by individuals or annuity brokers. We will discuss the number of providers in Chapter 9, but according to the FSA life insurance returns there are many more insurance companies selling compulsory annuities in 2005, than the number providing quotes in the Moneyfacts data-set. The 10 annuity providers identified as quoting annuity prices from the Moneyfacts database in August 2005 were AXA, Canada Life, Clerical Medical (HBOS), Friends Provident, Legal & General, Norwich Union (Aviva), Prudential, Scottish Equitable (AEGON), Scottish Widows (Lloyds TSB), and Standard Life. By comparing these providers with the sales of annuities in 2005 from the FSA returns, it would appear that our data-set contains price quotes from all the major providers.

Figure 2.9 provides a comparison of annuity rates in the compulsory market with long-term interest rates. It compares the annuity rate for 65-year-old males with the UK government 10-year bond yield. It can be seen that the two series clearly move very closely together, although the annuity rate is slightly smoother. In addition Figure 2.9 also plots the yield on corporate bonds from Datastream (an index of bonds of various qualities) and Merrill Lynch (an index of investment grade bonds).[17]

Descriptive statistics for annuity rates and bond yields are presented in Table 2.5 for the period as a whole, and for two sub-periods. As can be

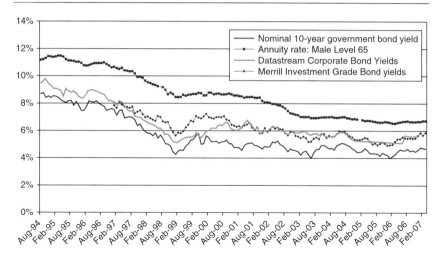

Figure 2.9. Comparison of annuity rates in CPA market with bond yields

seen, the series are highly correlated, but this correlation has decreased from 0.98 in the late 1990s to 0.57 over the last six years and the difference between the two series is falling over time. The annuity rate in the compulsory market was 9.9 per cent between 1994 and 2000, but had fallen to 7.2 per cent over the second half of the data-set for 2001–07. Table 2.5 also reports the yields on corporate bonds, and this has averaged

Table 2.5. Time series properties on compulsory annuity and 10-year bond rates 1994–2007

	Annuity rate (%)	10-year government bond yield (%)	Corporate bond yield (%)	Difference (%) in annuity rate and government bond yield
Panel A: 1994–2007				
Mean	8.59	5.61	6.52	2.98
St. Dev.	1.62	1.39	1.33	
Correlation	0.93			
Panel B: 1994–2000				
Mean	9.91	6.55	7.29	3.36
St. Dev.	1.10	1.39	1.42	
Correlation	0.98			
Panel C: 2001–07				
Mean	7.22	4.65	5.70	2.57
St. Dev.	0.65	0.29	0.41	
Correlation	0.57			

Note: This table presents descriptive statistics on the time series of average annuity rates, government rates, and corporate bond rates over the period 1994–2007 and for the two sub-periods.

about 90 basis points above the yield on government bonds. Using the corporate bond rate as the appropriate discount rate, or including the risk premium on corporate bonds, will therefore reduce the present value of annuity payments.

Notes

1. The FSA's 'Guide to Annuities and Income Withdrawal' (2004) provides a clear description for consumers of the types of annuity product available in the market.
2. It is also possible to purchase annuities that make payments at different frequencies such as annually, half-yearly, or every three months. Where the purpose of an annuity is to provide an income stream for immediate consumption (which is true in nearly all cases), such infrequent payments would obviously be inappropriate.
3. Discrimination on grounds of gender is legal in annuity markets in the United Kingdom and the USA (although this is not true in all countries). The most recent EU Directive on equal opportunities also allows discrimination on actuarial grounds (European Commission 2004). Discrimination on grounds of race is not practised, although it is likely that blacks in the USA could gain better annuity rates, since their life expectancy is shorter.
4. It is true that it is fairly straightforward to extend the model in Chapter 7, to include the possibility that the agent gains utility from bequeathing wealth to someone else. However, the guarantee period is a very clumsy and risky way of ensuring a bequest (since it is more likely than not that the annuitant will outlive the guarantee period). For this reason we hypothesize the motivation advanced in the text: that annuitants worry about dying early and hence earning a poor return on the annuity purchase *ex post*. Such a motivation more naturally falls within the area of modern economic psychological analysis, which we discuss in Chapter 8.
5. *Source*: UK Office of National Statistics.
6. Life expectancy would be about 18 years for a man aged 65, so the probability of dying before 12 years would be quite high.
7. Franzoni and Marin (2006) find that companies with large pension deficits are overvalued by the stock market.
8. Although the relative importance of interest rates of different maturities varies between annuities purchased for different ages.
9. A 'consol' is a government bond paying a total annual coupons of between $2\frac{1}{2}$ and $3\frac{1}{2}$ per cent on a par value of £100, with no redemption date: in principle, the government is allowed to re-purchase the bonds (dependent on the market price and sometimes after giving notice), but it has never done so. Historically there have been several conversions involving changing the coupon rate and

hence the effective par value, but the last of these was in 1888, and a consol is usually treated as a perpetual bond. The most recent issue of consols was an issue to fund the First World War with a coupon of $3^1/_2$ per cent (often referred to as the War Loan). In Figure 4.2, the consol rate is shown to be about 5 per cent at both the beginning and end of the period: this would imply that the market price of $2^1/_2$ per cent consols with a face value of £100 (i.e. paying £2.50 per year) was about £50.

10. If longevity increased so much that annuitants were immortal, the annuity rate and the consol rate would be the same, since the two products would be virtually identical.

11. We have been unable to test this hypothesis because the CMIR anonymizes the life offices it compares.

12. An alternative and more pessimistic view is that for some of our period we may be underestimating the spreads between worst and best annuities because we only have data on the better annuity prices quoted.

13. More substantial costs would be ceding costs (these are the administrative costs involved with closing the individual's account with an investment fund in preparation for the purchase of the annuity: they are borne by the life insurer and absorbed into the effective rate of return in the accumulation phase) and brokerage fees, typically 1 per cent or perhaps 2 per cent for impaired lives. Brokerage fees (paid to a financial adviser) would not affect the annuity rate offered, but would affect the amount of money an annuitant had to annuitize. In nearly all cases life insurers will only sell annuities through a financial adviser, mainly to avoid any problems with mis-selling.

14. For relative size of different companies see Chapter 10.

15. Some personal pension plans, connected with contracting out, have received preferential tax treatment on the condition that they are annuitized using unisex tables for a joint-life annuity (this has also needed to be an inflation-indexed annuity, although this requirement is being dropped from 2005). A male annuitant would rationally annuitize any pension fund not liable to these restrictions at the better male annuity rate (and might also prefer to avoid buying a joint-life annuity).

16. Data on annuity rates may also be obtained from the Anuity Bureau http://www.annuity-bureau.co.uk/ and from William Burroughs.

17. In their analysis of money's worth, Finkelstein and Poterba (2004) use the return on corporate bonds as a deflator rather than government bonds.

3

A short history of annuities

At this point we sketch the history of annuities drawing on accounts which typically place annuities within the context of life insurance as a whole. Our discussion will concentrate on the UK, which currently has the largest annuity market.[1] Until the early modern period an annuity market of sorts existed but it was not based on modern theories of probability or finance—since neither of these had yet been invented. From the late seventeenth century there were great advances in the understanding of business mathematics and in financial markets generally and this led to considerable evolution of the life insurance industry. From the late nineteenth century or early twentieth century the development of annuity markets was strongly influenced by increased state provision of pensions. We shall review these periods in turn before summarizing the most recent developments in the UK.

3.1. Annuities from Classical Times up to the Middle Ages

The existence of annuities can be traced back to Roman times when maritime insurance was also available. A contract called an annua consisted of a stream of payments paid either for a fixed term or for life and these were sold by the same people who sold maritime insurance: however, no records exist of the prices for such contracts (James 1947, quoted in Poterba 2005). The oldest available guide to pricing is that ascribed by Aemilius Macer in 220 AD to Domitius Ulpianus (Haberman and Sibbett 1995, vol. I, pt. 2). The common way of writing a valuation at this time was to express the purchase price as a multiple N of the annual income and refer to this as N years' purchase.

Table 3.1. Roman annuity rates

Age x	Ulpian's table	Macer's table
0–19	30	30
20–24	28	30
25–29	25	30
30–34	22	$60 - x$ i.e. between 30 and 26
35–39	20	$60 - x$ i.e. between 25 and 21
40–49	$59 - x$ i.e. between 19 and 10	$60 - x$ i.e. between 20 and 16
50–54	9	$60 - x$ i.e. between 10 and 6
55–59	7	$60 - x$ i.e. between 5 and 1
60+	5	undefined

Ulpian's table is reproduced in Table 3.1: Macer notes that in practice a simpler formula was often used: for someone over the age x of 30, the purchase price was calculated as $60 - x$, although he does not say how this was used for individuals whose age was close to or above 60. Macer's table is also reported in Table 3.1 and it is clear that the two tables are very similar except for the highest ages.

Both Poterba (2005) and Haberman and Sibbett (1995) note that it is uncertain whether these tables are based on life expectancies alone or whether they also include discounting of future income payments. In support of the former, Mays (1979) points out that the purchase prices are probably too high to be consistent with a true expected present valuation and argues that the figures are actually based on life expectancy alone. However, Macer reports that if income were left to the state (which would have been for 100 years) the income would have been valued at 30 years' purchase for a perpetuity, suggesting an interest rate of ~3.3 per cent and this was thus a legal maximum. Based on this Greenwood (1940) argues that both Ulpian's and Macer's tables just interpolate from the maximum purchase price of 30 years to arbitrary values of 5 and 0. Despite the problems with Ulpian's table, Haberman and Sibbett (1995) report that it was used to value life annuities by the Government of Tuscany as late as 1814.

The next point at which we have good information about pension provision is Europe in the Middle Ages. A useful review is provided by Lewin (2003), which refers to a fairly extensive literature based on primary sources such as Church accounts.

The Church had straightforward ways of providing pension income to employees who were too elderly to continue working. In monasteries an elderly monk just continued to live in the monastery until death.

A common solution for parochial clergy was to allow an elderly priest to receive a proportion of his parish income, some of which would have been in kind, and to appoint a chaplain to the parish church until the priest died. Sometimes the retired priest was allowed to continue living in the rectory. The income of the priest was often one-third of the total income and three-quarters had an income greater than a notional minimum income of £4 per year. However, the number of pensions awarded was not large: in the Diocese of Exeter (in the south-west of England) 10 per cent of parish posts had a pension paid when the post changed hands (Lewin 2003: 25). With these possibilities available to it, the Church did not need to have explicit annuitization of income.

Instead the Church was effectively a provider of pension income, unsurprisingly since it was one of only a few institutions whose existence in the future was beyond reasonable doubt. Monasteries sold corrodies to private individuals: these were effectively annuities providing a real income for life. For example, in 1316 Master William de Schokerwych paid £60 to the prior and chapter of Worcester to receive a room, stabling for a horse, and bread and beer everyday for life: in addition he received meat and fish when these would also be served to the monks (Lewin 2003: 39). The advantage to the monastery of such a transaction was that it allowed it to raise capital that might be needed for repairs or major building work; in addition Master William was a master mason and may have had links with the monastery before purchasing the corrody, so the monastery had some idea of his character and whether they wanted him living with them. From the point of view of the purchaser of the corrody, one of the biggest advantages was receiving a real income: although trend price inflation was negligible during most of the Middle Ages, year-on-year variation in prices was huge due to intermittent crop failures: the coefficient of variation for wheat prices was 0.34.[2] The corollary of this was that monasteries bore a very large amount of risk, in terms of both mortality risk and price risk. In addition the holder of a corrody could transfer it to a third party, possibly against the will of the monastery. The 1285 Statute of Westminster made it legally difficult for the monasteries to withdraw corrodians' benefits—an early example of pension consumer protection. Unsurprisingly, monasteries sometimes found themselves in legal difficulties if their liabilities exceeded their resources.

We know little about how corrodies were priced but Lewin (2003: 45) reports that St Leonard's Hospital, York, sold corrodies typically for 10 years' purchase and that the average length of time that the corrody was held was 11.4 years: after allowing for interest this suggests that pricing was reasonably fair. The Cathedral Church in Bath sold a joint-life annuity to a man and his son for 50 years' purchase in the late fifteenth century, which seems a very high price (Lewin 2003: 27), but Poterba (2005) quotes Murphy (1939) as reporting an annuity sold by the Abbot of St Denis in 1308 for only six years' purchase (although this contract was contested in 1323).

Smallholders would have been unable to purchase corrodies since they would have been too poor to raise the capital sum required. Instead they would give full use of their farmland to their son in exchange for a promise of an income for life and a room or rooms in which to live. These contracts were recognized legally and hence enforceable. However, they clearly tell us little about annuities per se, since they combine pension provision with a bequest from the elder to the younger generation.

One of the reasons for governments and the Church to sell life annuities during this period was the prohibition on usury, interpreted as either charging interest or charging excessive interest (these restrictions were steadily reduced or removed in the period from the reformation onwards). Life annuities were one means of circumventing the usury laws because they introduced a risk element (although a life annuity could still be declared usurious if the annuity rate were too high). From the twelfth century onwards the Italian city states were borrowing money through life annuities and this practice spread northwards to France, Holland, and Germany (Poitras 1996; Poterba 2005). Annuity rates varied considerably, largely due to the risk of default by the seller. These annuities were not tradable.

From the considerable evidence available it is clear that in the Middle Ages annuities were used both as a pension product and as a means of financing: in addition annuities were supplemented by corrodies which are a very specific form of annuity. In common with other financial products, however, annuity markets were constrained both by the usury laws and by an absence of financial mathematics.

3.2. Annuities in the period of developing financial markets

Over the period 1600–1850 financial markets in general underwent significant transformation: institutional innovations included joint stock companies in the seventeenth century, tradable government bonds in the eighteenth century, together with exchanges on which these could be traded (Dickson 1967); better understanding of monetary policy and the issue of coinage (Sargent and Velde 2002); the creation of central banks such as the Bank of Amsterdam (1609) and the Bank of England (1694) and the consequent greater use of paper currency. Alongside this process important mathematical tools were developed such as logarithms (published by Napier in 1614); probability theory (Huygens in 1657 and de Moivre in 1718); and actuarial life tables (published by Graunt in 1622 and Halley in 1693).

During this period a wide variety of life products were sold, some of which are no longer available. Two products that have not been considered in Chapter 2 are tontines and mortuary tontines. These were initially proposed by Lorenzo Tonti to Cardinal Mazarin in France in 1652, although they were not actually used until later when, in various parts of the Netherlands, a total of 13 tontines were issued between 1670 and 1680.

A tontine consists of a group of policyholders paying a lump sum into a closed fund, where each policy is based on the life of a nominee (which may be the same as the policyholder or may be a third party). At the end of each year the interest on the principle is paid out to holders of policies on nominees who are still alive: as the number of nominees dies the sum paid to each member rises until there is only one person remaining who receives all of the interest. When the last nominee dies interest payments cease. In the simplest case the principal is never repaid, since the purpose of the tontine is to raise money. From the point of view of the issuer, tontines have an advantage over life annuities in that the only uncertainty is the point of time at which the last nominee dies (since the total of payments up to that point is constant). When the last payment is likely to be a long time hence and when the discount rate is reasonable, the magnitude of this uncertainty is small. For a group of life annuities there is uncertainty about the total payment made to all surviving annuitants at every point of time, including periods of time that are relatively soon, and so the total uncertainty is larger.

A system of tontines was used by the French government in the eighteenth century, 46 per cent of whose national debt was financed by life-contingent assets in 1788 (Weir 1989). Between 1689 and 1759 France issued 10 tontines and these were largely successful in raising the funds projected. In contrast the first English state tontine of 1693 raised only 10 per cent of the expected £1 million and of the three tontines launched between 1757 and 1789 one was cancelled and the others were also poorly subscribed (an Irish tontine in 1773–77 was successful). No successful private tontines were launched in England thereafter (Clark 1999: 78).

Weir (1989) shows that the reason France successfully raised money on tontines was that internal rates of return on them were very high, especially for people at older ages. In fact the French government paid too much on tontines (relative to other forms of finance) and was forced into a partial default in 1770 when tontine policies were turned into life annuities. In England, however, internal rates of return on tontines were very low except for policies in the name of young children.

One perceived problem with tontines was the incentive for policyholders to hasten the death of other nominees to obtain a larger share of the interest payments. This theme is fully (and hilariously) developed in the 1889 book *The Wrong Box* by Robert Louis Stevenson and Lloyd Osborne (the 1966 film adaptation stars most of Britain's leading comic actors of the period), and has also been used by writers as diverse as P. G. Wodehouse and Agatha Christie. Tontines have been made illegal in some countries to avoid this problem.

A related idea is a mortuary tontine, which is similar to a tontine except that the annual payouts are made not to the holders of nominees who survive but on nominees who die. Thus this is a form of life insurance based on a mutual principle. Clark (1999) describes the founding of the Amicable Society for a Perpetual Assurance Office in 1706 which was based on this principle: policyholders paid 10 shillings (£0.50) to join and then £6 annually. With a projected 2,000 members and annual income of £12,000, payments were capped at £10,000 and the rest invested in a mutual fund. The Amicable Society also attempted to launch an annuity scheme in 1720, but this was prevented by the fallout from the collapse of the South Sea Bubble later that year.

During this period the British government issued life annuities, but these were not priced according to age—age-related pricing only began in 1808. However, this was not a large part of government borrowing, most of which was in the form of perpetuities called consols after the consolidation of the national debt in 1743. Private provision of life annuities was probably constrained by the presence of government annuities but may also have been due to a general lack of life insurance.

A rare exception is the scheme of reversionary annuities paid by the Mercers' Company of London starting in 1699, which is well documented by Clark (1999). By the end of the seventeenth century the Mercers' were in debt and needed ways of raising capital. William Assheton promoted a scheme, initially for clergy but later expanded, whereby men could provide an income for their wives. Men under the age of 60 could pay a single premium of between £50 and £300: if a man predeceased his wife then the wife would receive 30 per cent of the premium for life. If the wife predeceased the husband then there would be no payout. Assheton assumed that there was an equal chance of the husband or wife dying first and hence the average payout was 15 per cent, only a little higher than the rate on life annuities of 14 per cent (seven years' purchase). Given that the first payment of a reversionary annuity is likely to occur some time in the future (i.e. it is deferred), appropriate discounting would suggest that this was profitable. Indeed in the early years the scheme appeared successful. However, out of 1,104 policies issued between 1699 and 1745, only 221 had the wife die first. The Mercers' took a variety of steps to deal with this problem: the payment was reduced from 30 to 25 per cent in 1717 and to 20 per cent in 1723: at the same time a limit was placed on the difference in age between the husband and wife to exclude young wives. However, the scheme finally failed in 1745.

The fact that only 1,104 policies were sold over a 46-year period suggests a moribund life insurance market. Clark (1999) shows that from the time of the South Sea Bubble in 1720 to the middle of the eighteenth century life insurance in general was very limited in scope. The number of policies in the Amicable Society fell from 1,600 in 1725 to 680 in 1750 and the two main life insurers, London Assurance and Royal Exchange, had only about 300 policies in force at the latter date. The only successful annuity pension scheme was the Church of Scotland's scheme of reversionary annuities started in 1746, which had about 1,000 subscribers.[3] However, this exception was due to the fact that the Church of Scotland had excellent information on the mortality patterns of both church ministers and their wives and used very careful analysis to ensure correct pricing (Clark 1999).

This brings us to the point about how life-contingent products were priced in these periods. The first scientific pricing of annuities was by the Dutchman de Witt who was concerned that the Netherlands were selling annuities to individuals without pricing for their age. In 1671 he used rough-and-ready mortality figures to estimate that a life annuity purchased at age 3 when the interest rate was 4 per cent should be about 16 years' purchase (compared with a perpetuity, which would be 25 years' purchase). Further analysis based on mortality data of annuitants by Jan Hudde confirmed de Witt's figures (Poterba 2005).

In England analysis of mortality began with John Graunt's publication of mortality data for London and in 1693 Edmund Halley published his analysis of annuity rates using mortality data of the Silesian city of Breslau (Heywood 1985; Haberman and Sibbett 1995). Calculation of life expectancy actually occurred later than this, with Bernoulli in 1709. In 1730 John Richards published tables of prices for reversionary annuities on multiple numbers of lives (again using the Breslau mortality data), so it can be seen that quite sophisticated questions were being answered at a relatively early date. Poitras (1996) documents the history of progress made in both actuarial and financial mathematics and many of the original documents are reproduced by Haberman and Sibbett (1995).

Despite these advances in understanding, life insurers tended not to use actuarial methods and the first life insurer to do so explicitly in England was the Equitable Assurance Society in 1762. Clark (1999: ch. 4) reviews various explanations for this: first, a lack of understanding of the new methods; secondly, the fact that the new methods were not obviously correct at the time (that they appear so to us is due to the benefit of hindsight); thirdly, a lack of confidence in the precision of the numbers (which seems reasonable given the small samples on which they were based) and finally, that much of the motivation in life insurance was gambling or speculation and people in the market were not interested in correct calculation. On his own analysis of archival material, Clark rejects the last explanation and prefers a combination of the first three. For example, the Mercers' scheme of reversionary annuities did not even have such basic information on the number of its policyholders whose wives had already died.

In fact the result of selling life annuities without taking age into account led to strong selection effects. Alter and Riley (1986) show that most of the nominated lives for the Dutch annuities of the late sixteenth century were relatively young, with 80 per cent under the age of 20: for the seventeenth century annuities that were priced by age this proportion had fallen to 46 per cent, although Alter and Riley's analysis suggests that annuities were still priced slightly too generously for this age group. Poitras (1996) shows that French tontines of the eighteenth century had similar problems of atypical mortality. So clearly purchasers of life annuities realized the possibilities to benefit from selection.

Dissatisfaction with the practice of selling life insurance in this way led to James Dodson trying to set up a life insurance company on actuarial principles in 1756. Unfortunately Dodson died in 1757, but the result of his initial suggestion was the foundation of the Equitable Society in 1762 (Lewin 2003). By 1775 the Equitable had insured 900 lives and by 1777 the Amicable had succeeded in filling its subscribers to the maximum of 2,000. Clark (1999) estimates that, including the Church of Scotland scheme, the total number of life policies in force in 1775 was about 6,000. Alongside the Equitable, new companies such as the Westminster and Pelican led a revival of life insurance, helped by the publication in 1783 of updated life tables by Richard Price, whose Northampton Life Table was used widely until the mid-nineteenth century (Lewin 2003; Haberman and Sibbett 1995).

Another turning point in life insurance in the UK was the 1774 Gambling Act which made it illegal to take out life insurance on anyone in whom the policyholder did not have a genuine interest. This began a separation of pure gambling on other people's lives, which at that time could degenerate into tasteless or even illegal behaviour (fraud or murder), from genuine insurance. However, it was still legal to take out annuities in someone else's name and this continued to cause problems of selection in the annuity market. Mitchell and Mitchell (2004) document the problems that the UK government had in this regard.

Government life annuities were priced according to the age of the nominee after 1808, based on the Northampton Life Table (itself based on data from 1735 to 1780). These had been used by the Equitable, but since that firm had little competition it had tended to overcharge and therefore problems with overestimation of mortality were unimportant. For government life annuities these tables were completely inappropriate, since they were priced actuarially with no markup. The discrepancy between the assumed mortality and actual mortality of government life annuitants was noticed by Finlaison in 1819, who calculated that the government was losing £8,000 per month. Despite being appointed Government Actuary in 1822, his advice was not heeded until 1828 and annuities were priced on the basis of observed mortality of government annuitants from the period 1789 to 1822 (although this change in rates was only possible after an Act of Parliament in 1829).

Finlaison's analysis had not allowed for the possibility of selection and therefore overestimated mortality of the very elderly. The result was that large numbers of policies were purchased on nominated lives of septuagenarians in the early 1830s (even the poet Wordsworth purchased such annuities on others' lives). To foreclose this sort of speculation the government imposed the restriction that annuities could only be purchased on the lives of a nominee in whom the purchaser had an interest, thus bringing annuity regulation into line with life insurance.

Apart from problems of speculation, the government's main problem was in promoting the sale of both life insurance and annuities. In particular the government sold multiple premia deferred annuities (i.e. personal pensions) but take-up was low. Gradually the government began to be interested in this business not as a way of raising funds, but to assist the elderly poor. To increase sales it allowed sales through friendly societies (1819) or savings banks (1833) (Wilson and McKay 1941). Gladstone introduced legislation in 1864 to sell annuities and life insurance through the Post Office, primarily due to the financial weakness of savings banks (Morley 1903). Additional stimuli for the legislation were elements of empire building within the Post Office and paternalism towards the poor (Perry 1992).

The provision of government annuities through the Post Office meant that the government was engaged more directly in competition with both private life insurers and friendly societies. These companies were politically powerful enough to ensure that minimum and maximum limits were placed on life insurance sales to restrict effective competition, but the restrictions on annuity purchases were less important. However, sales of immediate annuities from 1865 to 1884 only numbered 13,897 and deferred annuities for the same period were even fewer, totalling 1,043 (Perry 1992). Even after the removal of the restrictions in 1882, sales remained poor: by 1907 the total number of insurance policies in force was 13,269 at the Post Office compared to 2,397,915 from life-assurance companies (Daunton 1985). This was despite government insurance being sold at better prices and being virtually immune to default risk. After continuing low sales of both forms of insurance and losses on government annuities, sales ceased in 1928.

There appear to be several reasons for the failure of Gladstone's scheme to sell government annuities. First, it was very difficult for most people to accumulate a pot of wealth for retirement or any other purpose. This was a general problem and posed equal problems to friendly societies which promoted thrift among the poor (Johnson 1985). Norwich Union stopped selling annuities in 1870, suggesting that demand for annuities was low (Wadsworth, Findlater, and Boardman 2001). Secondly, purchasing government annuities involved bureaucratic procedures, and there was both an absence of marketing and restricted availability, since annuities could not be purchased at all post offices. Finally, where life insurance was sold successfully it was due to the fact that private insurance companies had large sales forces to collect premiums and sign up new members. A very large number of policies lapsed soon afterwards, strong evidence of unscrupulous sales techniques (Wilson and Levy 1937). The costs of these insurance salesmen were very high, amounting to nearly half of the premiums that they collected, but insurance companies were able to offset this disadvantage compared with government policies by investing in assets with much higher returns.

The cessation of sales of government annuities may have had some effect on the private market (Norwich Union started selling annuities again in 1928; Dyson 1969), but by this time two further considerations also reduced demand for annuities. Many workers were now in either occupational pension schemes or state pensions. Among the more affluent middle classes, demand would have been reduced by the tax treatment of annuities: the entire annuity payment was treated as income and taxed accordingly, despite the fact that some of the annuity payment was implicitly a reduction in capital.

One obvious advantage that the government had over private life insurers in selling annuities is the relatively small possibility of default (the government is unlikely to default while life insurers may go out of business). Since an annuity is a promise to pay benefits for a long time into the future, in an unregulated annuity market, default risk is of considerable importance. The earliest regulation of private life insurance was that of the Dutch government in the period 1827–30, which forced life insurers to operate based on very conservative mortality assumptions. This regulation finished in 1880 and it was only after that date that Dutch life insurance began to grow again (Stamhuis 1988), demonstrating the fine line between ensuring life insurers' solvency and excessive regulation.

The UK took a different approach and from 1870 required all life insurers to provide returns to the Board of Trade detailing both their revenues and their balance sheets. This provided an element of information which would allow both customers and the government to monitor the health of insurance companies, and the Board of Trade returns continue to this day as the Financial Service Authority returns.[4]

3.3. Annuities and UK pension provision since 1945

State retirement pensions were first introduced in the UK in 1908, and became universal under the National Insurance Act 1946, which introduced the basic flat-rate pension. In 1975 the Social Security Pensions Act indexed pensions to the growth in earnings, and extended the basic state pension to include an earnings-related component (SERPS). Like the first tier, this second tier was also unfunded and compulsory, and guaranteed contributors an additional pension as a percentage of their earnings.

The third tier in the UK's retirement provision is provided by the private sector, and is made up of occupational pensions and individual personal pensions. The annuity market makes up part of the third tier.

After a long period of stagnation in the early twentieth century the UK annuities market was finally given a boost under the 1956 Finance Act which implemented the main recommendations of the 1954 Millard Tucker No. 2 Committee on the introduction of tax efficient personal pensions for the self-employed. This meant that the self-employed were treated the same as the employed sector who had enjoyed the benefits of tax efficient occupational pension schemes for a number of years.

Following the Act, individuals could obtain tax relief on contributions into an approved pension contract, and at retirement would be required to annuitize the fund that had been built up. Further, the returns to investments in the pension fund of life-assurance companies during the accumulation part of the pension contract would be exempt from tax. An additional part of the 1956 Act also affected the tax treatment of voluntary annuities: a fixed proportion of the annuity payment for purchased life annuities was to be regarded as a rundown of capital, and an annuitant would only be liable for income tax on the balance. These changes stimulated the demand for annuities in the UK, and Table 3.2 shows the sales of voluntary annuities averaged over five-yearly intervals from the 1950s onwards. The numbers of annuities purchased each year vary greatly, though the value of the lump sum used to purchase an annuity contract has grown steadily from £106 million in the late 1960s to £650 million in the first half of the 1990s. The overall trend increase during this period was due to the increase in private pensions that were reaching the point of retirement.

The 1956 changes introduced a new compulsory-purchase annuities market for those who had built up a personal pension fund, distinct from the existing voluntary annuities market. As recognized in Finkelstein and Poterba (2002), these are likely to be quite different markets: only individuals who expect to live for a long time are likely to purchase a voluntary annuity, whereas compulsory annuities are purchased as part of the terms of the pension contract. Typical voluntary annuitants are female and relatively old (over 70), whereas typical compulsory annuitants are male and recently retired (about 65).[5]

Hannah (1986) explains the evolution of tax-free lump sum of 25 per cent of the pension fund. 'The chapter of accidents which led in absurd progression to this situation, [the tax-free lump sum] which was

Table 3.2. Growth in number and value of purchased life annuities, pension annuities, and outstanding personal pension schemes 1954–2005: Annual averages over successive five-year periods

	1951/55	1956/60	1961/65	1966/70	1971/75	1976/80	1981/85	1986/90	1991/95	1996/00	2001/05
Panel A: New Purchased Life Annuities (Immediate and Deferred) (Voluntary Market)											
No. of new annuity policies per year (000s)				33.8	173.2	67.6	84.2	67.8	65.4	13.8	3.1
Premiums on new immediate annuity policies (£m)			106.0		235.3	159.6	394.5	432.2	650.4	444.8	163.7
Annuity payouts per annum (£m)	0.7	1.6		12.7	44.0	25.1	66.2	80.5	129.8	39.2	
Panel B: New Pension Annuities (Compulsory Market)											
Premiums on new immediate pension annuities (£m)									2,794.6	5,178.4	7,269
Pension annuity payouts per annum (£m)									276.4	446.2	
Personal Pensions in Force											
No. of Policies (000s)		83.9			620.0	1,309.4	3,151.4	8,835.2	17,916.0	20,810.2	22,900.8
Yearly premiums (£m)		10.6			68.0	212.6	758.1	2,451.6	4,876.2	6,497.6	9,236.0

Source: Life Offices' Association; Association of British Insurers.

initially desired by no one, began in the early years of [the 20th] century' (Hannah 1986: 115). He notes that at the turn of the last century, occupational pensions varied widely in whether they paid a pension as a lump sum or as an annuity. There were arguments that suggested a lump sum would ease the progression from working to retirement, but against this was the concern that a lump sum would be frittered away. The Radley Commission on the Civil Service said in 1888 'The payment... of a lump sum is open to the obvious objection that in the event of improvidence or misfortune in the use of it, the retired public servant may be reduced to circumstances which might lead to his being an applicant for public or private charity'. Tax-exempt (1921) Act occupational funds were not allowed lump sums by the Inland Revenue,[6] though they could be paid by the pension out of non-tax exempt funds. Meanwhile the Civil Service in 1909 had negotiated a tax-free lump sum, to ensure comparability with widows' pension rights in the railway pension schemes, and in the course of these negotiations the tax-free lump sum was extended to surviving pensioners at retirement age. The Inland Revenue, whose workforce would benefit, were asked to agree to this scheme, which they did! The 1947 Finance Act attempted to clamp down on the proliferation of schemes that had attempted to get round the 1921 Act, and abolished all tax-free lump sums except those that were 'reasonable'. The 1956 Act which introduced personal pensions explicitly did not allow for tax-free lump sums, but pressure from private sector schemes to mimic the 'reasonableness' of the Civil Service scheme meant that from 1970 all schemes were explicitly permitted to pay tax-free lump sums from untaxed funds. In 1971 one-third of private sector schemes paid a lump sum as part of the pension entitlement. This proportion had risen to more than 90 per cent by 1979. Attempts to remove the tax-free treatment of the lump sum in the 1980s were derailed by what the then Chancellor later described as 'the most astonishing lobbying campaign of my political career' (Lawson 1992: 368) and, in the face of such strong political opposition, UK pension policy has had to concentrate on limiting the anomaly of the tax-free lump sum to 25 per cent rather than the more obvious policy of abolishing it altogether.

Immediately after its introduction in 1956 the compulsory-purchase annuity market had zero sales, since it would have been the young working cohort in the late 1950s who would have started saving through a personal pension, and it is unlikely that this cohort would have annuitized immediately. By the 1990s this compulsory annuity market was 10 times larger than the voluntary annuities market, and will continue to grow as the percentage of the population with personal pensions grows. Table 3.2 also records the growth in personal pensions throughout the second half of the last century.

An important consideration is how private pensions interact with the state pension and how different private pensions can interact with each other. To discuss this, it is useful to characterize the UK pension system as having several components.[7]

The **Basic State Pension** (BSP) is paid weekly and payments depend upon the number of national insurance contributions made by a pensioner: for a married couple it depends on total contributions. The value of this in 2007–08 was £87.30 per week for a single individual, or £4,539 per year following 30 qualifying years of National Insurance contributions.[8] Since 1979 the BSP has increased in line with inflation rather than with earnings and has accordingly become increasingly small compared with income from other sources, although this tendency to decline relative to earnings has been attenuated by some discretionary increases since 1997.

The **State Second Pension** (S2P) is an additional unfunded state pension, which is compulsory unless one opts out either into a private pension scheme or into an occupational pension scheme. The addition to the BSP began in 1977 and was called the State Earnings Related Pension Scheme (SERPS). From 2002 the additional pension, S2P, was no longer wholly earnings-related, with benefits skewed towards those with low earnings and the inclusion of carers and disabled people. Unfortunately there have been several revisions both to how SERPS was administered and the degree to which the government of the day was committed to the scheme. The Pensions Commission (2004) characterizes these schemes as highly complicated and difficult to understand, even for professionals, and this contributed to mis-selling scandals when individuals were encouraged to opt out of SERPS who should not have done so.

The **Pension Credit** dates from 2003 and supersedes the Minimum Income Guarantee. This ensures that pensioners receive a minimum level of income, £119.05 per week (or £6,191 per year) in 2007–08 for an individual. There are additional credits for pensioners with income from savings or a private pension so that the pension credit does not imply a marginal tax rate of 100 per cent.

Occupational and personal pension schemes are usually funded and require contributions (out of pre-tax income) throughout the employees' working life. The fund accumulates over time, and then is converted into a pension on retirement. Occupational schemes are provided by an employer and may pay on a defined benefit (DB) or a defined contribution

(DC) basis. Defined benefit schemes offer a pension, guaranteed by the employer, usually defined in terms of some proportion of final year earnings, and are related to the number of years of employment. Defined contribution (or money purchase) schemes are always funded and convert the value of the individual's pension fund at retirement into an annuity. Under a defined benefit scheme, the employer bears the risk of fund underperformance, while under defined contribution schemes the pensioner bears the risk of fund underperformance. In addition a defined contribution plan also exposes the pensioner to the risk of converting the fund into an annuity at a particular point in time.[9] In contrast, in a defined benefit scheme the individual is promised a pension for each year of service, and this pension promise is equivalent to a deferred annuity.

Occupational pension schemes for public sector workers are different from those for private workers since some are unfunded and are paid out of taxation. Where public sector schemes are funded, there may be explicit guarantees from the government to make up any shortfall in the event of one occurring.

In the tax year ending in April 2005, 28.30 million people paid national insurance contributions which will entitle them to some part of the basic state pension at retirement.[10] The numbers of the working population covered by a private pension are given in Figure 3.1. This figure shows that out of about 35 million people of working age, roughly 25 million are in work, but of these, nearly 9 million people do not contribute to a private pension.

Up until the 1980s pension provision had been a major component of the welfare state. Concerns about the state's ability to pay for the state pension commitments coupled with demographic trends of an ageing population, resulted in a change of policy in the 1980s, with an emphasis on the private sector provision of pensions. The Government Green Paper in 1998 reported that in 1960 there were over four people of working age for every pensioner; but by 2060 it is projected that there will only be two and a half people of working age for every pensioner.[11] The implication is that a declining workforce will have to support a growing number of pensioners.

The Government Pension Green Papers of 1998 and 2002 both emphasize that the state provision of pensions will decline, and individuals will be expected to contribute to third-tier schemes.[12]

Those who are able to save for their own retirement should do so. For this, . . . the right schemes [need] to be available and affordable; to be able to cope with flexible

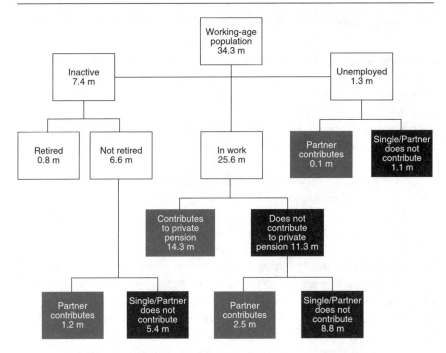

Figure 3.1. Participation in private pension schemes 2002–03, millions

Note: Those individuals with personal pensions who are only receiving contracted-out rebates have been counted among non-contributors since they will only accrue pension rights equivalent in value to the SERPS/S2P rights forgone (assuming that GAD calculations of approriate rebates are fair).

As the numbers of inactive and unemployed individuals contributing to Stakeholder Pensions are small (fewer than 0.1 m in FRS) they have been ignored for the purposes of this analysis.

Figures may not sum due to rounding.

Source: FRS (2002–03); The Pensions Commission (2004, 2005), © Crown Copyright.

working and variations in earnings... The current pension system does not meet these needs. Occupational pensions are usually good value and secure and are generally the best choice, but they are only available if the employer offers one, and can be unsuitable for those who move jobs frequently.... At the heart of our reforms are new stakeholder pension schemes. (DSS 1998: 5)

From the late 1980s, however, there has been a shift towards defined contribution occupational schemes. By 2000, around 16 per cent of private sector occupational scheme members, and nearly 70 per cent of all private sector occupational schemes, were based on defined contributions. The late 1980s also saw the launch of personal pensions. (DWP 2002: 51–2)

Concurrent with this government's view that pensions should be provided in the private sector, there has been a large decrease in the number of workers covered by occupational defined benefit pensions (The Pensions Commission 2004). This sudden reduction has arisen for several reasons.

First, the generosity in the 1990s of private occupational pensions was largely driven by a very strong stock market, which may have masked the extent to which underlying trends in labour markets were removing the incentives to employers to provide such schemes. Thus, the extent and speed of the fall in occupational pension provision is more obvious than might have been the case if the stock market had been less buoyant.

Secondly, the introduction of FRS17 reporting requirements making firms' pension liabilities explicit and the removal of Advanced Corporation Tax were further discouragements to the provision of occupational pensions, since they increased the risk to firms and raised costs.

Finally, changes in labour markets have made the provision of an occupational pension a less useful device for firms to motivate workers (McCarthy and Neuberger 2003: ch. 3), since occupational pensions are of less value to workers who expect to move firms more regularly. Conversely, more mobile workers would prefer a portable personal pension. Enthusiasm for occupational pensions may also have been undermined by instances of firms being unable to honour pension promises.[13]

The result of this has been a large transfer of occupational schemes from a DB to a DC basis. This will reinforce the underlying trend increase in demand for annuities arising from personal pension schemes, many of which will enter the decumulation phase in the near future.

The combination of the various forms of personal and occupational pensions, together with frequent changes in regulation and tax policy meant that the system of taxation for pensions was highly confusing by the beginning of the twenty-first century.[14] DWP (2002) recognized this confusion and the consequent 2004 Finance Act simplified the system: changes came into effect on 6 April 2006, commonly referred to as 'A-day', under which the tax system was changed to a lifetime allowance. At retirement the maximum pension fund which bears no additional tax liability was set at £1.5 million on A-day, rising annually thereafter. The maximum amount that could be paid into this pension fund was £215,000 per year. This means that an individual with a large number of pension schemes, which might have had different tax rules and annuitization requirements, is now able to aggregate the entire fund and buy a single annuity.

The compulsion to purchase an annuity was altered in several ways: it was strengthened by raising the minimum pension age to 55 (effective in 2010); but weakened by increasing access to pension funds through means other than an annuity. Following A-day, there are now three ways in which a tax-privileged pension may be accessed:

Secured Income involves purchasing an annuity in the compulsory-purchase annuity market. In addition to having the option of a guaranteed annuity, it is possible to have a value-protected annuity, where the difference between the original purchase price and cumulated payments made is received as a lump sum on death (this is taxed at 35 per cent). Value protection stops at age 75.

Unsecured Income (previously available as 'income drawdown') allows the pensioner to avoid annuitization until age 75 and to draw an income from the pension fund. The maximum amount drawn in each year is 120 per cent of the best level single-life annuity payment at the respective age and sex available in the compulsory-purchase market (these rates are collected and published by the FSA). At 75 the pensioner must switch to secured income or alternatively secured income. If the pensioner dies before 75, remaining funds may be repaid as a capital sum, subject to tax of 35 per cent, or transferred to a dependant's pension. In addition, a pensioner who opts for unsecured income may purchase term-certain annuities with a maximum term of 5 years.

Alternatively Secured Income (ASI) is a form of drawdown after age 75 allowing the pensioner to avoid formal annuitization at any age. The rationale for this provision was that some individuals might have religious objections to buying any form of life insurance product (although only one very small sect was ever referred to in parliamentary debate as having this objection). In the initial legislation annual payments could be drawn from the pension fund of up to 70 per cent of the best annuity rate at age 75 (there was no minimum withdrawal): on the pensioner's death, any remaining funds had to be transferred to a pension for a dependant, be paid to a nominated charity, or revert to the scheme provider. The fact that there was no need to draw any income at all meant that ASI was potentially a means of inter-generational transfer (which HMRC interprets as a form of tax avoidance). Demand for ASI in 2006 showed that many people were using it in this way. As a consequence the rules were changed so that it is compulsory to draw between 65 and 90 per cent of the best annuity rate aged 75 and payments made outside this range were taxed at 40 per cent. Any funds remaining on the death of the pensioner can now be taxed at a penal rate of up to 70 per cent: it is still possible for these funds to be passed to a dependant's pension or to a charity.

The justification for the compulsory annuitization is that savings in a personal pension are tax-advantaged, and that the reason for the tax break in the first place is to encourage individuals to save for a pension. This policy is unpopular, especially as annuity rates have fallen since the early 1980s, and appears to make pensioners particularly susceptible to annuity rate risk. Apart from the effects this has on people retiring now, it may also influence potential saving behaviour of people who will retire in the future.

Despite the apparent unpopularity of compulsory annuitization, the government remains committed to support the market for annuities for a number of reasons (DWP 2002; HM Treasury 2006): first, annuities pool people's risk, ensuring that they are the most financially efficient way of turning capital into an income stream; secondly, annuities make sure that people continue to receive an income from their savings no matter how long they live; and finally, tax relief on pension contributions is provided so people can save for an income in retirement, not for other purposes.

There are serious concerns about the magnitude of the pensions, in terms of both the welfare consequences for pensioners and the total demand for annuities. Figure 3.2 and Table 3.3 show the distribution of

Table 3.3. Pension annuity sales by size of fund

Size of fund	Number of pension annuities sold					
	2001	2002	2003	2004	2005	2006
Less than £5,000	79,740	94,834	106,599	116,671	71,808	92,381
£5,000–£9,999	35,738	43,290	50,926	48,272	54,308	70,621
£10,000–£19,999	42,167	51,118	58,753	57,406	68,523	96,475
£20,000–£29,999	22,156	26,583	29,898	29,525	36,486	52,918
£30,000–£39,999	12,565	15,520	17,517	16,971	20,555	27,961
£40,000–£49,999	7,663	9,348	10,631	10,764	13,026	16,178
£50,000–£59,999	5,012	6,322	7,247	6,988	8,408	9,941
£60,000–£69,999	3,460	4,293	5,008	4,745	5,685	6,661
£70,000–£79,999	2,405	3,198	3,690	3,602	4,168	4,667
£80,000–£89,999	1,831	2,434	2,624	2,517	3,098	3,483
£90,000–£99,999	1,455	1,811	2,008	1,922	2,299	2,463
£100,000–£124,999	2,467	3,189	3,419	3,233	3,705	4,109
£125,000–£149,999	1,351	1,742	2,038	1,739	2,111	2,350
£150,000–£174,999	812	1,221	1,294	1,183	1,396	1,380
£175,000–£199,999	598	745	840	880	905	959
£200,000–£249,999	713	903	1,008	895	1,056	1,207
£250,000–£299,999	411	497	543	528	602	645
£300,000–£349,999	268	334	369	321	333	385
£350,000–£399,999	178	202	234	203	237	255
£400,000–£449,999	123	134	149	125	140	155
£450,000–£499,999	76	118	100	101	103	114
£500,000 and above	338	369	374	291	379	393
Total	221,526	268,205	305,270	308,882	299,331	395,699

Source: Association of British Insurers.

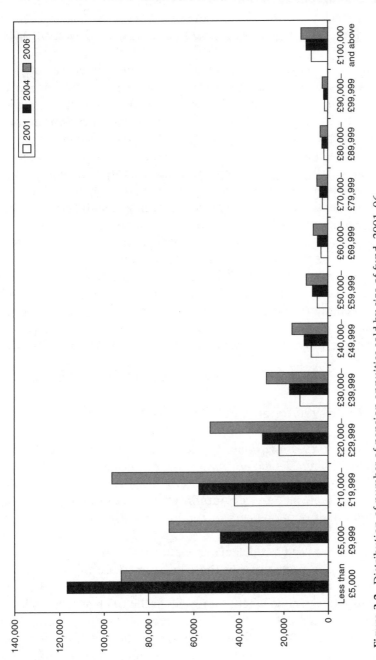

Figure 3.2. Distribution of number of pension annuities sold by size of fund, 2001–06

Source: Association of British Insurers.

annuity fund sizes from 2002 to 2006. The distribution is similar in every year, and is highly skewed. In 2006 around 42 per cent of pension funds were less than £10,000, and another 24 per cent were between £10,000 and £19,999.

An annuity purchase of £10,000 in 2006 would only provide an income of about £500 per year or £10 per week. Although many pensioners may have more than one pension and thus have total incomes much higher than this, the message from Figure 3.2 is that personal pensions may be insufficient to provide pensioner income, although this is due to a failure in the accumulation phase of the pension, rather than the decumulation phase. Oliver, Wyman, and Company (2001) identify a 'savings gap' of £27 billion between pension needs and pension provision in the UK. The Pensions Commission (2004) suggests that around 9 million people are making insufficient provision for retirement income.

Following A-day, individuals with a total pension fund of less than £15,000 were exempt from compulsion to annuitize (called the 'trivial commutation rule').[15] Figure 3.2 suggests that this rule applies to more than half of pension funds, but these account for only about 25 per cent of total premiums. Stark (2003) reports that 30 per cent of annuitants had more than one fund, so 25 per cent is only an upper bound for the proportion of new annuity business falling under this exemption.

3.4. Recent developments in UK financial markets

As we have discussed elsewhere, annuities in the UK are typically provided by life insurers, which are part of the much larger financial service industry, nearly all of which is regulated by the government (since 2002 through the Financial Services Authority). In this section we look at several important developments in the industry over the last 20 or so years.

This period has been a problematic one for UK financial services, particularly from the perspective of the consumer. Three major problems that have occurred have been mis-selling of personal pensions in the late 1980s, mis-selling of endowment mortgages in the 1990s and the collapse of Equitable Life in 2000. Although not a pension product, endowment mortgages were usually provided by life insurers during this period and they are therefore relevant in terms of the effect on consumer perceptions and on calls for political intervention. Furthermore, a series of mergers and acquisitions has resulted in some life insurers being owned by banks[16] or selling products through bank branches and it is thus appropriate to treat the financial service industry as a block rather than as separate components.

As documented in the previous section, personal pensions were introduced in 1987. This created the opportunity for workers to opt out of the State Earnings Related Pension Scheme (SERPS) to take up a private pension with a life insurer. For many people this opt-out was inappropriate because it would almost certainly make them worse off. However, salesmen for life insurers sold pensions to such people anyway, referred to as mis-selling. Mis-selling may have arisen for a variety of reasons, including salesmen being insufficiently trained and consumers having poor financial understanding. The fact that many salesmen were paid on a commission basis led to suspicion that they wilfully mis-sold pensions. The problem of mis-selling only became apparent much later, by which time it was too late for purchasers of personal pensions to take action to ensure they had a sufficiently large pension. According to the FSA (2002) by January 2002 over 1 million people had been offered payments totalling £9 billion to compensate for pensions mis-selling by a total of 345 firms.

The endowment mortgage problem was similarly due to consumers receiving bad advice or possibly incorrect information. FSA (2006) reported that ten firms had been fined for mis-selling and that compensation of £2.7 billion had been paid by September 2006. In the UK it was common to buy a house with an interest-only mortgage, which involved paying a bank or building society[17] interest throughout the term and then having to repay the entire principal on maturity of the mortgage. The final payment was achieved by making contributions to an investment fund called an endowment, usually with a life insurer recommended by the bank. So long as sufficiently high returns were made on the endowment policy there would be at least enough money to pay off the mortgage on redemption. However, the rates of return assumed for most of these mortgage policies assumed relatively high inflation and were consequently much higher than the nominal returns actually experienced during the 1990s. This resulted in endowments falling short of their target and homeowners being unable to repay their mortgages.[18]

The final problem to hit the life insurance industry was the collapse of the mutual life insurer Equitable Life. This is fully documented in *The Report of the Equitable Life Inquiry* (2004), usually referred to as the Penrose Report after the report's author.

From the 1950s to the 1980s Equitable Life sold pension products which contained a guaranteed minimum annuity rate, which was much lower than the actual annuity rate. This ceased to be the case as interest rates fell in the late 1980s and early 1990s. Ballotta and Haberman (2004) use simulations to suggest that the option value of the guarantee was positive from as early as 1991. In 1993 an Equitable Life actuary raised the issue, but no substantial steps were taken until 1998. Penrose (2004) suggests that financial reserves to deal with the value of guaranteed annuities should have been put in place in about 1994. Of course, since Equitable Life is a mutual society, doing this would have been a redistribution of funds away from pensioners without the guarantees.

Equitable Life's alternative solution was based on manipulating the size of the pension fund of those pensioners who had guaranteed annuities. Thus if an individual was guaranteed an annuity rate of $A_{(\text{g'teed})}$ and the actual annuity rate at the point of retirement was A_t, then it would be possible to honour the guarantee if the pension fund were adjusted down by a ratio of $A_t/A_{(\text{g'teed})}$. Equitable Life would be able to do this because the pension funds were invested in financial products referred to as 'with-profits'. These are long-term retail savings vehicles which smooth investment returns from year-to-year (and imply some redistribution between savers): every year an annual bonus is added to the size of the savings fund which is guaranteed by the life insurer, so that the consumer is insured against negative investment returns in subsequent periods. This results in the life insurer taking on more risk, so annual bonuses are typically set at a relatively low level and after $n - 1$ years of a savings product lasting n years, the cumulated annual bonuses are usually considerably less than would have been obtained by investing in another financial product. However, when the savings product matures the life insurer adds a terminal bonus, which results in the total return being good value. Equitable Life decided to pay lower terminal bonuses to pensioners who had guaranteed annuities, on the argument that the annuity guarantee was effectively a guarantee of a pension rather than a guaranteed annuity rate.

Equitable Life's decision was opposed by some policyholders. Confident that its position was correct, Equitable Life initiated legal action against a sample policyholder (Alan Hyman) resulting in a favourable decision for the life insurer in the High Court in September 1999. However, this was reversed on appeal in January 2000 and the highest court of appeal (the House of Lords) upheld this decision in August 2000. A consequence of this was that Equitable Life ceased offering new business: an attempt to sue its auditors (Ernst & Young) was eventually dropped.

One important finding of the Penrose report was ambiguity in the role taken by actuaries. Accordingly the government immediately set up a Review of the Actuarial Profession (Morris 2004, 2005). The interim report in 2004 was highly critical of the actuarial profession, on the grounds that the profession was insular, insufficiently transparent, and had failed to make explicit the risks involved in pension planning. One suggestion was that actuaries should lose their reserved role: that is the requirement that only a qualified actuary could value pension liabilities. The final report of 2005 was more conciliatory, but recommended a variety of changes in procedures including independent oversight of the profession.

The Morris Review was only one of a series of major government enquiries into various aspects of UK pensions and savings: it accompanied the Myners Report (2001) on institutional investment in the UK; the Sandler Review (2002) on medium and long-term saving in the UK; the Pickering Report (2002) on the simplification of pensions, and the Pensions Commission (2004, 2005, 2006). In addition, DWP and HMRC (2002) and HM Treasury (2006) explicitly consider the annuity market. The UK government, having also produced Green Papers on pensions in 1998 and 2002, and a White Paper in 2006, cannot be faulted for a deficiency of official enquiries into the whole area of pensions and savings. Together these provided a series of recommendations for changes in the way that the whole gamut of pensions should be provided and regulated.

Notes

1. Poterba (1997, 2005) also provides an introduction to the history of the annuity markets in the USA and Europe.
2. Figure based on authors' calculations and English annual wheat prices from the period 1259 to 1400 taken from Rogers (1866).
3. Another form of life insurance at this time was insuring lives of slaves lost in shipment from Africa to America: the fact that it attracted legislation suggests that this market was significant, but no data are available. In 1788 it became illegal to provide insurance for deaths of slaves jettisoned at sea and this was later extended to death by natural causes or ill treatment. With the abolition of the slave trade such forms of insurance became illegal in 1807 (Clark 1999).
4. In the post-war period the Board of Trade was renamed the Department for Trade and Industry: responsibility for regulation of insurance companies was transferred to the Financial Services Authority in 2002.

5. Evidence for this can be found for an example life assurer in Finkelstein and Poterba (2004), discussed in Chapter 9, Section 9.1. Crude calculations based on the Continuous Mortality Investigation Bureau reports confirm that this generalizes to other companies.

6. The Inland Revenue has now been subsumed into Her Majesty's Revenue and Customs (HMRC).

7. There is some overlap with our characterization and that of the 1994 World Bank Report *Averting the Old Age Crisis*, which defines a first pay-as-you-go pillar; a second compulsory and funded pillar; and a third voluntary and funded pillar. The most recent World Bank thinking has suggested two more pillars: a basic income and minimum health care (Holzmann and Hinz 2005). The first of these two additional pillars corresponds partly to the UK minimum income guarantee, although the UK MIG is means-tested.

8. Details of pension payments are taken from DWP A Guide to State Pensions, NP46, April 2005. National Insurance contributions are a tax on labour income: so long as contributions have been made for a sufficient number of years (regardless of the income earned) agents receive the BSP. Individuals not in work may still be credited with NI contributions: e.g., parents bringing up children full time or people who are registered unemployed.

9. The 1995 Pensions Act allows a pensioner to defer the conversion of the fund into an annuity up to the age of 75, and in the meantime 'draw-down' the fund to provide an income. There are limits on the speed at which the fund can be decumulated in this period. The administrative costs of drawdown means that it is only an option for the better off.

10. Annual Abstract of Statistics (2007: table 10.2).

11. Department for Social Security (1998). The DSS was later renamed the Department for Work and Pensions (DWP).

12. Department for Work and Pensions (2002).

13. The Pension Benefit Guaranty Corporation in the USA (founded 1974) and the Pension Protection Fund in the UK (founded 2004) partly insure employees against this possibility.

14. Pemberton (2006) argues that UK pensions policy has had a particular tendency to become highly complicated since governments usually introduce new legislation without resolving all of the problems of previous pensions. Of course, one reason for this is the difficulty in changing the terms of pensions (either in accrual or in payment) which are already in existence.

15. A trivial commutation rule existed before A-day, but only applied to much smaller pension funds.

16. Of the large life insurers selling annuities, Scottish Widows is owned by LloydsTSB. Cannon and Tonks (2004*b*) document mergers and takeovers of insurance companies over the second half of the twentieth century.

17. Building societies were heavily regulated mutual organizations, which raised money through retail deposits to lend for purchasing domestic property:

during this period regulation was relaxed and many societies were demutualized to become banks. In principle the primary obligation of mutual societies was to their members, but many of the building societies were as guilty of mis-selling as the banks.

18. There may have been a problem of poor financial literacy on behalf of consumers. Sandler (2002: 138) questions whether the standards of knowledge of some financial advisers is appropriate.

4

Modelling life expectancy

In this chapter we shall review the relevant actuarial background for the annuity market. This chapter is intended primarily for readers who do not have an actuarial training and readers with a knowledge of actuarial science may wish to skip many sections of this chapter or read it very briefly. We start with a brief review of actuarial notation before describing mortality data. We then consider how projections of life expectancy have evolved over the last 20 or so years.

4.1. Definitions, concepts, and actuarial notation

The mathematical notation used by economists and writers in the area of finance tends to follow certain norms (such as using i or r to denote the interest rate), but there is no completely uniform set of notation. The situation is rather different in actuarial practice where there is an agreed set of notation based upon that adopted at the Second International Actuarial Congress in London 1898 and revised in the Third Congress of Paris 1900. The issue of further revision was raised at the Eleventh Congress in 1937 and after the hiatus of the Second World War this was adopted in the UK in 1950 (Institute of Actuaries 1949). The presence of such a consistent notation allows a wide variety of life insurance products to be summarized very briefly.

For example, the present value of an annuity paying £1 per year starting one year hence is denoted by the symbol a in actuarial notation, but then qualified with additional subscripts to determine the form of annuity. A term-certain annuity is denoted by putting a ⌐-shaped bracket around the variable representing the term of the annuity, while a life annuity has no such bracket:

$a_{\overline{n}|}$ Present value of a term-certain annuity lasting n years.

a_x Expected present value of a life annuity for someone
       currently aged x.

With a constant interest rate of r a term-certain annuity (really just a specific form of bond) can be rewritten straightforwardly as

$$_{r}a_{\overline{n}|} = \sum_{j=1}^{n} (1+r)^{-j} \qquad (4.1)$$

where the additional subscript denotes the interest rate. More complicated formulae would be needed for the expected present value of a life annuity where the payments are conditional on the probability of being alive. Similarly q_x is the probability of someone aged x dying in the next year and $p_x \equiv 1 - q_x$ is the probability of them living for at least one more year. In what follows we shall not stick slavishly to actuarial notation and will write present value formulae such as these in full.

In these definitions, notice that 'mortality' is used to refer to the probability of dying. 'Morbidity' is used to refer to the different concept of the probability of becoming seriously or terminally ill. The latter concept is important for health insurance, particularly long-term health care insurance.

From these definitions it is possible to calculate other relevant values: the probability of someone currently aged x still being alive j years hence (the survival probability) is

$$s_{x,j} = p_x \times p_{x+1} \times \cdots \times p_{x+j-1} \equiv \prod_{i=0}^{j-1} p_{x+i} \qquad (4.2)$$

and the probability of living to age j exactly is

$$P_{x,j} \equiv p_x \times p_{x+1} \times \cdots \times p_{x+j-1} \times (1 - p_{x+j}) \equiv (1 - p_{x+j}) \prod_{i=0}^{j-1} p_{x+i} \qquad (4.3)$$

This implicitly assumes a discrete time model, where individuals' deaths are potentially at one-year intervals. For expositional purposes we shall use this approach for nearly all of the book. The continuous-time analogue is the probability of dying at a point in time, usually denoted μ_x and referred to as the 'mortality'.

Given the survival probabilities we can now define life expectancy. A simple approximation can be obtained from equation (4.2): if we ignore

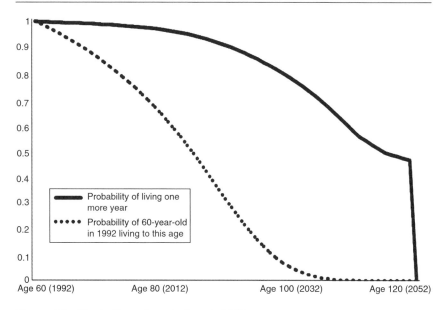

Figure 4.1. Illustration of survival probabilities

the fact that someone can die at any point in the year, then the life expectancy would be

$$l_x \approx \sum_{j=1}^{\infty} s_{x,j} = \sum_{j=1}^{\infty} j P_{x,j} \tag{4.4}$$

(a more accurate formula would be obtained using the continuous-time analogue). These concepts are illustrated in Figure 4.1, where we have used forecasted mortalities for male pensioners in the UK: the projection method assumes that no one lives beyond 120 years (we shall discuss these projections below). Life expectancy for a male pensioner aged 60 with these probabilities was just under 24 years (i.e. they are expected to live to age 83 years, 11 months). The most likely—or modal—age at which this person will die, however, is the value for which $P_{x,j}$ is maximized (this is the point at which the survival probability curve, $s_{x,j}$, switches from being concave to the origin to being convex to the origin, sometimes called the 'Lexis point') and this is about 89 years.

It is possible to supplement life expectancy with a summary statistic representing the variability of life length—for example the range of ages over which one would be most likely to die might be decreasing. This phenomenon is referred to as rectangularization and is illustrated stylistically

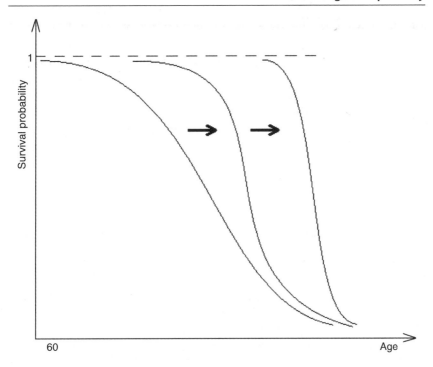

Figure 4.2. Illustration of the rectangularization hypothesis

in Figure 4.2, which shows that the S-shaped curve gets steadily steeper over time. One possible rationale for the rectangularization hypothesis is that life expectancy is increasing but there is a maximum age to which people live and this is not increasing (or is increasing more slowly than life expectancy). The combination of these two effects would result in a compression of ages at which people were likely to die. However there is no reason to believe that there is a relatively constant maximum age and we view changes in the shape of the survival curve as a purely empirical matter.

Using long-run historical data from Sweden, Japan, and the USA, Wilmoth and Horiuchi (1999) find clear evidence of rectangularization when analysing deaths at all ages in the period 1870–1950. This was predominantly because infant mortality fell dramatically, but also because mortality was falling at all ages, including those pre-retirement. Since 1950, however, they find no quantitatively important changes in the variability of life length and hence no evidence for continued rectangularization. In Chapter 7 we shall see that the variation in life length is not a useful statistic in making economic decisions about annuity purchase and for this reason we do not explore this line of analysis any further.

We now turn to how these probabilities can be used to price annuities. Consider an annuity which pays £1 annually while the annuitant is alive (starting one year hence): if the annuitant dies as little as a day before the due payment date then no additional payment is made to the estate.[1] The probability of an annuity payment being made is then equal to the probability of the annuitant being alive and assuming a constant interest rate r the expected present value of the annuity stream is

$$_r a_x \equiv \frac{s_{x,1}}{1+r} + \frac{s_{x,2}}{(1+r)^2} + \cdots = \sum_{j=1}^{\infty} \frac{s_{x,j}}{(1+r)^j} \qquad (4.5)$$

This assumes that there is just one interest rate, but in practice there is a range of interest rates available at any point in time. Interest rates usually depend upon the timing, or term to maturity, of the payments of the financial assets. Information on the full set of interest rates is called the term structure of interest rates and a graph of the interest rate plotted against term is called the yield curve.

We illustrate this with a numerical example. A financial asset promising to pay just £1 in one year's time might be trading for 90 pence, in which case the one-year interest rate r_1 would be defined by

$$1 + r_1 \equiv \frac{1}{0.9} \approx 1.111 \qquad (4.6)$$

and the one-year interest rate would be about 11.1 per cent. A financial asset promising to pay just £1 in two years' time might be trading for 78 pence, in which case the two-year interest rate (expressed as the return per year) would be defined implicitly by

$$(1 + r_2)^2 \equiv \frac{1}{0.78} \Rightarrow 1 + r_2 = \sqrt{\frac{1}{0.78}} \approx 1.132 \qquad (4.7)$$

and hence would be 13.2 per cent. An alternative way of writing the two-year rate introduces the concept of a forward rate $f_{1,2}$ using the formula

$$(1 + r_2)^2 \equiv (1 + r_1)(1 + f_{1,2}) \Rightarrow 1 + f_{1,2} = \frac{(1 + r_2)^2}{(1 + r_1)} = \frac{1/0.78}{1/0.9} \approx 1.154 \qquad (4.8)$$

Since we know it is possible to earn 11.1 per cent for one year, earning 13.2 per cent for two years corresponds to earning 15.4 per cent in the second year. Both the basic interest rates r_i and the forward rates $f_{i,j}$ are more complicated to calculate in practice because most financial assets consist of promises to make multiple payments at different points in the future. However, agencies such as the Bank of England calculate and publish the term structure regularly, so the information is readily available.[2]

With this information, we may rewrite the expected present value of the annuity as

$$\frac{s_{x,1}}{(1+r_1)} + \frac{s_{x,2}}{(1+r_2)^2} + \cdots = \sum_{j=1}^{\infty} \left(1+r_j\right)^{-j} s_{x,j} \tag{4.9}$$

When divided by the annuity premium (or 'consideration'), this gives a measure of the value of the annuity (in financial rather than utility terms) compared with the price: this measure is widely referred to as the 'money's worth': in a perfectly competitive market with no transactions or administrative costs, this would be equal to unity.

$$\text{Money's worth} \equiv \frac{\sum_{j=1}^{\infty} \left(1+r_j\right)^{-j} s_{x,j}}{\text{Premium}} \tag{4.10}$$

Typically the money's worth will be less than or equal to one: we shall discuss this measure in more detail in Chapter 5.

As we have seen in Chapter 2, it is also possible to buy annuities where the payments are either escalating or inflation-protected. The value of an escalating annuity where the first payment is £1 and thereafter payments rise by g per cent per year requires a straightforward extension to the formula in equation (4.9):

$$\frac{s_{x,1}}{(1+r_1)} + \frac{s_{x,2}\,(1+g)}{(1+r_2)^2} + \frac{s_{x,3}\,(1+g)^2}{(1+r_3)^3} + \cdots = \sum_{j=1}^{\infty} \left(1+r_j\right)^{-j} (1+g)^{j-1} s_{x,j} \tag{4.11}$$

The valuation of an inflation-protected annuity is more complicated, since future inflation is unknown. In the UK and the USA, it is possible to purchase government bonds where all of the payments are automatically adjusted for inflation.[3] This means that there is a real interest rate available, which makes it possible to fully insure the annuity provider from inflation risk. The real interest rate would be less than the nominal interest rate, since, approximately, it equals the nominal interest rate minus expected inflation. To emphasize that we are using a real interest rate we denote this in the rest of this section as $\tilde{r}_j$, so that the formula for an inflation-linked annuity is simply

$$\sum_{j=1}^{\infty} \left(1+\tilde{r}_j\right)^{-j} s_{x,j} \tag{4.12}$$

Where no inflation-linked bonds are available, then it is necessary to form expectations about future inflation. If we write expected inflation in j periods' time as π_j^e and use r_j to mean the nominal interest rate then the expected net present value of an inflation-linked annuity is approximately[4]

$$\frac{s_{x,1}\left(1+\pi_1^e\right)}{(1+r_1)} + \frac{s_{x,2}\left(1+\pi_1^e\right)\left(1+\pi_2^e\right)}{(1+r_2)^2} + \cdots = \sum_{j=1}^{\infty}\left(1+r_j\right)^{-j} s_{x,j} \prod_{k=0}^{j-1}\left(1+\pi_k^e\right)$$

(4.13)

In practice valuation of annuities requires more detailed mortality information than p_x because annuity payments are often made more frequently than on an annual basis: when forming a pension, monthly payments would be more convenient for many annuitants. As the frequency of annuity payment increases, it becomes convenient to value the annuity using the continuous-time measure of mortality μ_x.

The interest rates in the denominator of the annuity valuation formulae have been taken to be the relevant government risk-free interest rates. Life insurers should match assets and liabilities, and since their liabilities are certain, they should be matched with low risk assets such as government bonds (Exley, Mehta, and Smith 1997). In addition, life insurers are regulated, and the regulatory system requires that they have sufficient resources to honour their promised payments. As we will see in Chapter 10, annuity providers have increasingly backed their annuity payments with high-grade corporate bonds and even riskier assets, which we can see from Figure 2.3 have a slightly higher rate of return than government bonds to allow for credit risk. However, when life insurers value such risky assets, they adjust their rates of return for risk and the resulting risk-adjusted rates are usually very similar to the government bond yields.

4.2. Mortality data in the UK

In this section we illustrate the range of mortality data that exist. We do this by describing pensioner mortality data from the UK. Other than the USA, no other country has such a rich variety of data for such a long time period.[5] For various reasons, some countries do not have their own mortality data, or have obtained it only recently, and use mortality data from other countries, possibly with adjustments. For example,

Canadian actuaries tended to use US data until recently since there was no Canadian inter-company collection of annuitant mortality data (Howard 2006).[6]

We distinguish pensioner mortality from population mortality because people with pensions need not be representative of the population as a whole. Pensions can be divided into private sector pensions—whose mortality data is analysed by the Institute of Actuaries—and UK government pensions—whose mortality is analysed by the Government Actuaries Department (GAD).[7] Mortality tables are usually divided by certain categories: for example, men and women experience such different rates of mortality that it is usual to treat them separately.

Since 1924 the Continuous Mortality Investigation Bureau of the Institute of Actuaries has collected UK data on mortality for both life insurance and pensioners/annuitants from major life insurers and pools the data.[8] An extensive discussion of the CMI Committee's methods can be found in Forfar, McCutcheon, and Wilkie (1988) on which we draw heavily in this section. The CMI publications include four sorts of material:

1. Summaries of the entire data are published for every quadrennium (four-year period): the more detailed data available to the CMI Bureau is not published to preserve anonymity. These data are compared with previous quadrennia and existing projections of mortality to see whether mortality improvements are greater or less than might have been expected. These comparisons are typically presented as the ratio of actual to expected deaths (A/E ratios), which are comparisons of actual deaths compared to expected deaths from the 'standard tables'.

2. Graduations of mortality experience are published more infrequently based on statistical analysis of the full data-set. A graduation is a smooth curve fitted to the actual data (we discuss this in Section 4.3).

3. Standard Tables containing both graduations and suggested projections of mortality. However, in the most recent set of mortality tables (the 00 series) the CMI has not committed itself to any single set of projections.[9]

4. In the last few years the CMI has also published articles on developments in actuarial methodology.

The results of the CMI were published in the *Journal of the Institute of Actuaries* until the 1970s and thereafter in individual CMI Reports: more recently CMI Standard Tables have been accompanied by a software

Table 4.1. CMI studies of UK pensioner mortality

Mortality experience	Report	Publication date
1967–70	CMIR 1	1973
1971–74	CMIR 3	1978
1975–78	CMIR 5	1981
1979–82	CMIR 8	1986
1983–86	CMIR 11	1991
Revision of 1983–86	CMIR 13	1993
1987–90	CMIR 14	1995
1991–94	CMIR 16	1998
1995–98	CMIR 19	2000
1999–2002	CMIR 21	2004

package for calculating certain functions based on the mortality data. Since 2000 the CMI has also produced Working Papers to supplement the Reports: part of the reason for this is to disseminate information in a more timely manner and also because Reports have a semi-official status (e.g. being recognized by the regulatory authorities) and Working Papers are a means of promoting discussion without putting a formal *imprimatur* on the analysis therein. The relevant tables for the sub-periods in our sample are described in Table 4.1.

The life insurance and pensioner/annuitant data are treated separately since experience has shown that they differ from each other as well as from the overall UK population—a phenomenon referred to as a selection effect. This is unsurprising since people who purchase pensions and annuities may be expected to be disproportionately long-lived (either because they are richer than the population as a whole or because they have private information about their mortality).[10] Occasionally additional information is published on additional classes of risk, such as smokers or people in Self-Invested Personal Pension plans (SIPPs). Also on an infrequent basis the CMI provides some information showing how mortality experience differs between life insurers.

Apart from distinguishing male mortality from female mortality, the CMI separates the mortality of lives and amounts, unless insufficient data are available. Not only is the life expectancy of pensioners quite different from that of the population as a whole, but there is substantial variation by purchase price: unsurprisingly since we know that wealth is correlated with longevity and size of pension is likely to be correlated with total wealth. Data measured by lives (more strictly policies) is a simple average of mortality of all pensioners: this is probably a good measure of a 'typical' pensioner's mortality. Amounts data is weighted by the size of policy—since this is strongly affected by a relatively few rich individuals it is less good as a measure of the typical pensioner, but it is the appropriate measure for assessing life insurers' profitability.

A further complication is that annuitants' mortality is often lower in the period immediately following the purchase of an annuity: for practical purposes the relevant period is often taken to be one year. For example, actuaries would distinguish between:

1. the probability of dying for a 65-year-old who has purchased an annuity in the last year (called the select period and notated $q_{[65]}$);
2. the probability of dying for a 65-year-old who purchased an annuity more than one year ago (called the ultimate mortality and notated q_{65}).

The fact that $q_{[x]} < q_x$ in some mortality tables is probably because individuals have more information about their chances of dying in the near future than the distant future and those with a high likelihood of dying soon avoid annuitization.[11]

After allowing for splitting the data by males and females and by lives and amounts, the CMI publishes data for the following sets of pensioners:

Immediate Annuities (I), referring to annuitants who have purchased voluntarily in the purchased life annuity market.

Retirement Annuity Contracts (RAC), referring to annuitants in an early version of personal pensions introduced in 1957, primarily designed for self-employed workers. This was so that the self-employed could receive the tax privileges available to employees in company pension schemes. This is a subset of the compulsory-purchase market.

Personal Pensions (PP), referring to the personal pensions introduced in 1987 and for which the data-set is small until about 1995 (most such pensions are still in accrual rather than in payment). These data would also apply to the compulsory-purchase market.

Life Office Pensioners (P), which are company pension schemes administered by life insurers and for which the most comprehensive data are available. These are only a subset of the company pensions in the UK—small firms that are unable or unwilling to run their own pension schemes contract their administration to life insurers. Strictly speaking these data are irrelevant for the annuity market but Finkelstein and Poterba (2002) suggest using them to measure compulsory purchase annuitant mortality. When Finkelstein and Poterba were writing the PP mortality data were

Year	60	61	62	63	64	65	66	67	68	69
1990	✓	✓	✓	✓	✓	✓	✓	✓	✓	✓
1991	✓	✓	✓	✓	✓	✓	✓	✓	✓	✓
1992	✓	✓	✓	✓	✓	✓	✓	✓	✓	✓
1993	✓	✓	✓	✓	✓	✓	✓	✓	✓	✓
1994	✓	✓	✓	✓	✓	✓	✓	✓	✓	✓
1995										
1996										
1997										
1998										

Figure 4.3. Period and cohort life tables

unavailable and the RAC are not available by amounts. With the benefit of hindsight the PP data resemble the P data more than the RAC data.

Self-Administered Pensions (SAP), which are company pension schemes, typically for large companies, which are run by the company without recourse to life offices (although they would be advised by actuarial consultancy firms).[12] Although the number of lives covered is roughly double the lives covered by life office pensioners, the CMI has started collecting these data only very recently so it is not yet possible to project trends from these data.

Summary statistics of some of these data are shown in Table 4.2, which illustrates the small size of the voluntary annuity market, the relatively large size of the RAC market and the phenomenal growth of the PP market. The table shows the number of annuitants by annuity type and the associated crude death rates for each group (which clearly depend largely on the age composition of the exposed to risk).

A final consideration is whether mortality data is a period or a cohort life table. Clearly someone aged x in period t will be aged $x + 1$ in period $t + 1$. Life tables usually report the mortality on a period basis, so that mortality is displayed for people of different ages at one point in time: hence it includes people born in different years, belonging to different cohorts.

This difference is illustrated in Figure 4.3, which shows an extract of a life table for ages 60–69 for years 1990–98. Suppose data are available on mortality for years up to 1994 (as it was for the CMI 92 Standard Tables): data is available for all cells containing a tick (✓). The period mortalities are obtained by reading a horizontal row in this table, which clearly involves taking data for people of different cohorts.

Table 4.2. CMI estimates of numbers of annuitants and death rates for various categories of annuity types

	Males				Females			
	1987–90	1991–94	1995–98	1999–2002	1987–90	1991–94	1995–98	1999–2002
Panel A: Immediate annuitants								
Exposed to risk (000)	50	40	31	36	101	74	52	53
Crude death rate	0.081	0.075	0.074	0.072	0.076	0.082	0.086	0.082
Panel B: Retirement annuities in accrual								
Exposed to risk (000)	6,358	4,511	3,795	3,880	1,097	829	672	679
Crude death rate	0.003	0.003	0.003	0.003	0.002	0.002	0.002	0.002
Panel C: Retirement annuities in payment								
Exposed to risk (000)	648	641	638	893	134	151	156	291
Crude death rate	0.035	0.032	0.03	0.033	0.018	0.018	0.016	0.016
Panel D: Personal pensions in accrual								
Exposed to risk (000)	1,332	3,831	6,043	8,563	593	1,883	2,998	4,327
Crude death rate	0.001	0.002	0.002	0.002	0	0.001	0.001	0.001
Panel E: Personal pensions in payment								
Exposed to risk (000)	2	50	207	692	0.6	20	84	294
Crude death rate	0.013	0.011	0.012	0.014	0.003	0.006	0.005	0.006

Source: CMI 21 (2004).

Someone born in 1930 and hence aged 65 in 1995 would experience mortality shown by the cells with the dashed edges, not all of which are known in 1995. In pricing an annuity for this person, a life insurer could use the data available up to 1994, since that contains mortalities of people of very similar ages and similar cohorts. However, that would only be appropriate if the 1930 cohort were similar to cohorts from the late 1920s. If there were evidence that cohorts born in 1926 and earlier were substantially different from those born in 1927, then the life insurer would find mortality data from the pre-1927 cohorts less useful: these cells are shaded grey in the table. The appropriate method of mortality projection requires knowledge of whether mortality is primarily dependent upon age-and-period or age-and-cohort (or some more complicated combination). We turn to this in the next section.

4.3. Patterns of mortality

In this section we consider how to describe the relationship between mortality and age. Except at very young ages (in the few years after birth) mortality rises with age and we shall confine most of our discussion to the mortality of the relatively elderly.

Forfar, McCutcheon, and Wilkie (1988) provide a comprehensive review of mortality estimation techniques up to the 1980s. The simplest scenario is to estimate mortality for a group of people of the same age. Suppose we observe R annuitants (R is the 'exposed to risk'), all aged exactly x at the start of the year t, and the number that die within the year is D. The obvious estimator of $q(t, x)$ is just $D(t, x)/R(t, x)$ which, if the deaths are independent from each other, is the maximum likelihood estimator and has variance $q(1-q)R$.

One problem with this approach is that the data used by the CMI will double- (or triple- or more) count those individuals who have more than one policy. Fortunately this has no implications for estimation of the mortality figures, but it does affect the variance of the estimator, the standard errors and any statistical tests.

In practice we usually have data for groups of individuals of different ages at different points of time. This means that we can use information from ages close to x and time periods close to t in our estimation $q(t, x)$. There are three possibilities that we could consider. First, mortality typically changes slowly over time. For example the mortality of a 65-year-old in 2006 (i.e. someone born in 1941) is similar to the mortality of a 65-year-old in 2007 (i.e. someone born in 1942). Second, mortality is usually similar for similar ages. For example the mortality of a 65-year-old in 2006 (i.e. someone born in 1941) is similar to the mortality of a 66-year-old in 2006 (i.e. someone born in 1940). Finally, mortality usually changes slowly for a cohort of people as they get older. For example the mortality of a 65-year-old in 2006 (i.e. someone born in 1941) is similar to the mortality of a 66-year-old in 2007 (i.e. someone also born in 1941). It is possible that all three are true, but we may wish to give emphasis to one or other of these smoothing assumptions.

CMI Standard Tables typically emphasized the second sort of smoothness. For a given quadrennium of data (i.e. data for a given short interval of time) a smooth curve was fitted, a technique referred to as graduation (Forfar, McCutcheon, and Wilkie 1988). It is not possible to fit a linear relationship between mortality and age, since the relationship is clearly non-linear, so it is necessary to choose a functional form which is both flexible and capable of delivering the correct 'shape'. A simple formula was used in the a(55) Standard Tables which analysed data up to 1950 and were widely used by actuaries until about 1980 for mortality projections:

$$q_x = \frac{a_1 + a_2 \exp\{a_3 x\}}{1 - a_4 \exp\{a_3 x\}} \qquad (4.14)$$

A more flexible functional form used from the 1970s onwards was referred to the Gompertz–Makeham function, defined as

$$GM^{r,s}(x) \equiv \sum_{i=1}^{r} a_i x^{i-1} + \exp\left\{\sum_{i=1}^{s} a_i x^{i-1}\right\}, \quad r > 0, \ s > 0$$

$$GM^{0,s}(x) \equiv \exp\left\{\sum_{i=1}^{s} a_i x^{i-1}\right\}, \quad s > 0 \qquad (4.15)$$

$$GM^{r,0}(x) \equiv \sum_{i=1}^{r} a_i x^{i-1}, \quad r > 0$$

The GM formula is just the sum of a polynomial in x and the exponent of a further polynomial: experience shows that only relatively low power polynomials are needed to fit the data. Since the GM function can take any value it is only suitable for modelling μ_x; for variables that must lie in the range [0,1], such as q_x or m_x it is often preferable to use the Logistic Gompertz–Makeham function

$$LGM^{r,s}(x) \equiv \frac{GM^{r,s}(x)}{1 + GM^{r,s}(x)}, \qquad (4.16)$$

which always lies in the appropriate range. Estimation of the parameters can be undertaken by maximum likelihood methods; it is possible to check the validity of the graduation by testing for an absence of residual correlation and an optimal choice of r and s can be made using the Akaike criterion or some similar measure: larger values of r and s obviously lead to slightly better fit, but at the expense of loss of degrees of freedom and the Akaike criterion is just one way of determining a trade-off between these two.

The disadvantage of this approach is that it emphasizes smoothness across ages and completely ignores the possibility of smoothness over time or by cohort. An alternative approach was suggested by Lee and Carter (1992) who proposed that mortality $m(t, x)$ in year t for age x was simply

$$\ln(m(t, x)) = \beta_0(x) + \beta_\kappa(x)\kappa(t) \tag{4.17}$$

where $\beta_0(x)$ and $\beta_\kappa(x)$ are two functions of age and $\kappa(t)$ is a function of time: all three of these functions need to be estimated. In principle both of these functions could be estimated parametrically using functional forms such as those described above. However, completely flexible non-parametric functions could also be estimated and it is common to do this in practice.

Suppose we have data for exposed to risk $R(t, x)$ and actual deaths $D(t, x)$ for 60- to 85-year-olds for the period 1991–2000 inclusive, so that we have a total of 260 observations. Clearly we could estimate 260 death rates for each age in each year using $D(t, x)/R(t, x)$ as described above, but this would make no use of the structure of the data. Using the Lee–Carter method both of the functions $\beta_0(x)$ and $\beta_\kappa(x)$ would be estimated as 26 parameters [one each for the 26 ages $\beta_0(60), \beta_0(61), \ldots, \beta_0(85)$ and $\beta_\kappa(60), \beta_\kappa(61), \ldots, \beta_\kappa(85)$] and $\kappa(t)$ needs 10 parameters (for the 10 years), making a total of 62 parameters to be estimated. However, consider the alternative parameter functions defined as follows:

$$\begin{aligned}\tilde{\beta}_0(x) &= \beta_0(x) + \theta\beta_\kappa(x) \\ \tilde{\beta}_\kappa(x) &= \beta_\kappa(x)/\varphi \quad \varphi \neq 0 \\ \tilde{\kappa}(t) &= \varphi\{\kappa(t) - \theta\}\end{aligned} \tag{4.18}$$

Clearly if equation (4.17) is true then it is also true that

$$\ln(m(t, x)) = \tilde{\beta}_0(x) + \tilde{\beta}_\kappa(x)\tilde{\kappa}(t) \tag{4.19}$$

and thus not all of the parameters are identified. Trivial re-parameterizations of this type can be avoided by using restrictions such as

$$\sum_x \beta_\kappa(x) = 1 \qquad \sum_t \kappa(t) = 0 \qquad (4.20)$$

and thus the total number of parameters to be estimated is only 60, clearly feasible with 260 observations.

A consequence of the Lee–Carter model is that changes in log-mortality at different ages are perfectly correlated. To see this note that from equation (4.17) the change in log-mortality is

$$\Delta \ln(m(t, x)) \equiv \ln(m(t, x)) - \ln(m(t - 1, x)) = \beta_\kappa(x) \{\kappa(t) - \kappa(t - 1)\} \qquad (4.21)$$

One of our identifying restrictions is $\sum_t \kappa(t) = 0$, so the sample variance and covariance of the change in log-mortality at ages x and y are

$$\begin{aligned}
\mathrm{var}\left[\Delta \ln(m(t, x))\right] &= \left\{\beta_\kappa(x)\{\kappa(t) - \kappa(t - 1)\}\right\}^2 \\
\mathrm{var}\left[\Delta \ln(m(t, y))\right] &= \left\{\beta_\kappa(y)\{\kappa(t) - \kappa(t - 1)\}\right\}^2 \\
\mathrm{cov}\left[\Delta \ln(m(t, x)), \Delta \ln(m(t, y))\right] &= \beta_\kappa(x)\beta_\kappa(y)\{\{\kappa(t) - \kappa(t - 1)\}\}^2
\end{aligned} \qquad (4.22)$$

from which it follows that $\Delta \ln(m(t, x))$ and $\Delta \ln(m(t, y))$ are perfectly correlated. This is clearly a very strong assumption and one which is not observed in the data. For this reason several generalizations to the Lee–Carter model have been proposed.

Renshaw and Haberman (2006) propose introducing a cohort effect so that the model becomes

$$\ln(m(t, x)) = \beta_0(x) + \beta_\kappa(x)\kappa(t) + \beta_\gamma(x)\gamma(t - x) \qquad (4.23)$$

In our illustrative example of 60- to 85-year-olds for the period 1991–2000, there would be a total of 35 cohorts with people present born in every year from 1906 to 1940 inclusive and hence there would be 123 parameters in total. However, to identify these parameters it is necessary to make four restrictions so the number of free parameters to be estimated would only be 119. A simpler version of this model is

$$\ln(m(t, x)) = \beta_0(x) + \kappa(t) + \gamma(t - x) \qquad (4.24)$$

Currie (2006) estimates this model using a technique called P-splines so that the functions $\beta_0(x)$, $\kappa(t)$, and $\gamma(t - x)$ are relatively smooth, but it is also possible to estimate a full set of parameters (71 in our example) as is done by Cairns et al. (2007).

Building on Cairns, Blake, and Dowd (2006), Cairns et al. (2007) suggest a further set of alternatives based on a logistic function such as

$$\frac{q(t, x)}{1 + q(t, x)} = \kappa_0(t) + \kappa_1(t) \times \{x - \bar{x}\} \tag{4.25}$$

Further generalizations allow for cohort effects and greater curvature in age. One of the problems in comparing these models is that they contain vastly different numbers of parameters and models with more parameters are always likely to fit data better through over-fitting. Using the BIC criterion to overcome this problem, Cairns et al. (2007) find a strong cohort effect in population data for England and Wales, with a steep fall in mortality for cohorts born just before 1930 (there are other cohort effects, but this is the most important for age groups purchasing annuities now). However, while the cohort effect is statistically significant, Cairns et al. (2007) report that the effect on annuity prices is economically small: using the model without cohort effects from equation (4.25) the value of a life annuity for a man aged 65 was 11.449 (an annuity rate of 8.73 per cent) while models with cohort effects suggested annuity values of 11.451 and 11.427 (8.73 and 8.75 per cent respectively). Similar analysis on US data suggested no systematic cohort effect at all.

4.4. Projecting mortality in the future

There are two approaches that can be used to project future mortality. First, one could rely upon the smoothness of mortality over time and age discussed in the previous section and use various methods of extrapolation. We shall devote most of our discussion to this approach since it is currently the one most widely used in practice.

Alternatively, one could estimate causal models for different groups of people using explanatory factors such as current health status, whether or not people are smokers, diet, and—although this will be more important only in the future—genetic information. Since there is potentially a lot of such information available for people on the verge of buying an annuity, this could be used to estimate future mortality both for a group of people or even for individuals (allowing for personalized annuity rates).

One of the problems with a causal model is identifying the causal effects because many of the possible explanatory variables are highly correlated and there are also issues of reverse causation. Perhaps unsurprisingly, there is a strong correlation between life expectancy and wealth at an individual level (Attanasio and Hoynes 2000; Attanasio and Emmerson 2003). However, it is unclear whether individuals are unhealthy because they are poor or whether they are poor because they use up wealth to compensate for bad health. Furthermore, it is uncertain whether the effect on individuals' health is due to absolute or relative wealth. Using data from the British Retirement Survey, Attanasio and Emmerson (2003) find that there is evidence that at least some of the causality runs from wealth to health, but it is impossible to determine whether this is absolute or relative wealth. The latter question is crucial for making projections about future mortality: with positive economic growth, absolute wealth is rising over time, but at the same time both the UK and the USA have experienced large increases in inequality, so that many individuals are experiencing falling relative wealth. Since one cannot obtain clear identification of which sort of wealth determines mortality, the effect on future mortality is ambiguous.

Alternative causal models use other possible explanatory variables such as smoking. But Adda and Cornaglia (2006) observe that smoking is correlated with wealth and there are likely to be other correlations of this sort (perhaps including diet). So again there are issues of both identification and reverse causation.

For this reason we now return to extrapolative models of mortality. Of course, it is well known that extrapolation is often a superior form of projection for more complicated methods in fields other than demography. Many economic forecasts rely upon some degree of extrapolation as does weather forecasting. Surveys of the literature agree that the best means of projection is based on a log-linear (i.e. multiplicative) extrapolation of mortality (Benjamin and Soliman 1993, quoted in Willets 1999; Wong-Fupuy and Haberman 2004).

Details of CMI Standard Tables are summarized in Table 4.3: the two most recent that included projections are the 80 and 92 Tables (so-called because they extrapolated from base years of 1980 and 1992 respectively). For base year B they both used the following deterministic formulae:

$$q(t + B, x) = RF(t, x)\, q(B, x)$$
$$RF(t, x) \equiv a(x) + [1 - a(x)] \times [1 - f(x)]^{t/20} \tag{4.26}$$

The interpretation of these formulae is as follows: mortality rates would eventually converge to $q(\infty, x) = a(x)\, q(B, x)$ so that $a(x)$ can be interpreted as the limiting reduction in mortality. In both tables it was assumed that mortality rates of people aged 110 and above would remain constant

Table 4.3. Summary of UK Life Tables

Table	Publication	Publication date	Based on data up to year
80 Table	CMIR 10	1990	1982
92 Table	CMIR 17	1999	1994
92 Table interim adjustment	CMI WP 1	2002	1999
00 Table	CMIR WP 22	2006	2002
Stochastic projections	CMI WP 25	2007	2003[a]

[a] This was based not on mortality of annuitants but of insured lives (i.e. life insurance data).

[so that $a(110) = 1$], while the limiting mortality rates of 60-year-olds would fall to either half their initial value (1980 Table) or 0.13 of their present value (1992 Table). Between ages 60 and 110 the limiting reduction factor was linearly interpolated so that

$$a(x) = \begin{cases} c & x < 60 \\ 1 + (1 - c)\left(\dfrac{x - 110}{50}\right) & 60 \leq x \leq 110 \\ 1 & x > 110 \end{cases} \tag{4.27}$$

1980 Table: $c = 0.5$ 1992 Table: $c = 0.13$

While $a(x)$ determines the limiting reduction in mortality, the function $f(x)$ determines the speed of convergence to this limit. In the 1980 Table this is constant, while in the 1992 Table it is age dependent:

1980 Table: $f(x) = 0.6$

$$\text{1992 Table:} \quad f(x) = \begin{cases} 0.55 & x < 60 \\ \dfrac{0.55 \times (110 - x) + 0.29 \times (x - 60)}{50} & 60 \leq x \leq 110 \\ k & x > 110 \end{cases} \tag{4.28}$$

Both of these tables viewed mortality as being based on age and time and thus ignore the cohort effects discussed in the previous section. Willets (1999) first drew attention to the apparent discontinuous drop in mortality in cohorts born around 1926, based on life insurance (rather than pensioner) data and this led to UK actuaries to begin to look for more sophisticated extrapolative models.

In the first instance, the Institute of Actuaries published in 2002 a set of 'interim adjustments' to the 92 Tables based on the Male life insurance

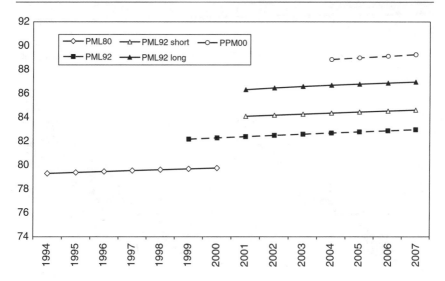

Figure 4.4. Revisions to life expectancy in the UK

Source: Authors' calculations based on various CMI publications.

mortality data (lives rather than amounts).[13] The size of the revision depended upon the size and dating of the cohort effect and this cohort effect was difficult to estimate precisely on the data available. Accordingly three different assumptions were made and three corresponding sets of revisions produced, called respectively the 'short', 'medium', and 'long' cohort assumptions.[14] This was the first time in the UK that a range of mortality projections were published rather than just a central projection.

To give some idea of the magnitude of the revisions in the CMI tables, the life expectancy of a 65-year-old man (based on the projected mortalities) is illustrated in the Figure 4.4, based on the 80 and 92 Tables, the interim amendments. Also for comparison we show the life expectancy based on the personal pensioner (PPM) tables, based on the 2000 base tables and projected forward using the long cohort reduction factors from 2000 onwards.

Alongside the concerns raised by the possibility of substantial cohort effects, more recent research has concentrated on the uncertainty of the projections. One immediate consequence of this was that the 00 Tables (published in 2006) did not contain any suggested projections into the future at all.

Dowd, Blake, and Cairns (2007) suggest a possible way of presenting uncertainty about future mortality by using fan charts. These are diagrams

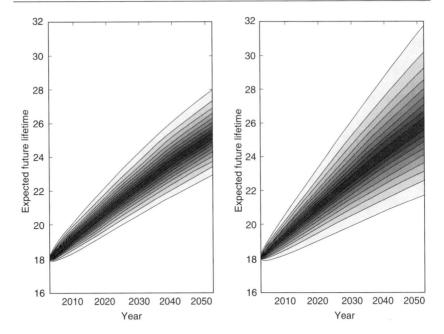

Figure 4.5. Mortality fan charts

Source: Dowd, Blake, and Cairns (2007).

with a darkly coloured band showing the central projection for mortality and increasingly lighter-coloured bands for future mortality which is less likely. Figure 4.5 shows mortality projections from 2002 onwards, based upon the model estimated in Cairns et al. (2007). The left-hand diagram shows projections based on the parameter estimates from the model, taking the parameter estimates as correct. The right-hand diagram explicitly includes the uncertainty about the parameter estimates and hence has wider bands.

Although useful for presentational purposes, it is necessary to go back to the underlying model to estimate either life expectancy or the value of an annuity. Suppose we are selling an annuity to a 65-year-old man, in which case we will need to use our forecasts of mortality for both 70-year-old men five years and 71-year-old men six years hence [respectively $\hat{q}(5, 70)$, and $\hat{q}(6, 71)$]. These forecasts will be correlated and, since the formula for the present value of an annuity involves products of mortality rates [as can be seen from equations (4.4) and (4.5)], we need to know this correlation to calculate the expected present value. This underlines the

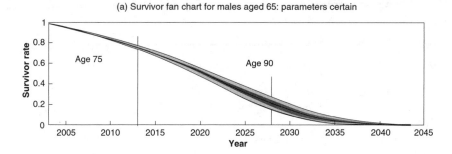

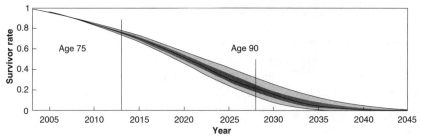

Figure 4.6. Survival fan charts

Source: Blake, Dowd, and Cairns (2007).

necessity of estimating a mortality model which explicitly incorporates these correlations.

After allowing for these correlations, Blake, Dowd, and Cairns (2007) report that the greatest uncertainty over survival probabilities occurs for ages just over 90 and this is illustrated in Figure 4.6. They do not report confidence intervals for the fair value of an annuity, but using a slightly different methodology (P-spline rather than Lee–Carter) CMI Working Paper 20 (2006) reports the following results for two variants of the P-spline method of projection, one assuming cohort effects ('Age-Cohort') and one assuming no special cohort effects ('Age-Period'). Table 4.4 shows the appropriate annuity rates based on the central projection of mortality and also the 95 per cent confidence interval.

The first row of the table shows the annuity rate based upon the original medium cohort interim adjustments to the 92 Tables, based upon an underlying 4.5 per cent interest rate (i.e. assuming 4.5 per cent interest rates at all maturities: a flat term structure); the revised medium cohort figure updates these projections to take account of the mortality data from

Table 4.4. Annuity rates with uncertain mortality

	Male, 65		Female, 65	
	Estimate	Confidence interval	Estimate	Confidence interval
Initial medium cohort	7.254%		6.750%	
Revised medium cohort	7.331%		6.905%	
Age-cohort	6.365%	6.236%	6.712%	6.572%
		6.487%		6.847%
Age-time	6.369%	6.167%	6.704%	6.483%
		6.554%		6.910%

Note: Figures are for 2004 with 4.5% interest rates.
Source: Tables M3 and F3 in CMI (2006*a*) and authors' calculations.

2003 (recall that the interim adjustments were calculated on data up to 2002). Using the P-spline methodology leads to much lower central estimates of the appropriate annuity rate for Males (although not Females), regardless of whether the Cohort or Time effect is deemed to be more important. However, the Age–Cohort estimates fit the data slightly better and thus have narrower confidence intervals, suggesting a 95 per cent confidence interval of about one-quarter of a percentage point. The key point, however, is that the entire 95 per cent confidence interval lies beneath—for Males considerably beneath—the annuity rate suggested by the medium cohort projections.

We conclude this section by noting that actuaries have only explicitly modelled uncertainty in mortality forecasts relatively recently. Valuing this uncertainty has important implications for the money's worth calculations in the next chapter, and in the valuation of pension liabilities for annuity providers which we discuss in Chapter 10.

Notes

1. Some annuity contracts pay a proportional amount of the last year that the annuitant died to his or her estate, referred to as with proportion, but for simplicity we ignore that here. It is also possible for a payment to be made very shortly after the pensioner's death because notification of death did not arrive in time for the payment to be stopped (the requirement to repay this is frequently waived).

2. The Bank of England uses sophisticated methods to calculate the full UK term structure on a daily basis and publishes it on its website (Anderson and Sleath 1999): retrospective calculations go back to 1980. Up to about the mid-1980s the published data were cruder and estimates of the yield curve in the 1950s

and 1960s were probably based more on interpolation of rates calculated at different maturities. Cannon and Tonks (2004a) discuss this issue in their calculations of the money's worth of annuities for 1957 onwards. A financial asset, such as a bond, making multiple payments can potentially be split up into multiple assets each making one payment—these are now traded on financial markets and are called gilt strips in the UK (a gilt is another name for a UK government bond).

3. In the UK these are called index-linked bonds, in the USA Treasury Inflation-Protected Securities (often abbreviated to TIPS).

4. This is only an approximation because it ignores the problem of having to compound risky future inflation rates: the true calculation would involve an expectation of a non-linear function of inflation, which differs from a non-linear function of expected inflation (by Jensen's inequality).

5. Historical population mortality for a range of countries is easily available on the Internet from the *Human Mortality Database* hosted by the University of California, Berkeley (www.mortality.org), and the Max Planck Institute for Demographic Research (www.humanmortality.de).

6. MacDonald (1997) reports that several countries used population rather than pensioner mortality. Portugal used French mortality data.

7. The UK government is responsible for both (unfunded) state pensions and a variety of occupational pensions. Pensions for civil servants are unfunded and paid out of receipts from general taxation. Pensions for other employees in the state sector (such as school teachers) are funded, but may be underwritten (explicitly or implicitly) by the government. The Government Actuaries Department is responsible for valuing these liabilities. None of these cases would involve the purchase of annuities and we do not discuss them further.

8. The Institute of Actuaries is the professional organization of actuaries in England: the Scottish analogue is the Faculty of Actuaries. The CMI is a joint venture.

9. The 00 Tables are published in CMI (2006b).

10. The situation is more complicated for life insurance: on rationally economic grounds selection would suggest people with a higher mortality, but purchasers tend to be drawn from the richer parts of the population, suggesting a lower mortality: to complicate matters further some life insurance is compulsory or bundled with other goods such as mortgage products. A priori we cannot say which effect dominates. Selection effects in annuity markets are discussed in Chapters 8 and 9.

11. This means that formulae need to distinguish select and ultimate mortality when calculating annuitant survival probabilities and equation (4.2) needs to be amended to become $s_{x,j} = p_{[x]} \times p_{x+1} \times \cdots \times p_{x+j-1}$. With this revised definition of $s_{x,j}$, the formulae in equations (4.5) and (4.9)–(4.13) are unchanged.

12. Self-Administered Pension schemes (SAPs) are those self-administered by the company and should not be confused with Self-Invested Personal Pensions

(SIPPs) which are a form of personal pension, primarily for the very wealthy, where investment decisions are taken by the pensioner.

13. Population data from GAD was also used to produce these adjustments: the adjustment were published in CMI (2002).

14. The short cohort projections assume that the mortality improvements observed in the post-1926 cohort cease to occur after 2010: the medium cohort projections assume 2020 and the long cohort projections assume 2040. The difference between the projections has more impact on the value of pensions in accrual rather than pensions in payment and thus is not so important for annuity valuation.

5

Annuity markets around the world

In this chapter we will examine how annuity markets function in other countries apart from the UK. In particular we are interested in comparing annuity markets in different countries with respect to the types of annuity products available, the size of the annuity market, the costs of annuities, the characteristics of annuity providers, and the regulatory framework.

In most countries annuity providers are companies within the insurance industry, and their supply is often linked together with the provision of life insurance. Life insurance, in return for contributions, provides a cash payout to the insured in the event of death. In contrast in return for a cash payment, an annuity pays out an income which ceases in the event of death. So life insurance and annuities can be viewed as mirror-image insurance contracts concerning the death event.

Although we cannot obtain a direct cross-country comparison of annuity markets, we can compare the penetration of the life insurance industry in selected countries, illustrated in Table 5.1 and Figure 5.1. Penetration is defined by OECD as the ratio of direct gross premiums in the life insurance industry to Gross Domestic Product, to represent the relative importance of the life insurance industry in the domestic economy. The UK has the highest penetration ratio, emphasizing that the UK's long tradition in life insurance products is related to why the UK's annuities market is the most developed.

We now provide a brief description of the pension systems and annuity provisions across a number of countries. At the start, we note that annuity rates (annual payment per unit currency of premium) differ widely between countries. However, James and Vittas (2000) and James and Song (2001: 4) find that money's worth of annuities is high 'above 95 per cent in almost every case' across all the countries that they survey, suggesting that these differences in annuity rates are almost all due to corresponding

Table 5.1. Size of life insurance industry in selected countries (annual gross life premiums as percentage of GDP)

Country	1994	1999	2004
United Kingdom	7.2	10.1	9.8
Korea, Republic of	7.9	8.9	6.9
Switzerland	6.2	8.0	6.8
France	5.4	5.3	6.7
Japan	6.3	5.5	5.4
Netherlands	4.5	5.2	5.2
United States	4.0	5.4	5.2
Denmark	3.0	4.1	5.1
Italy	1.2	3.2	5.0
Sweden	3.3	4.6	4.7
Australia	—	6.1	4.1
Germany	2.9	3.2	3.9
Canada	2.8	3.4	3.4
Spain	2.1	2.8	2.4
New Zealand	1.4	1.2	—
Mexico	0.5	0.8	0.8
Turkey	0.1	0.2	0.3
EU15: European Union of fifteen	3.6	4.9	5.7
OECD—Total	4.2	5.2	5.2
NAFTA	3.7	5.1	4.8

Source: OECD Insurance Statistics (2006).

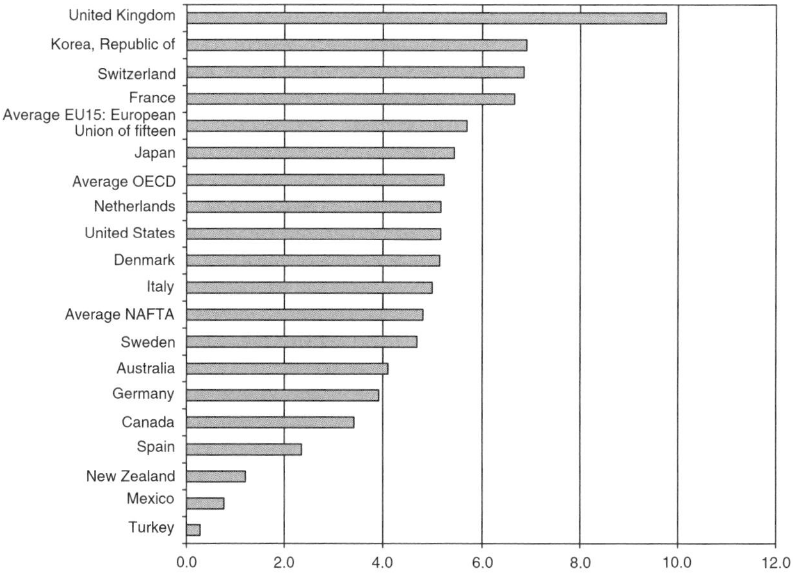

Figure 5.1. Importance of life insurance across countries: life insurance premiums as a percentage of GDP by country

Source: OECD Insurance Statistics, 2006.

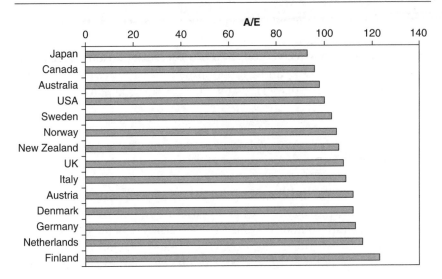

Figure 5.2. A/E metrics for 65-year-old males in selected OECD countries

Source: McCarthy and Mitchell (2004).

differences in interest rates and mortality rates. McCarthy and Mitchell (2004) illustrate the differences in mortality between countries using the A/E metric. This is a ratio of the weighted average probabilities of death for Actual Deaths compared with Expected Deaths (taken from a base mortality table):

$$A/E = 100 \times \frac{\sum_x w_x m_x^*}{\sum_x w_x m_x} \tag{5.1}$$

where m_x^* is the death rate at age x according to the mortality table for that country, m_x is the death rate at age x according to some base table and w_x is the proportion of the population of age x in the base table. The A/E metric is illustrated in Figure 5.2 for a number of countries, comparing the actual mortalities in that country with respect to the expected drawn from US 1991 life tables, so the US A/E metric is 100 by definition, and the mortality tables for other countries are computed relative to the USA. Japan has a much lower male population mortality rate, and European countries tend to have higher mortality rates.[1]

Cardinale, Findlater, and Orszag (2002) note that many of the issues and problems with annuities markets are common across countries, including inadequate supply of suitable backing assets (long-term index-linked fixed income securities); the unpopularity of annuities with consumers (the annuity puzzle); the over-reliance on level annuities, when other products are available; and regulatory rigidities. We now provide a comparison of annuity markets in selected countries. Further comparisons of international annuities markets can be found in James and Vittas (2000), James and Song (2001), Cardinale, Findlater, and Orszag (2002), and Cardinale and Orszag (2002).

5.1. Australia

Bateman, Kingston, and Piggott (2001: ch. 5 and Appendix 1) provide a comprehensive description of retirement policy in Australia with a chapter on annuity markets. The Australian pension scheme consists of the three standard pillars, although the second mandatory pillar was introduced as recently as 1992 when the Superannuation Guarantee was set up. The first pillar is the universal 'age pension' which began in 1909. The age pension is means tested according to a person's income or wealth, whichever determines the lowest rate of pension, and acts as a safety net for the elderly. The single-rate age pension is legislated to be equal to 25 per cent of male total weekly average earnings. This translates into a replacement ratio of 37 per cent.

The Superannuation Guarantee represents the second pillar and requires employers to make pension contributions at 9 per cent of earnings on behalf of their employees into individual personal pension accounts. Accredited occupational defined benefit schemes can count towards the Superannuation Guarantee obligations. The accumulated funds in the superannuation fund can only be accessed at the statutory preservation age. This is currently 55 increasing to 60 over the period to 2025. At the preservation age the accumulated funds can be taken as a lump sum or as a pension. According to Bateman, Kingston, and Piggott (2001), 75 per cent of retirement benefits were taken as a lump sum in 2001, even though there are tax and means-tested incentives to take the benefits as a pension. The third pillar consists of voluntary group and individual pension savings.

As well as the lump sum option at retirement, there are three main categories of retirement income: (*a*) superannuation pensions, traditionally paid by DB schemes; (*b*) annuities offered by insurance companies, which could be life or term annuities; and (*c*) allocated pensions (or phased withdrawals), representing a rundown of the accumulated individual's pension fund, and is offered by various financial institutions. According

Table 5.2. Size of the Australian annuity market

Income product	A$ billion				
	Dec.-94	Dec.-95	Dec.-96	Dec.-97	Dec.-98
Allocated annuities and pensions	5.776	6.54	8.139	11.73	15.259
Term-certain annuities	3.215	4.225	4.858	5.942	6.429
Life annuities	1.354	1.515	1.967	2.374	2.989
Total funds backing annuity products	10.345	12.28	14.964	20.046	24.677
Total superannuation assets	206.44	240.143	271.27	325.722	377.367
Assets backing annuities as a percentage of superannuation assets	5.01%	5.11%	5.52%	6.15%	6.54%

Source: Knox (2000).

to Knox (2000), although the Australian annuity market is poorly developed, 10 life insurance companies provide annuity quotes including the 6 largest insurance companies.

Table 5.2 shows the funds under management for the categories of annuity retirement income. Allocated annuities (offered by insurance companies) or allocated pensions (offered by a superannuation fund) are investment products where the accumulated capital from the superannuation fund is invested in a fund, from which income must be paid every year subject to maximum and minimum limits. The maximum that can be paid is set to ensure that the fund does not reduce to zero before the age of 80, and the minimum is the capital sum in the fund divided by life expectancy of the pensioner's age. As Table 5.2 shows, these allocated annuities, which offer no protection against longevity risk, are very popular, with over 60 per cent of retirement assets in this category.

Table 5.3 shows the assets of life insurers in 1998 split over the various life products that they offer. It can be seen that life annuities are a small proportion of life insurers' business.

Following the introduction of the Superannuation Guarantee in 1992, the most pressing policy issue remains the form that retirement benefits should take. While informed commentators stress that benefits should be taken as an income stream, the general public prefer to take their retirement benefits as a lump sum—'the so-called *lump sum mentality*' (Bateman and Pigott: 13). In addition the interaction between the means-tested first-pillar age pension and private retirement income is unresolved,

Table 5.3. Data on Australian life insurance industry

Product	Assets at Dec. 98	Single premiums Jan.–June 2008
Investment Linked		
Individual	48.649	4.412
Group	31.088	2.64
Investment Account		
Individual	15.818	0.724
Group	9.836	0.917
Allocated Annuities		
Individual	10.184	1.368
Group	0.676	0.071
Term-certain annuities	5.266	0.7
Life annuities	3.685	0.056
Group annuities	0.015	0.0
Conventional, risk, and other products	36.101	0.119
Total	161.318	11.007

Note: All figures are A$ billion.
Source: Australian Prudential Regulation Authority (1999) unpublished from Knox (2000).

leading to concerns of 'double-dipping', whereby an individual retires early, consumes all the lump sum, and then falls back on the age pension.

There are both solvency and capital adequacy requirements imposed on annuity providers in Australia. The first-tier Solvency Requirement is set by the Life Insurance Actuarial Standards Board, and ensures that the firm has sufficient capital to honour its liabilities. The insurance company must value its liabilities under prescribed rules concerning investment rate assumptions and mortality tables (derived from the UK's CMI database). The second tier of capital adequacy requirements, assessed by the firm's actuary, is intended to ensure the financial soundness of the firm as a going concern to ensure that the reasonable expectations of the policy-holders can be met. The capital adequacy requirement adds an additional buffer of capital above the solvency requirement, though this additional buffer may not be necessary.

5.2. Chile

Rocha and Thorburn (2006) describe the recent development of annuity markets in Chile in detail. Chile undertook a substantive pension reform in 1981, under which the public pay-as-you-go system was gradually

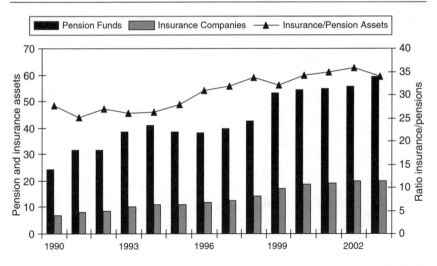

Figure 5.3. Pension and insurance assets in Chile (percentage of GDP), 1990–2003
Source: Rocha and Thorburn (2006).

replaced by a fully funded defined contribution private scheme. In the new scheme workers are mandated to contribute 10 per cent of their wages/salaries into an individual pension account. Employees pay an extra 2.2 per cent to pay for disability and survivorship insurance. These accounts during the accumulation phase are managed by pension fund administrators, called Administradoras de Fondos de Pensiones (AFPs) on a defined contribution basis. Rocha and Thorburn (2006) estimate that 55 per cent of the workforce were enrolled in a pension system by 2004, of which 97 per cent were enrolled in the new system. The result of this switch from the pay-as-you-go system to a funded DC system has resulted in a substantial growth in pension fund assets, from 25 per cent of GDP in 1990 to almost 60 per cent in 2003, illustrated in Figure 5.3.

Although the pension scheme is operated by the private sector, the government provides four guarantees to protect the individual: (*a*) a minimum relative return guarantee with respect to the AFP, so that if the particular AFP underperforms relative to the industry average, the state will restore the returns to the minimum; (*b*) insurance of the disability and death risks if the AFP defaults on its obligations; (*c*) a minimum pension guarantee (MPG); (*d*) a guarantee to the pensioner if the annuity provider defaults.

Under the post-1981 system, at retirement the pensioner uses the accumulated capital to purchase combinations of three retirement products:

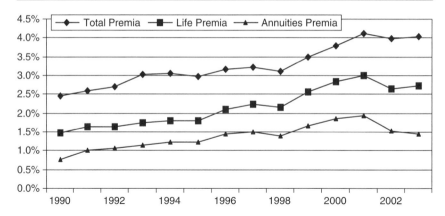

Figure 5.4. Insurance premia in Chile: Total, life, and annuities (percentage of GDP), 1990–2003

Source: Rocha and Thorburn (2006).

an annuity; a phased withdrawal; or a temporary withdrawal combined with a deferred annuity. Annuities of different types are purchased in the open market from insurance companies, though married males have to buy a joint annuity. The pensioner can only purchase an annuity provided the annuity is greater than the government's minimum pension guarantee. Otherwise the pensioner purchases a phased withdrawal, and receives the MPG from their accumulated funds until they are exhausted, after which they receive the MPG from the state.

The number of pensioners under the new scheme has increased to 520,000 in 2004 and this has resulted in a large growth in the demand for annuities and phased withdrawals. Figure 5.4 shows the strong growth in annuities and life insurance over the period 1990–2002. Total insurance premiums increased from 2.5 per cent of GDP in 1990 to 4.0 per cent of GDP in 2002, predominantly due to the growth in annuities: by 2001 the premiums on immediate life annuities had reached 2.0 per cent of GDP. The ratio of life insurance premiums to GDP in 2001 was over 4 per cent, which compares with the average ratio of 5.2 per cent in OECD companies: the mandatory retirement system has led to the development of these financial institutions.

The pensioner can also take a lump sum provided the remaining capital can finance a pension of at least 120 per cent of the MPG and at least 70 per cent of the pensioner's real wage in the 10 years preceding retirement. Similarly the pensioner can retire early if he or she has an accumulated pension fund sufficient to support a pension in retirement,

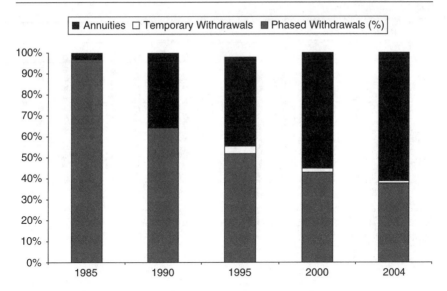

Figure 5.5. Stock of pensions by product type in Chile

Source: Rocha and Thorburn (2006).

without the risk that the funds will become exhausted and the pensioner resort to the MPG (funded by the state). Rocha and Thorburn (2006) note that these early retirement restrictions were tightened in 2004, because of concerns that the conditions were too liberal.

Figure 5.5 shows the percentages of retired pensioners purchasing each of the three retirement products. There has been a dramatic increase in the percentage buying a life annuity, switching out of purchased withdrawals. By 2005, 61 per cent of pensioners were purchasing annuities: a very high rate of annuitization.

Figure 5.6 shows the market structure for both annuities and pensions. Pensions are accumulated through AFPs, and this industry is much more concentrated than the annuity industry.

Figure 5.7 shows the changing measures of market concentration in the pensions and annuities markets. Again, the numbers illustrate that the pensions industry is much more concentrated than the annuity industry, and that the relative levels of concentration have diverged over time.

Walker (2006) examines the relationship between annuity rates and government bond yields. He observes that over the period 1993–2003 this

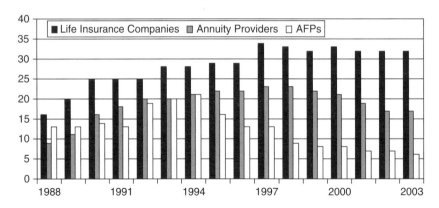

Figure 5.6. Number of life insurers, annuity providers and pension providers in Chile, 1988–2003

Source: Rocha and Thorburn (2006).

relationship changed. In Figure 5.8 the spread between the internal rate of return on an annuity for a 65-year-old male and a 20-year inflation-indexed Chilean government bond switches from being negative up to the year 2001 to positive afterwards. Walker (2006) estimates the long-run elasticity of annuity rates to changes in interest rates, and finds that the value increases over the sample and after 2001 is close to unity.

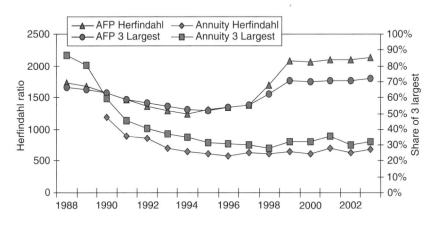

Figure 5.7. Market concentration indices of annuity and pension providers in Chile

Source: Rocha and Thorburn (2006).

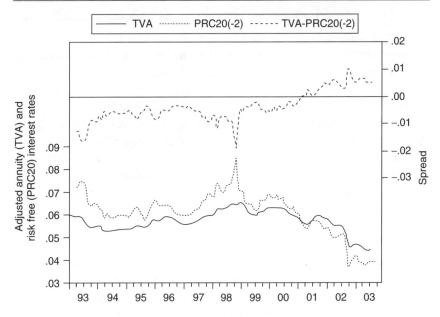

Figure 5.8. Annuity rates and government bond yields in Chile

Source: Walker (2006).

He argues that quoted annuity rates include an excessive broker's commission, which was simply a device to induce individuals to purchase annuities, since the commission was used by the brokers to offer illegal lump sums to the annuitants. A consequence of this system was that competition between insurance companies was reduced and annuity rates were relatively uncompetitive. From 2001 onwards Congress proposed legislation (finally enacted in 2004), to put a cap on these commissions. This story is consistent with the money's worth initially being low and then rising, which is observed in the data.

AFPs are regulated by the Superintendencia de Administradoras de Fondos de Pensiones (SAFP) and life insurance companies are supervised by the Superintendenciade Valores y Seguros (SVS). There are two sets of regulations imposed on annuity providers: investment regulations and capital regulations. Investment regulations relate to the types of financial instruments life insurers may hold to back their annuity liabilities, and include restriction on low-grade corporate debt, foreign assets, mutual funds, and real estate. Capital regulations include a minimum level of capital of UF90,000 (equivalent to US$2.4 million) and a minimum gearing or solvency margin of 1/15 or 6.67 per cent. The solvency margin is the ratio of shareholder capital, retained earnings, and CALCE reserves to annuity liabilities (technical reserves). This means that when an insurance company writes annuity business it must have sufficient capital (of at least 6.67 per cent) to back these liabilities. Alternatively the gearing ratio tells the insurance company the maximum amount of annuity business it may write given its shareholder capital. The CALCE reserves were introduced in 1990 and address the risks of asset–liability mismatches: since annuity liabilities are essentially long-term, reinvestment risk is minimized if assets are of similar duration. CALCE computes the reserves required to compensate for any mismatch.

5.3. Germany

The German pension system is a traditional 'continental model' first-pillar pay-as-you-go state-provided scheme coving 85 per cent of the labour force. Demographic concerns have resulted in some changes. Under the pension reforms of 1992 and 2001, the replacement ratio of public pensions will fall from 70 to 64 per cent, and Schnabel (2004) predicts further cuts are inevitable. Given the reliance on generous state pensions, occupational pension schemes in the second pillar are small, and make up only 5 per cent of average retirement incomes. The Reister reforms of 2001 also encouraged second- and third-pillar occupational and voluntary schemes through tax subsidies.

Contributions into a Reister plan, which may be occupational or individual, are tax deductible for both an employer and an employee. Capital gains during the accumulation phase are not taxed, but benefits received during retirement are taxed. Reister plans must be authorized by a federal institution, and a minimum return of 0 per cent is guaranteed at the end of the accumulation phase, meaning that the pension fund must be at least equal to the sum of contributions at retirement. If the contributor or pensioner leaves Germany permanently, the subsidies and tax benefits must be repaid (though this may transgress EU law). At retirement, 80 per cent of the accumulated funds must be annuitized, with up to 20 per cent taken as a lump sum. Annuitization must occur before the age of 85. Schnabel (2004) estimates that 3 million Reister plans had been sold by insurance companies by the end of 2002. Average annual contributions of employees were €175, which together with a subsidy of €120, makes an

Table 5.4. Private annuities and public pensions in Germany

Year	Life annuities paid by insurers (€ billion)	Main insurance benefits paid by insurers (€ billion)	Payments from public old-age insurance (€ billion)
1998	1.7	25.8	171.5
1999	2.1	29.4	167.8
2000	2.5	32.8	177.8
2001	2.7	35.4	183.4
Increase 1998–2001	57.90%	37.10%	6.90%
Average annual increase	12.10%	8.20%	1.70%

Source: Schnabel (2004).

overall annual plan contribution of €295. At this stage few Reister plans will have reached maturity, and so it is not possible to assess this 'pensions annuity' market.

Germany's private annuity market is very small (Von Gaudecker and Weber 2004) and Table 5.4 illustrates this by showing that annuities formed only 1 per cent of pensioners' incomes in 1998, rising to 1.5 per cent in 2001. This means that the rate of increase is large (58 per cent) and the effect of the Reister plans will fuel this growth further.

Most life annuities are single level annuities and may be guaranteed (referred to in Germany as 'with refund'). Annuities may have constant or escalating participation, which depends on whether bonuses from equity investments are included in the payments to the annuity holder.

5.4. Italy

Borella, Fornero, and Ponzetto (2004) describe the Italian pension system.[2] Italy has one main earnings-related social security pension scheme covering the whole population, providing old-age, early retirement, disability and survivors' pensions. Everyone entering the labour market since 1996 falls under a Notional Defined Contribution (NDC) scheme and there are transitional schemes for workers in the labour market before 1995.

An NDC system is a type of PAYG scheme, but where individual pension rights are identified with a notional capital value, accumulating at an imputed rate of return. At retirement the notional capital value is converted into an income stream. Other countries which have NDC schemes include Sweden (discussed below), Poland, and Latvia. An NDC has the advantage that individuals can see the build-up of their pension entitlement, but the government has two tools to ensure that the system remains in balance: the imputed rate of return on notional capital in the notional accumulation phase, and the terms of the annuity capitalization in the notional decumulation phase.

The NDC scheme in Italy replaced a previous DB pension scheme. In addition there is a first-pillar means-tested social assistance pension for those who would otherwise have less than the minimum level of the earnings-related pension. Within the third pillar there are both voluntary occupational and individual supplementary schemes.

The Italian annuity market has historically been very thin. The public pension system (first pillar) is characterized by both high contribution rates (often in excess of 30 per cent for dependent workers) and high replacement ratios (75 per cent) (Miles and Timmermann 1999). So workers have few spare resources to save for a pension and little incentive to buy one. However, a further feature of the Italian labour market is that most workers receive mandatory severance pay called Trattamento di Fine Rapporto (TFR). This is a form of deferred salary and could be an additional source of retirement savings. However, until recently annuitization of TFR has been discouraged by unfavourable tax treatment.

Under the pension reforms of 2004, this situation is likely to change because the reforms, while mainly directed at correcting the financial imbalances of the public pillar, have also boosted the private funded pillar in order to restore the pre-reform replacement ratios. According to the Italian Private Pension Legislation (Legislative decree 124/1993 and subsequent modifications), the private pillar is characterized by voluntary participation with a defined contribution formula for private pension schemes, tax deductability on contributions, and investment returns taxed at favourable rates, with taxation payable on retirement income. The reforms also require compulsory annuitization of at least 50 per cent of the retirement wealth accumulated. Before 2000 annuitization represented only an option attached to insurance contracts, usually overcome by allowing lump sum withdrawals. From January 2008 the TFR will automatically be diverted to a managed pension fund, unless an employee opts out. By June 2007 about 2.7 million employees had an additional private pension (Fornero and Piatti 2007), a substantial increase from the previous year. Once the quasi-compulsory diversion of TFR takes effect, it is likely that the demand for private pension schemes will increase.

On the supply side, private pensions are offered through occupational (close-end) pension funds; open-end pension funds; and (since 2000) insurance policies. These policies may be 'revaluable' policies and unit-linked policies. Under the 2000 reforms, the two types of insurance product are eligible as individual pension plans. In this case, they are deferred annuities.[3]

In order to price annuities, most insurance companies use the mortalities and projected mortalities from the RG48 tables provided by the Ragioneria Generale dello Stato corrected for selection effects on the basis of UK insurance market experience. The technical rate used by insurance companies is governed by the national supervisory agency (ISVAP).

5.5. Singapore

Social security support in Singapore is limited and operates in the context of an ageing population, since it is estimated that 20 per cent of Singapore's population will be over 65 by 2030.[4] The second pillar is a mandatory defined contribution pension scheme called the Central Provident Fund (CPF) started in 1955, with contributions into the individual's CPF account from employers and employees. Contributions into the CPF are made monthly and since 2003 have been 20 per cent of earnings for employees and 13 per cent for employers, though these rates change depending on macroeconomic conditions. The long-term CPF contribution rate varies between 30 and 36 per cent for employees aged below 50. These are very high contribution rates and explain why Singapore has one of the highest savings rates in the world. However, the CPF funds can be used to finance housing and a large percentage of funds are used for this purpose. Given high house prices in Singapore, the amounts left in the CPF to fund retirement are relatively small. The 1999 CPF Annual Report stated that 50 per cent of CPF members who reached 55 in 1999 had gross CPF balances of less than S$146,000. Because of concerns that the CPF was not providing sufficient funds for retirement there has been a Minimum Sum Scheme since 1995, under which CPF members reaching 55 must set aside S$94,600 (in 2006, rising to S$120,000 in 2013), though a portion of this can be pledged with a property.

In December 2006 the CPF had 3.1 million members, of whom 57,129 members were brought into the Minimum Sum Scheme in 2006. Of these, 27,456 pledged their properties, 2,358 bought annuities, and 13,297 left their Minimum Sum either with the banks or the CPF. The remaining

14,018 comprised members who had no Minimum Sum to set aside as they had small balances and those who were exempted from the scheme because they were terminally ill, had withdrawn from the CPF under medical grounds, had died, had their own annuities, had left the country permanently, or were pensioners in receipt of a monthly pension.

The official retirement age is 62, after which an individual can annuitize their CPF fund or leave it to accumulate further. According to a survey of the nine CPF-approved insurers in 2001 by Fong (2002), 20 per cent of retirees purchase an annuity, a fairly high rate of voluntary annuitization; 93 per cent of these annuities are deferred, being purchased at age 55 with a first payment at age 62; 87 per cent of annuity contracts are purchased using the CPF Minimum Sum. Annuities may be participating or non-participating. A non-participating annuity pays a nominal fixed amount each period; a participating annuity includes a non-guaranteed bonus that depends on the investment performance of the insurance company.

Table 5.5 lists the nine insurers and details the contract features of their annuity plans. As documented in other countries, payouts vary across life insurers, ranging from $468 to $600 for a male purchaser and $444.60 to

Table 5.5. Annuity contract features in Singapore by CPF-approved insurers

Insurance company	S&P rating	Annuity rate at age 55 (S$ per month)		Guarantee details
		Male	Female	
Non-Participating Annuities				
American International Assurance	AAA	468	444.60	15 years
Asia Life	BBB	573.65	534.82	$91,461 less annuity payments made
Great Eastern Life	AA-	585.00	555.00	15 years
Insurance Corp. of Singapore	BBB	575.00	510.00	Return of original capital plus interest less total annuity payments made
Keppel Insurance	BBB	551.00	504.00	15 years
Overseas Assurance Corp.	BBB	573.17	538.85	15 years
Prudential Assurance	A	566.03	496.53	Return of original capital plus interest less total annuity payments made
UOB Life Assurance	Not rated	600.00	555.00	15 years
Participating Annuities				
NTUC Income	AA	552.5	523.90	15 years

Source: Fong (2002).

$555 for a female purchaser. Given their longer life expectancy, female purchasers receive lower payouts.

5.6. Sweden

The Swedish pension system is described by Sundén (2006) and the Pensions Commission (2005). Sweden has a standard three-pillar pension system, but with a variety of second pillars. The first pillar is a minimum guarantee benefit (FP, introduced in 1913) designed for people with low lifetime earnings: entitlement is based on years of residence in Sweden, and is financed out of central government spending. Until its pension reforms of 1998, the second pillar in Sweden was a standard defined-benefit earnings-related pay-as-you-go system (ATP, introduced in 1960). These two pillars produced an average replacement ratio of 65 per cent. In addition the second pillar also includes a series of occupational schemes that provide an extra 10 per cent in income replacement. Following the recommendations of the Parliamentary Working Group on Pensions in 1994, Sweden has revised its second pillar to a Notional Defined Contribution (NDC) system, which we have already described in Section 5.4.

In Sweden the contribution rate to the NDC is 16 per cent of earnings (shared between employers and employees). The rate of return on the notional accumulated capital value in the NDC is normally the growth of average earnings, and from age 61 onwards individuals can annuitize the notional capital sum at a rate that reflects the age of retiring and the life expectancy of that cohort. The system is subject to 'Automatic Balancing Mechanism' (ABM) to protect against changes in economic performance and demographics. Under the ABM, the present value of future contributions is compared with the present value of future pension liabilities and the rate of return on capital, and the annuity rate is adjusted to ensure that the system remains in balance. Table 5.6 shows the financial balance for the Swedish NDC system over the period 2001–04. The system's assets are the capitalized values of the contributions, and the current value of the buffer stock. The system's liabilities are the present value of the pension promises, under the current assumptions about pension rights. The ABM is triggered when the balancing ratio falls below unity, in which case the indexation is reduced, decreasing the value of the pension liabilities. Over the period 2001–04 the balance ratio has been just above unity. The buffer funds allow for gradual adjustments to demographic shocks.

Table 5.6. Assets and liabilities in the Swedish NDC

	2001	2002	2003	2004
Contribution assets	5,085	5,293	5,465	5,607
Buffer funds	565	488	577	646
Total assets	5,650	5,781	6,042	6,253
Pension liabilities	5,432	5,729	5,984	6,244
Ratio of assets to liabilities	104%	101%	101%	100%

Note: Except for the last row all numbers are in billions of Swedish Kronor. Over the period 2001–04 the exchange rate was approximately kr9 to €1.
Source: Sundén (2006).

An additional second pillar is a compulsory funded defined contribution Premium Pension Plan under which individuals contribute a further 2.5 per cent of earnings into individual accounts, which may be invested at the discretion of the plan-holder. A government agency, the Premium Pensions Agency (PPM), administers the accumulated contributions in the plans, transferring the contributions into the nominated investment fund. There are about 700 investment funds, managed by fund management companies, registered with the PPM, with half of these funds investing in international equities. Individual plan members are responsible for selecting their own personal diversified portfolio from the list of registered funds. The average fund management fee is 0.43 per cent of assets under management, and the PPM charges an administrative fee of 0.3 per cent, making a total annual fee to the plan member of 0.73 per cent. From the age of 61, benefits accumulated in an individual's Premium Pension Plan can be accessed by annuitization which is mandatory via the PPM using unisex life tables.

Finally Sweden has a funded system of semi-mandatory occupational pension schemes, which constitute a combination of second and third pillars. There are four occupational pension systems which, as a result of national pay bargaining, cover 90 per cent of the workforce.

5.7. Switzerland

The Swiss pension system is described by Bütler (2004) and Bütler and Ruesch (2007). Switzerland has a traditional three-pillar pension structure, with a small pay-as-you-go first-pillar supplemented by a mandatory second-pillar occupational pension scheme, and a third-pillar voluntary system. The first-pillar AHV[5] was introduced in 1948 and is a pay-as-you-go unfunded scheme. Although Switzerland has a long tradition of occupational pensions, the second pillar was only made mandatory in 1985 with the introduction of the BVG/LPP.[6] The second pillar is mandatory but organized through occupational schemes, which may be run as independent pension funds, or via a contract with an insurance company. Typically the institution that organizes the accumulation phase of the pension also administers the decumulation phase.

At retirement employees are allowed to withdraw at least 25 per cent of the accumulated funds as a lump sum, with the remaining funds paid out as an annuity for life. Bütler and Teppa (2005) analyse the factors affecting the fraction of accumulated pension taken as a lump sum. They find that small balances are much more likely to be taken as a lump sum, possibly due to differential mortalities, and income support ('double-dipping'). For very high balances the fraction cashed-out is higher, probably due to a combination of bequest motives, investment opportunities, and preferential tax treatment.

BVG/LPP law imposes a conversion factor at which the accumulated capital sum in the second pillar is converted into a life annuity. This conversion factor is not related to market conditions, gender or income, and a single conversion factor is used for both men and women, and for married and single persons. The conversion factor was set at 7.2 per cent up to 2004 falling to 6.8 per cent by 2014. When the BVH/LPP was introduced most occupational pensions were defined benefit, but by 2006 85 per cent of schemes were defined contribution. However the fixed conversion factor has the effect of changing an apparent defined contribution scheme into something more like a defined benefit scheme. The high conversion factor compensates the employee for low returns during the accumulation phase. Bütler and Ruesch (2007) note that the failure to adapt the conversion ratio to market conditions will make the system unsustainable in the long run.

Given the full annuitization under the first pillar and 80 per cent annuitization under the second pillar, there is very little demand for additional annuitization. Early retirement is allowed at an actuarially fair reduction of the conversion factor.

Table 5.7 and Figure 5.9 show the growth in the Swiss annuity market in the second pillar over the last few years. Both the amounts of annuity payments and the amounts of the lump sums taken have increased substantially to about 5 per cent of GDP by 2002. This growth has occurred both through an increased number of recipients and the average value of

Table 5.7. Size of Swiss annuity market

	1987	1992	1994	1996	1998	2000	2002
Annuity payments (CHF million)	5,503	9,000	10,751	12,533	14,492	16,292	18,127
Capital payments (CHF million)	948	1,830	2,320	2,842	2,993	3,910	3,525
Total payments (CHF million)	6,451	10,830	13,071	15,375	17,485	20,202	21,652
Annuity payments (% of GDP)	2.09%	2.57%	2.92%	3.35%	3.71%	3.92%	4.21%
Capital payments (% of GDP)	0.36%	0.52%	0.63%	0.76%	0.77%	0.94%	0.82%
Average annuity payment (CHF)			17,628	19,368	20,854	21,777	22,572
Number of recipients of annuity payments			609,875	647,111	694,912	748,124	803,064
Number of recipients of capital payments			29,684	30,342	29,145	31,164	28,308

Source: Bütler and Ruesch (2006).

the payments increasing. Bütler and Ruesch (2007) suggest that the slight fall in lump sums in 2002 may be due to the increased incidence of early retirements that require annuitization. Given the size of the mandatory second pillar, the third-pillar annuity market is very small.

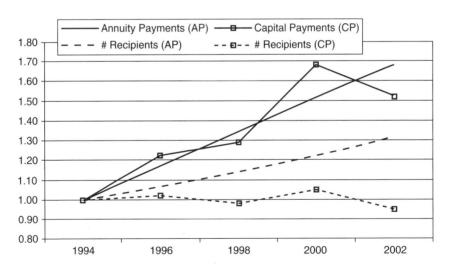

Figure 5.9. Growth in Swiss annuity market
Source: Bütler and Ruesch (2007).

Table 5.8. Size of US annuity market: Annuity premiums received

Type of annuity	Annuity premiums received ($ million)		
	2004	2005	2006
Individual annuities	172,140	167,032	187,083
Group annuities	104,537	110,084	115,645
Term-certain annuities	24,352	25,479	26,344
Total	301,029	302,596	329,071

Source: ACLI tabulations of National Association of Insurance Commissioners data.

5.8. United States of America

Poterba (2001*a*) provides a description of annuity markets in the USA. The size of the US market for life annuities is difficult to determine because in the USA the term annuity is also used to include the accumulation phase of a pension scheme through a form of deferred annuity which encompasses the accumulation phase. Fixed annuities are deferred annuities with the funds invested in fixed-interest securities providing for a stable capital sum, whereas variable annuities are invested in equity products and produce more volatile returns, and hence a more volatile capital sum. Poterba (2001*a*) notes that variable annuities are very popular, but these are not necessarily life annuities. At retirement these deferred annuity payments may be taken as a life annuity, a term-certain annuity, or as a lump sum. Data from the American Council of Annuity Lenders on contributions into annuities include both deferred and immediate annuities.

Table 5.8 shows that the total amount of annuities sold in the USA in 2005 was around $300 billion, but in addition to individual annuities, this includes sales to group or occupational pensions, and term-certain annuities. According to Reno et al. (2005) around $10 billion of the total annuity sales are life annuities.

According to Poterba (2001*a*) annuities have been sold by insurance companies for over two centuries in the USA, and he reports that by the end of the 1990s, 40 per cent of life insurance payouts were annuity payouts. Sales of group annuities were much greater than sales of individual annuities throughout the 1950s and 1960s, but the decline in defined benefit pension plans has resulted in an expansion of individual annuity products.

Notes

1. The Human Mortality Database at http://www.mortality.org/ provides historical and cross-country information on population mortalities.
2. We are grateful to Elsa Fornero for supplying us with information for this section on Italian annuities. Brugiavini and Galasso (2004) also describe the Italian pension system.
3. According to the Italian Private Pension Legislation (D.lgs. 124/1993), retirement wealth accumulated through private pension plans (closed- or open-end funds and insurance products) ought to have at least 50 per cent annuitized.
4. This section draws on Fong (2002), and information provided by the CPF board which can be found at http://mycpf.cpf.gov.sg.
5. AHV = Alters- und Hinterbliebenen-Versicherung (old-age insurance).
6. BVG = Berufliches Vorsorge-Gesetz (Occupational Benefit Plan) in German; LPP = Loi sur la Prévoyance Professionnelle in French.

6

Money's worth calculations

The most common way to compare the value of annuities with other assets is to use a measure called the money's worth.[1] The money's worth of an annuity is the value of the expected annuity payments that would be received if the annuity were purchased with £1. If the money's worth is £1 then the annuity is perfectly fairly priced in actuarial terms (and the life-insurance company receives no money for administrative costs or profit). Given that the life-insurance company incurs some costs and has to make some profit, we should expect the money's worth to be a little less than one.

Warshawsky (1988) and Mitchell et al. (1999) have used the money's worth procedure to analyse the annuities market in the USA and similar exercises have been conducted by various authors in annuity markets around the world, summarized later in this chapter. For a general discussion of the calculation of the money's worth, see the introduction to the collection of papers in Brown et al. (2001).

To calculate the money's worth of an annuity for a person of age 65: define $A_{t,65}$ as the annuity rate (annuity payment divided by premium) for an annuity purchased in year t by a 65-year-old. Following on from the definition in equation (4.9), the money's worth is

$$\mathrm{MW}_{t,65} = A_{t,65} \left\{ \sum_{j=1}^{\infty} s_{t,65,j} (1 + r_{t,j})^{-j} \right\} \tag{6.1}$$

where $r_{t,j}$ is the j-term spot rate of interest in period t and $s_{t,65,j}$ is the survival probability of someone born in year t-65 surviving to age $65 + j$ having reached age 65 by period t.

Analogous formulae can be used to calculate the money's worth for annuitants at different ages. An arbitrary T is set as the maximum longevity. With a five-year guaranteed annuity the first five years' payments are made regardless of the annuitant's death, so in this case the expected present value is

$$\text{MW}_{t,65}^{\text{5-year g'tee}} = A_{t,65} \left\{ \sum_{j=1}^{5} (1 + r_{t,j})^{-j} + \sum_{j=6}^{\infty} S_{t,65,j} (1 + r_{t,j})^{-j} \right\} \quad (6.2)$$

The money's worth is the ratio of the present discounted value of the expected annuity payments to the price. The formula makes no allowance for load factors representing costs incurred by the annuity provider. These include administrative costs of the sale, payments system costs, transactions costs of purchasing assets to match the liability incurred by the insurance company, regulatory costs relating to prudential regulation of insurance company business, and an element of normal profit.

An annuity contract is fairly priced if the premium set by the annuity provider is equal to the present discounted value of the expected annuity payments plus the load factor. The degree of fair pricing may be assessed by examining the money's worth of an annuity. With a zero load factor and fair pricing, the money's worth would be exactly equal to unity ($\text{MW}_{t,65} = 1.0$). This can be expressed alternatively as 100 per cent or 100 pence in the pound. However, any positive load factor will result in the money's worth being less than unity. If data were available on the size and components of the load factor, then it would be possible to compare the money's worth with the load factor to assess the degree of fair pricing. But in the absence of information on load factors, we may instead compare the money's worth of annuities with similar financial and insurance products to assess whether annuities are fairly priced.

6.1. Evidence on money's worth of UK annuities

Murthi, Orszag, and Orszag (1999), Finkelstein and Poterba (2002, 2004, 2006), and Cannon and Tonks (2004a) have examined the money's worth of UK annuity markets. Finkelstein and Poterba (2002) estimate money's worth for both the voluntary and compulsory annuity markets based on a cross-sectional sample of annuity rates in 1998. Murthi, Orszag, and Orszag (1999) estimate money's worth in the compulsory market for both open-market options and compulsory annuities using a cross-sectional sample of annuity rates in 1999. We follow the discussion of money's worth calculations for UK voluntary annuities in Cannon and Tonks

(2004*a*) using the time series of annuity quotes in the voluntary purchased life annuity market from 1957 to 2002, which we have updated to
2007.

There are two ways to implement these money's worth calculations,
which we refer to as *ex ante* and *ex post*. *Ex ante* implementation uses
expectations of interest rates and survival probabilities that were available
at the time when the annuity was sold, that is, historic expectations
information. Since life-insurance companies usually back their annuity
liabilities with bond assets of appropriate maturity, it is anyway probably
appropriate to use historic yield curves for the interest rates.[2] The Bank
of England does not publish detailed yield curve data for years before
1980 and Cannon and Tonks (2004*a*) reconstructed the relevant figures
from contemporaneous term structures data available in hard copy. So,
for example, the interest rates used to value an annuity sold in 1957 are
the implicit rates in 1957 yield curve. Apart from consistency across time,
the approach has the advantage that it can be compared directly with
Mitchell et al. (1999), Murthi, Orszag, and Orszag (1999), and Finkelstein
and Poterba (2002), who all estimated money's worths at given dates using
the forward-looking appropriate yield curves.

Ex ante mortality projections were taken from the various tables (four
in the period 1957–2002) published by the Continuous Mortality Investigation Committee. Finkelstein and Poterba (2002) calculate the money's
worth using two sets of mortality statistics: one based on 'Lives' (IML),
calculated as a simple average of mortality experience and one based on
'Amounts' (IMA), calculated as a weighted average of mortality experience
where the weights are the size of the policy. Because of selection and
socio-economic effects, we should expect the money's worth calculated
on Lives mortality to be lower, which is borne out in the analysis of both
Finkelstein and Poterba (2002) and ourselves.

Cannon and Tonks's (2004*a*) estimates of the money's worth over the
period 1957–2002 are reproduced in Table 6.1, and this data has been
updated to include the more recent evidence in the 2002–07 purchased
life annuity quotes. The money's worth is computed over different sub-
samples, depending on the relevant actuarial tables, and in all cases the
money's worth is very close to unity, implying that annuities were sold
at a rate which was approximately fair in actuarial terms. The annuity
quote data over the period 1957–73 were obtained for five-year guaranteed
annuities, whereas post-1972 the quote data related to annuities without
any guarantees. To obtain a single statistic on the money's worth over

Table 6.1. *Ex ante* money's worth of UK annuities, male, lives, aged 65

Years	Type of annuity	Actuarial table	Mean MW	95% Confidence interval	*p*-value
Panel A					
1957–73	no g'tee	a(55)	1.034	0.996–1.072	0.078
1972–2002	5-year g'tee	various	0.979	0.957–1.001	0.062
1972–80	5-year g'tee	a(55)	1.004	0.938–1.070	0.894
1978–91	5-year g'tee	a(90)	0.978	0.955–1.001	0.057
1990–99	5-year g'tee	IM80	0.985	0.955–1.015	0.296
1999–2002	5-year g'tee	IML92	0.938	0.891–0.984	0.023*
1957–2002	No g'tee spliced with 5-year g'tee	various	0.977	0.958–0.996	0.018*
2001–07	No g'tee	IML92 long cohort	0.928	0.847–1.009	0.072
Panel B					
1972–2002	5-year g'tee	Population	0.956	0.937–0.975	0.000**

Panel A computes the money's worth over different sub-samples of the data-set. The *p*-value reports a two-tailed t-test for whether the average money's worth is significantly different from unity. *, ** denotes significance at the 5% and 1% levels, respectively. Confidence intervals and *p*-values are robust to serial correlation. Panel B computes money's worth using population life tables to assess the degree of selection.

Source: Cannon and Tonks (2004*a*) updated and revised.

the sample 1957–2002, it is necessary to splice together the guaranteed and non-guaranteed annuity series. These money's worth calculations are based on annuity rates which are themselves a simple average of different companies' prices: the money's worth for the companies quoting the highest rates would have been very good indeed.

These results are similar to the cross-sectional analysis of Finkelstein and Poterba (2002) and Murthi, Orszag, and Orszag (1999). The former found the money's worth in the voluntary market to be 99 pence and the latter 93 pence in the open-market options, compared with our figure in the voluntary market of 99 pence in 1998. Murthi, Orszag, and Orszag (1999) also provide estimates of 100 pence in 1990 and 92 pence in 1994: our analogous figures are 98 pence and 89 pence.[3] But our evidence is that over the whole period, the average money's worth is much closer to unity than the snapshot evidence of the earlier work for specific years in the 1990s.

As in Finkelstein and Poterba (2002), Cannon and Tonks (2004*a*) also calculate the money's worth using population rather than annuitant mortality, and also find that this shows a much lower money's worth. This follows directly from the fact that population mortality is higher than annuitant mortality (conversely population life expectancy is lower than annuitant life expectancy). This could be due to adverse selection

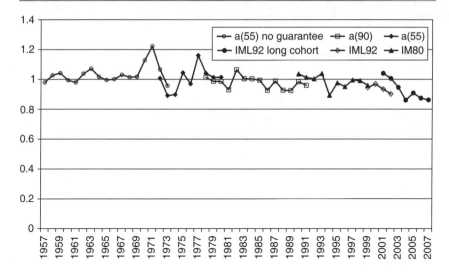

Figure 6.1. Money's worth for voluntary annuities, male, lives, aged 65

Source: Cannon and Tonks (2004*a*) updated by the authors to include IML92 long cohort projections for 2001–07.

or merely due to the fact that annuitants tend to be richer, and hence healthier, than the general population. Since Cannon and Tonks (2004*a*) are analysing the voluntary-purchase market, both adverse selection and wealth/health effects are likely to be present. Finkelstein and Poterba (2002) suggest that there may also be some adverse selection effects in the compulsory-purchase market, although it may not be so severe: in the latter market it is likely that wealth and health effects are quantitatively more important. We shall discuss this point in more detail below.

As can be seen in Figure 6.1, the more recent revisions to the mortality projections have shown increases in the money's worth, because the revised projections of life expectancy have increased. It is noteworthy, however, that actuaries have not always underestimated increases in longevity and the improvements projected in the a(55) tables were not realized.[4]

In addition to the *ex ante* estimates of the money's worth, Cannon and Tonks also calculate *ex post* money's worth using the actual one-year interest rate and actual mortality experiences of annuitants. The corresponding *ex post* money's worths are shown in Figure 6.2 for comparison and also suggest that the historical norm is about £1.

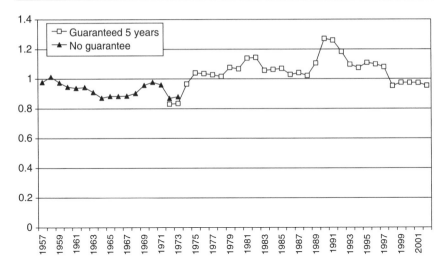

Figure 6.2. *Ex post* money's worth for voluntary annuities, male, lives, aged 65

Source: Cannon and Tonks (2004*a*).

6.2. Evidence on money's worth in the UK's compulsory annuities market

We now present the results of calculating the money's worth of UK annuities in the compulsory market using the data on annuity quotes 1994–2007 outlined in Chapter 2. We calculate the money's worth using our *ex ante* expectations of interest rates and survival probabilities that were available at time *t*. We estimate expectations of future interest rates from the term structure of interest rates, following the same methods as we discussed in the calculation of voluntary money's worth. This means that the 1994 interest rates used to value an annuity sold in 1994 are the implicit rates in the 1994 yield curve.

With respect to assumptions of life expectancy over the period 1994–2007, clearly annuities are (or should be) priced on future life expectancy of annuitants, so we are dealing with past values of expectations about the then future (much of which is still in the future). The period since 1994 has seen major revisions to actuarial projections and this means that changes in life expectations are the important causes of changes in annuity rates.

Summary statistics of some of these data was displayed in Table 4.2, showing the number of annuitants by annuity type over various quadrennia, and the associated death rates for each group. In an ideal world we would use the Personal Pensions life expectancy data in our money's worth calculations, since it is the most relevant to the compulsory-purchase market. However, as can be seen from Panel E in Table 4.2, it is only recently that significant numbers of individuals have been monitored by the CMI and so these data alone would be unsatisfactory for projection into the future. Furthermore, they were first published only in 2004 (although a smaller sample had been available before then) and so are unavailable for most of the period.

An alternative would be to use the RAC life expectancy, but Panel C in Table 4.2 suggests that the death rate of such pensioners is twice as high as the death rate of personal pensioners (looking at pensions in payment rather than in accrual) and hence the life expectancy is much lower. In fact, these summary statistics exaggerate the difference, since the average age of RAC pensioners is higher than PP pensioners, but differences remain even when we disaggregate the data by age. This difference in life expectancy may be because the two groups have different socio-economic characteristics, which is plausible if the RACs were self-employed. Since the number of RAC pensioners in accrual has fallen from 7.5 to 4.6 million over the period, coinciding with an increase of PP pensioners in accrual from 1.9 to 12.9 million, it is almost certain that some individuals who would have taken up RACs are now taking up PPs (as we would have expected), but this movement from one group to another has apparently been insufficient to mask the difference in life expectancy.

Given the problems with RAC and PP life expectancy it seems prudent to follow Finkelstein and Poterba (2002) and resort to a larger and more consistent set of data, namely the Life Office Pensioners, of whom there were over one million in 1999–2002 and for whom a long run of data are available in the past. Use of the Life Office Pensioner data has the additional advantage that life expectancy is available on both a lives and an amounts basis. The former shows the life expectancy of each life (or more accurately of each policy—if a pensioner has more than one policy then he or she may be counted twice). The latter basis re-weights the life expectancy by the size of the pension so that richer pensioners have a higher weight—unsurprisingly life expectancy of amounts is longer than life expectancy of lives since richer people tend to live longer. From the point of view of the Life Office, what matters is the amounts measure, since that is what determines the profitability of the life business: from the point of view of a 'typical' pensioner the lives basis may be more relevant in terms of the 'value for money' of the annuity.[5]

Table 6.2. Money's worth for compulsory annuities, male, 65, level

Year	PML80 ('Lives')	PML92 ('Lives')	PML92 short cohort ('Lives')	PML92 long cohort ('Lives')	PNML00 short cohort ('Lives')	PNML00 long cohort ('Lives')	Overall MW (combined 'Lives')	Overall MW (combined 'Amounts')
1994	0.900						0.900	0.940
1995	0.912						0.912	0.953
1996	0.886						0.886	0.924
1997	0.901						0.901	0.943
1998	0.888						0.888	0.933
1999	0.865	0.936					0.936	0.993
2000	0.878	0.955					0.955	1.015
2001		0.916					0.916	0.969
2002		0.864	0.923	0.979			0.951	0.994
2003		0.825	0.883	0.940			0.912	0.953
2004			0.827	0.879			0.853	0.891
2005			0.838	0.894	0.835	0.891	0.863	0.895
2006			0.829	0.885	0.826	0.883	0.855	0.886
2007			0.829	0.885	0.826	0.883	0.854	0.885

The final two columns show the overall money's worth obtained by combining the life tables based on 'Lives' (PML tables) and combining the life tables based on 'Amounts' (PMA tables).

The results on the money's worth calculations over various sub-periods of the data sample are presented in Tables 6.2–6.5 and illustrated in Figures 6.3–6.7. The general evidence *is that money's* worth has fallen since the year 2000, but the level of the money's worth and the extent

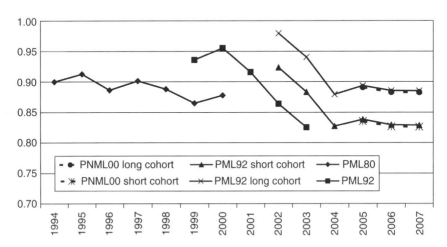

Figure 6.3. Money's worth for compulsory annuities, male, 65, level, using 'Lives' mortality over different mortality tables

Table 6.3. Money's worth for compulsory annuities, male, level, various ages

Year	60-year-old PML80	60-year-old PML92	60-year-old long cohort	65-year-old PML80	65-year-old PML92	65-year-old long cohort	70-year-old PML80	70-year-old PML92	70-year-old long cohort	75-year-old PML80	75-year-old PML92	75-year-old long cohort
1994	0.916			0.900			0.880					
1995	0.928			0.912			0.892					
1996	0.895			0.886			0.871					
1997	0.920			0.901			0.878					
1998	0.909			0.888			0.863			0.837		
1999	0.886	0.955		0.865	0.936		0.842	0.911		0.817	0.884	
2000	0.905	0.982		0.878	0.955		0.844	0.918		0.813	0.883	
2001		0.938			0.916			0.886			0.857	
2002		0.880	0.960		0.864	0.979		0.846	0.995		0.823	0.977
2003		0.834	0.913		0.825	0.940		0.811	0.963		0.796	0.961
2004			0.865			0.879			0.889			0.887
2005			0.887			0.894			0.905			0.906
2006			0.882			0.885			0.890			0.886
2007			0.878			0.885			0.888			0.890

Table 6.4. Money's worth for compulsory annuities, female, 65, level, lives

Year	PFL80	PFL92	PFL92 short cohort	PFL92 long cohort	PNFL00 short cohort	PNFL00 long cohort	Overall MW (combined 'Lives')
1994	0.915						0.915
1995	0.932						0.932
1996	0.898						0.898
1997	0.925						0.925
1998	0.920						0.920
1999	0.896	0.923					0.923
2000	0.925	0.958					0.958
2001		0.924					0.924
2002		0.882	0.925	0.976			0.950
2003		0.845	0.888	0.940			0.914
2004			0.846	0.894			0.870
2005			0.846	0.896			0.871
2006			0.836	0.887	0.828	0.878	0.853
2007			0.840	0.892	0.832	0.882	0.857

of the fall depends upon assumptions made about the appropriate life expectancy tables.

We first provide a comparison of money's worth based on mortality of male lives, using the contemporary actuarial tables based on 'lives' discussed above, in Table 6.2 and Figure 6.3. Since it is impossible to date the precise point at which one should move from one life table to another we allow overlap years. The main feature of this graph is one which we shall find in the other graphs too: for any given life table, money's worth appears to be falling over time: for example, using the PML80 table, the money's worth falls from 90 pence to 88 pence over the period 1994–2000. However, on moving to the PML92 table, the money's worth rises

Table 6.5. Money's worth for compulsory annuities, male, 65, real, lives

Year	PML80	PML92	PML92 short cohort	PML92 long cohort	PNML00 short cohort	PNML00 long cohort	Overall MW (combined 'Lives')
1999	0.812	0.895					0.895
2000	0.778	0.860					0.860
2001		0.820					0.820
2002		0.796	0.862	0.938			0.900
2003		0.779	0.845	0.922			0.884
2004			0.770	0.841			0.806
2005			0.741	0.812	0.739	0.810	0.774
2006			0.719	0.790	0.717	0.789	0.753
2007			0.710	0.782	0.708	0.780	0.744

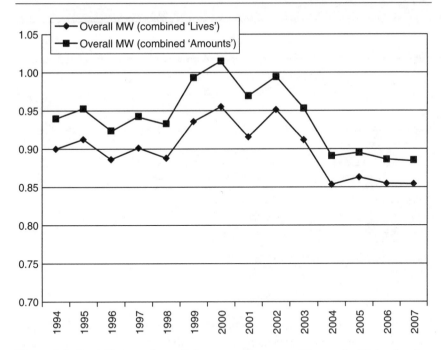

Figure 6.4. Overall money's worth for compulsory annuities, male, 65, level, using combined 'Lives' and combined 'Amounts' mortality

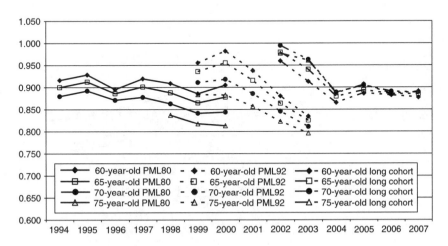

Figure 6.5. Money's worth for compulsory annuities, male, level, different ages, using 'Lives' mortality

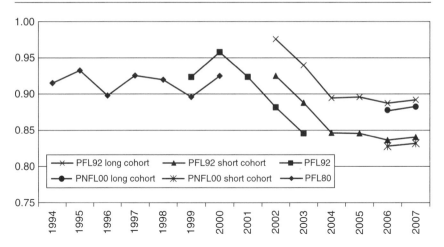

Figure 6.6. Money's worth for compulsory annuities, female, 65, level, using 'Lives' mortality

from 88 pence to 96 pence in 2000. Almost certainly the gradual decline we appear to observe when using the PML80 table is due to life insurers pricing in higher life expectancy and anticipating the newer mortality tables on the basis of private information. The only new mortality table which makes little difference is the 00 Table, but this is unsurprising since

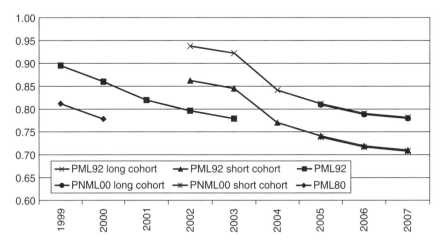

Figure 6.7. Money's worth for compulsory annuities, male, 65, real, using 'Lives' mortality

it follows on so quickly from the interim adjustments to the 92 Table.[6] In Figure 6.4 we plot our estimate of the overall money's worth of 65-year-old males using the combination of life tables, from Figure 6.3, to give our estimate of the change in money's worth over the sample.

Once we allow for the discrete arrival of revised mortality projections, the decline in money's worth appears to be very small and is itself uncertain because of the uncertainty in which mortality projections to use. If we take the interim short cohort adjustment as the appropriate basis for pricing annuities, the money's worth falls from 90 pence in 1994 to 83 pence in 2007, but if we use the interim long cohort adjustment then the money's worth only falls to 88 pence.

In the last column of Table 6.2 and illustrated in Figure 6.4 we present the money's worth numbers based on mortality calculated from amounts (the size of annuity policies) from the PMA tables. As discussed above, richer people tend to live longer and so when we take an expectation of life weighted by pension size, the life expectancy is longer and the money's worth is higher. Using the PMA tables, the money's worth is 94 pence in 1994, falling to between 87 pence and 92 pence, depending on whether one uses the short or long cohort assumption. This is uniformly considerably higher than for the figures obtained using the PML tables. From the point of view of the life insurers' profits, it is the money's worth weighted by pension size that matters and these figures suggest that annuity business has not been excessively profitable. It is difficult to gauge whether the fall in money's worth is 'justified' by market conditions, but the change could be consistent with annuities being deemed as more risky due to greater uncertainty over life expectancy (and greater recognition of that uncertainty).

To get some idea of the significance of the improvement in mortality for our money's worth calculations, we can consider what money's worth we should estimate if we had the wrong mortality tables. If the 80 Tables were still being used in 2007, the apparent money's worth would be 70 pence, suggesting a fall in value of over one-fifth. Of course, it would be entirely inappropriate to use such a table because the cumulative effect of raised life expectancy is between six and nine years.

Table 6.3 and Figure 6.5 show the corresponding money's worths for different ages. As reported in Finkelstein and Poterba (2002) it initially appears that the money's worth is lower at older ages, but this ordering rather dramatically disappears or even reverses when using the long cohort adjustment (the short cohort adjustment, which is omitted from the graph for clarity, does not suggest such a reversal). It is also the case that at the older ages, and using the relatively optimistic long cohort adjustment, there has been no fall in money's worth at all: for example for 70-year-olds the money's worth is 88 pence in 1994 and 89 pence in 2007.

Table 6.4 and Figure 6.6 illustrate similar results for women, although, interestingly women always tend to have higher money's worths.

Table 6.5 and Figure 6.7 turn to inflation-linked or real annuities, for which we only have data for 1999 onwards. The money's worth is always lower for such annuities: compare the money's worth of 94 pence for a nominal and 90 pence for a real annuity for a 65-year-old man in 1999. Finkelstein and Poterba (2002) suggest this is due to selection effects, as longer-lived people would be more likely to choose real to nominal annuities (see Chapter 9). However, the discrepancy has more than doubled since 1999: using the 92 table with the long cohort projection, the money's worths are 89 pence for nominal and 78 pence for real. It is implausible to suggest that this is entirely due to changes in selection effects and this raises the question of whether other issues, such as higher costs of inflation-linked annuities, are the major cause of the difference in the money's worth.

The most recent revisions to mortality projections by the actuarial profession have been published (in provisional form) in CMI Working Paper 20 which we summarized in Table 4.4. These projections attempt to model the forecast uncertainty by reporting confidence intervals. The estimated 95 per cent confidence interval for annuity prices (the reciprocal of the money's worth) is about 6 per cent: that is, the money's worth could be up to 3 per cent higher or lower than the central projection. This is clearly a large range of uncertainty, but whether it is appropriate is the subject of ongoing actuarial research as discussed in Chapter 4.

As a final robustness check on our results, we considered two separate assumptions with respect to the annuity rate and the appropriate discount rate. So far we have used the average annuity rate quoted each month across the sample of annuity providers. However, these quotes may be stale or an annuity provider who wishes to manage the risk of their annuity book may quote uncompetitive rates. In addition the open-market option means that an annuitant could obtain the maximum of the annuity rates quoted and therefore the maximum annuity rate each month may be a better indicator of the money's worth. We repeated our money's worth calculations for 65-year-old males purchasing level annuities, and we used the PML92 (long) tables for the whole sample, and compared the money's worth from using the average annuity rate with that from the maximum annuity rate. The money's worth increased from an average value of 98 pence to 103 pence. So we may conclude that using the maximum annuity rate increases the money's worth by 5 pence.

As a second robustness check, instead of using the yields on government bonds to calculate money's worth, we use the corporate bond yield as the appropriate discount rate. From the information in Table 2.5, we infer that the risk premium on corporate bonds averaged 0.9 per cent over the sample. We repeated our money's worth calculations for 65-year-old males purchasing level annuities, and we used the PML92 (long) tables for the whole sample, and compared the money's worth from discounting the average annuity rate at the government bond yields with a discount rate that imposed a 0.9 per cent risk premium. We found that the money's worth decreased from an average value of 99 pence to 92 pence. The implication is that imposing a corporate bond risk premium in the discount rate reduces the money's worth by 7 pence.

6.3. Evidence on international money's worth

International evidence on money's worth is provided by James and Song (2001), who construct consistent money's worth figures across a number of countries, and a summary of their results are presented in Table 6.6. In order to ensure that these numbers are comparable across countries, these authors ensure that the mortality tables and discount rate assumptions are consistently defined.

The surprising aspect of this table is that although annuity payments differ widely across countries, and by gender, the money's worth numbers are very similar and very high. This suggests that any dispersion in annuity payments can be explained by differences in the appropriate discount rates, and differences in mortality assumptions. Money's worths using annuitant mortality experience are typically around 97 per cent in all categories (except index-linked). Switzerland appears to have the highest value-for-money annuities, with money's worth above 100 per cent. The money's worth ratios are lower if population tables are used implying that there are some selection effects at work. The one category that does have lower money's worths is indexed-linked annuities, and again this might be explained by the difficulty of matching these promised payments with index-linked assets, since the supply of such assets is limited.

Table 6.6. International evidence on money's worth of annuities in 1999

Panel A: Males 65 in 1999: Money's worth of nominal annuities using risk-free discount rate

Life tables	Canada		USA		Australia		UK		Switzerland		Singapore	
	Pop.	Ann.	Pop.	Ann.	Pop.	Ann.	Pop.	Ann.	Pop.	Ann.	Pop.	Ann.
Single level	0.914	0.981	0.858	0.974	0.911	1.01	0.912	0.983	0.916	1.082	0.996	1.024
10-year guarantee	0.928	0.974			0.915	0.996	0.944	0.993	0.945	1.08		
Joint	0.939	0.98	0.864	0.951	0.867	0.936	0.933	0.988	0.902	1.013		

Panel B: Males 65 in 1999: Money's worth of index-linked annuities using risk-free discount rate

Life tables	UK		Chile		Israel	
	Pop.	Ann.	Pop.	Ann.	Pop.	Ann.
Single level	0.817	0.894	0.865	0.967	0.769	0.882
10-year guarantee			0.887	0.954	0.797	0.877
Joint	0.818	0.88	0.905	0.985		1.092

Panel C: Females 65 in 1999: Money's worth of nominal annuities using risk-free discount rate

Life tables	Canada		USA		Australia		UK		Switzerland		Singapore	
	Pop.	Ann.	Pop.	Ann.	Pop.	Ann.	Pop.	Ann.	Pop.	Ann.	Pop.	Ann.
Single level	0.95	0.976	0.871	0.954	0.915	0.984	0.926	0.974	0.969	1.057	1.008	1.039
10-year guarantee	0.955	0.973			0.912	0.972	0.949	0.987	0.982	1.057		

Panel D: Females 65 in 1999: Money's worth of index-linked annuities using risk-free discount rate

Life tables	UK		Chile		Israel	
	Pop.	Ann.	Pop.	Ann.	Pop.	Ann.
Single level	0.813	0.867	0.861	0.949	0.73	0.869
10-year guarantee			0.878	0.942	0.756	0.866

Source: James and Song (2001), table 6.

The conclusion from Table 6.6 is that annuities seem remarkably good value for consumers in all annuity markets. In fact given the very high money's worth ratios that are observed across international annuity markets, once we take into account administration costs of running an annuity business, it appears that insurance companies are losing money on the annuity business that they write. James and Song (2001) argue that the only way insurance companies can make positive profits is on the spread between the risk-free rate and the returns on an equity portfolio: insurance companies invest the annuity premiums received in a portfolio of risky assets. They then engage in risk-reducing and risk-shifting strategies to lock-in the higher returns. We now look in more detail at money's worth evidence in specific countries.

Mitchell et al. (1999), following the methodology in Warshawsky (1988), compute money's worth values for annuities in the USA. They compute money's worth ratios using life tables for the general population and for people who purchase annuities. The general population life tables are based on mortality tables created by the Office of the Actuary at the US Social Security Administration in 1995. The set of annuitant life tables are based on expected mortality probabilities of the subset of the population that purchase annuities, made available by the Society of Actuaries. The results are presented in Table 6.7. Using a discount rate derived from the yield curve for US government bonds, and annuitant life tables, they estimate money's worth ratios of around 93 per cent for males and females of different ages. There is evidence of selection effects, since the money's

Table 6.7. Money's worth of US annuities in 1995

Life tables	Treasury yield curve		Corporate yield curve	
	Pop.	Ann.	Pop.	Ann.
Men				
Age 55	0.852	0.934	0.773	0.84
Age 65	0.814	0.927	0.756	0.853
Age 75	0.783	0.913	0.743	0.86
Women				
Age 55	0.88	0.937	0.791	0.838
Age 65	0.854	0.927	0.785	0.847
Age 75	0.846	0.919	0.796	0.861
Joint and survivor				
Age 55	0.889	0.93	0.792	0.824
Age 65	0.868	0.929	0.792	0.841
Age 75	0.846	0.922	0.791	0.857

Source: Mitchell et al. (1999).

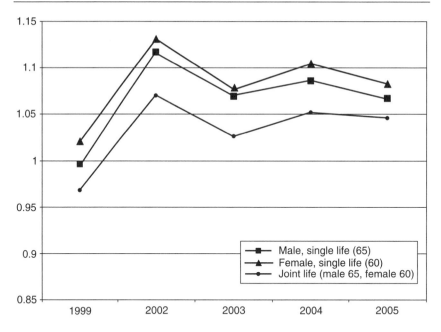

Figure 6.8. Money's worth of annuities in Chile 1999–2005

Source: Rocha and Thorburn (2006)

worth ratios from population life tables are significantly lower. There is also evidence that money's worth declines with age.

Rocha and Thorburn (2006) report money's worth figures for annuities in Chile across a range of products, for different ages. We illustrate the figures for level annuities for males aged 65 and females aged 60 in Figure 6.8. Rocha and Thorburn note that annuities have been very good value for consumers, with money's worth consistently higher than unity. They also find that money's worth of joint annuities is less than single annuities; money's worth for males are less than for females; money's worth of guaranteed annuities are smaller than non-guaranteed; and money's worth for older annuitants are higher than for younger ones. In addition, Rocha and Thorburn (2006) have information on 5,137 individual annuity contracts issued over the period 1999–2005, and compute the money's worth for each individual contract, so that they can then relate money's worth to individual characteristics. They regress MW$_{it}$ of individual i in period t on gender, age, size of premium, and dummies for guarantees and deferment. The regression specification explains around 65 per cent of the variation in the pooled sample, and they find that money's worth was positively and significantly related to age, size of

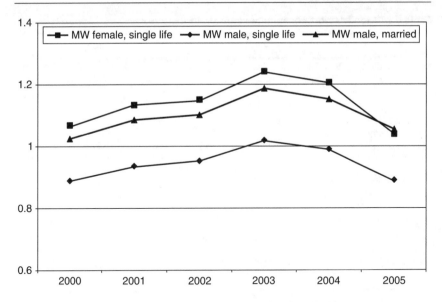

Figure 6.9. Money's worth of annuities in Switzerland 2000–05

Source: Bütler and Ruesch (2007)

premium, and deferment; and negatively associated with longer guarantee periods.

Bütler and Ruesch (2007) calculate money's worth for Swiss annuities illustrated in Figure 6.9, and conclude that these are very good value for consumers. For both females and married males, money's worth is greater than unity. Although for single males money's worth is less than unity, this is because by law in Switzerland single males are offered the same annuity rates as married males, and in the subsequent pooling equilibrium, married males are much better off than single males.

Money's worth values for Australian annuities are taken from Knox (2000). Table 6.8 Panel A reports money's worth for males and Table 6.8 Panel B for females, for three different annuity products: level, level with a 10-year guarantee, and index linked at 5 per cent in 1999. There are two sets of mortality assumptions: (*a*) A95–97Imp use population life tables based on deaths from 1995–97 prepared jointly by the Australian Bureau of Statistics and the Office of the Australian Government Actuary with imputed mortality improvements; and (*b*) UK's CMI IM80 tables for annuitants, updated to Australian conditions by multiplying by 0.6. Annual spot rates of interest rates are taken from the yields on government bonds.

135

Table 6.8. Money's worth of annuities in Australia in 1999

Age	Age 60			Age 65		
Mortality tables	A95–97 Imp	0.6*IM80	A95–97 Imp	A95–97 Imp	0.6*IM80	A95–97 Imp
Interest rates	Spot	Spot	Spot + 1% (Corporate)	Spot	Spot	Spot + 1% (Corporate)
Panel A: Males						
Type of annuity						
Level	0.923	0.964	0.845	0.914	0.986	0.846
Level with 10 year certain	0.922	0.957	0.845	0.919	0.975	0.852
Indexed at 5% pa	0.896	0.977	0.796	0.893	1.016	0.809
Panel B: Females						
Type of annuity						
Level	0.915	0.956	0.831	0.914	0.970	0.839
Level with 10 year certain	0.912	0.946	0.828	0.913	0.960	0.839
Indexed at 5% pa	0.871	0.946	0.763	0.880	0.979	0.786

Source: Knox (2000).

The Australian money's worth figures are predominantly above 90 per cent. Males have higher money's worth ratios than females. The use of the annuitant life tables increases the money's worth, implying that there are selection effects in the Australian annuity market. The extra 100 basis points in the discount rate to reflect a corporate bond yield also has the effect of reducing money's worth. Indexed annuities offer lower money's worths.

Table 6.9 shows the money's worth for Singapore annuities taken from Fong (2002). The table reports money's worth figures for 55-year-old males and females based on annuity quotes from nine insurance companies in 2000. For the discount rate, it is assumed that there is a flat term structure on a long-term Singapore government bond, which at that time was 4.6 per cent. In addition, Table 6.9 gives the money's worth for the official discount rate of 5 per cent, which, under the 1992 Insurance

Table 6.9. Money's worth of annuities in Singapore in 2000 for 55-year-olds

Life tables	Males 65		Females 65	
	Pop.	Ann.	Pop.	Ann.
4.6% (Govt. bond yield)	0.986	0.997	1.009	1.014
5% (Statutory rate)	0.923	0.933	0.94	0.944

Source: Fong (2002).

Table 6.10. Money's worth of German annuities in 2002

Life tables	Males 65		Females 65	
	Pop.	Ann.	Pop.	Ann.
No guarantee				
Constant participation	0.886	0.98	0.938	1.012
Escalating participation	0.864	0.968	0.921	1.008
10-Year guarantee				
Constant participation	0.902	0.969	0.94	1.001
Escalating participation	0.885	0.963	0.923	0.997

Source: Von Gaudecker and Weber (2004).

Regulation Act, insurers are required to use to value annuities. The life tables in the first column are for the general population of Singapore, and in the annuitants' column, make use of the UK's CMI a(90) tables for annuitants, adjusted to Singapore population experience.

The money's worth figures for Singapore are very high. Females have higher money's worth than males, but the difference in using annuity mortalities rather than population mortalities has very little effect. Fong (2002) concludes that this is evidence that there are few selection effects in the Singapore annuity market, possibly because of the mandatory aspect of the second tier pension scheme.

Money's worth results for Germany are given in Table 6.10. The difference between constant and escalating participation depends on whether bonuses from equity investments are included in the payments to the annuity holder.

As can be seen, for German annuities using annuitant life tables, the money's worth is 98 per cent for male non-guaranteed annuities, falling slightly for annuities with guaranteed payments. The money's worth figures for females are even higher and are greater than unity. There is evidence of some selection effects since the money's worth ratios for population tables are lower.

How does the money's worth of annuities compare with the value of other insurance products? The Association of British Insurers has provided us with estimates of the premiums paid and the claims made for a number of insurance markets: motor, domestic property, and commercial property insurance over the period 1994–2005. The ratio of the value of claims to premiums paid is a crude measure of the money's worth of these insurance products. We plot these ratios for each year, for level annuities for 65-year-old males, and for the three general insurance products, in Figure 6.10. It

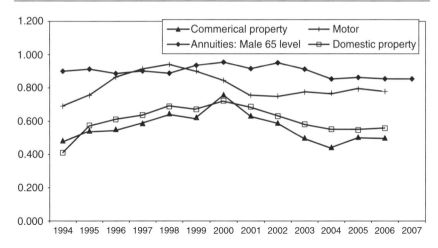

Figure 6.10. Money's worth of compulsory annuities ('Lives') and claims ratios for motor, domestic, and commercial property insurance

Source: ABI and own calculations.

can be seen that the money's worth of annuities is consistently higher than the other insurance products. There was only a brief period in the late 1990s when motor insurance was better value than annuities.

James (2000) examines the cost of investing in a variety of retail investment products in the UK, and finds that to get the market rate of return on £1, a consumer would have to invest £1.50 in a managed fund, and between £1.10 and £1.25 in an index tracker. These figures imply a money's worth of 66 pence for a managed fund, and less than 91 pence for a tracker. This suggests that it is during the accumulation phase that charges from pension providers have a significant reduction on the effective rate of return and not in the decumulation phase.

Notes

1. A less commonly used method is to calculate the internal rate of return implied by an annuity rate. The advantage of this approach is that it is necessary only to project life expectancies and no assumptions about interest rates are necessary.
2. For a discussion of this, see Chapter 7.
3. The figure of 98 pence for 1990 is based upon the money's worth calculated using the a(90) table. Using the IM80 table, which was just available in that year, the figure would be 103 pence.

4. These improvements (for both male and female mortality rates) were based upon the actual improvements in female annuitant mortality over the period 1880–1945: the data for male mortality over this period was too variable to be used for a projection. Note that the number of female annuities in force over that period was considerably larger than the number of male annuities.

5. However, we cannot assume that an individual with lower life expectancy than average will necessarily get less additional utility from purchasing an annuity (based on average life expectancy) than an individual with higher life expectancy. We discuss this in Chapter 7.

6. As we have noted already, the 00 Table does not have projections: to calculate these figures we apply the interim adjustments to the realized mortality in 2000. This is a further reason why our two sets of projections are so close.

7

Annuity demand theory

In this chapter and the next we turn to economic theories of annuity demand. This chapter presents the important theoretical result of Yaari (1965), which demonstrates that complete annuitization is optimal for individuals who have an uncertain lifetime, suggesting that demand for annuities should be high. As we have discussed in earlier chapters, the evidence is that annuity markets are actually quite small and this disparity between theory and practice is referred to as the 'annuity puzzle'. Clearly the simplest version of Yaari's theory is wrong: the challenge is to work out why it is wrong and the consequences which we return to in Chapter 8.[1]

To introduce the theory, we start the chapter with a simple diagrammatic exposition of the annuity purchase decision. This model is a deliberate simplification of the problem facing a pensioner, but is designed to introduce the basic framework and issues. This model can be extended easily to address a variety of additional issues and we use it extensively when discussing reasons for the annuity puzzle in the next chapter.

In the course of discussing Yaari's result (1965) we need to clarify what is meant by 'annuitization' and consider more carefully the actual choices available to people when they retire. Accordingly we incorporate the discussion of annuity products from Chapter 2 to provide a more realistic theory of annuity demand.

We also need to understand the methodology used by economists to analyse savings decisions, namely expected-utility maximization. We provide a detailed critique of this approach for both economists and non-economists to determine where the theory might be inapplicable. This allows us to quantify the benefits of annuitization under a range of assumptions. Our analysis provides an appropriate benchmark against which we can consider the annuity puzzle in Chapter 8.

7.1. A Simple model of annuity demand

One of the most important reasons for purchasing an annuity is to insure against uncertain length of life, so in this section we simplify the issue by ignoring all other forms of uncertainty. In particular, we shall assume that there is no inflation. Implicitly this is the same as assuming that individuals are purchasing index-linked annuities.

In practice someone retiring at 65 might live for a short period or live for another 40 years. Again, we simplify by assuming that in fact there are only two possibilities: the pensioner will live either for one period or for two periods. The individual will definitely be alive in period 0 (the current period) and will be alive in period 1 with probability p.

Suppose also that the individual has pension wealth W_0, no other wealth and no other source of income. The individual can choose to hold any positive proportion of his wealth in an annuity (which only pays a return if the individual is alive) or in another savings product which is not life-contingent, which we shall call a bond (in practice this is more likely to be a savings account in a bank or building society). We do not consider the possibility of holding some wealth in equity, either directly or indirectly. The individual has no heirs and no desire to leave a bequest.

The related questions facing this individual are: first, how much to consume in each period; and secondly, what proportion of wealth to annuitize?

Suppose that for each £1 invested in an annuity the annuitant receives a per-period payment of A: the first such payment is certain and the second occurs with probability p (if the individual is still alive). We shall refer to this as a 'conventional' annuity since it makes the same (real) payment in both periods. The expected net present value of these payments is the money's worth:

$$A + p\frac{A}{1+r} = \frac{A(1+r+p)}{1+r} = \text{money's worth} \qquad (7.1)$$

where we use r to denote the real interest rate.

Rearranging equation (7.1) we obtain the per-period payment received in exchange for £1 purchase price (which we refer to as the annuity rate)

$$A = \frac{(1+r)}{1+r+p} \times \text{money's worth} \qquad (7.2)$$

For simplicity of exposition we shall assume for the rest of this chapter that the money's worth is unity. Given this assumption, an individual who uses a proportion θ of his wealth to purchase an annuity (where $0 \le \theta \le 1$) will receive a total per-period annuity payment of

$$A\theta W_0 = \frac{(1+r)\,\theta W_0}{1+r+p} \tag{7.3}$$

and still has $(1 - \theta)W_0$ which has not been invested.

An important assumption that we shall make is that the individual is unable to borrow against future annuity payments. Although there is no reason in principle why individuals could not do this, in fact financial institutions would be wary of lending money against a future uncertain payment and would be suspicious that the individual had private information that he was going to die and that the future contingent payment would thus not be forthcoming. We discuss this issue in more detail in Chapter 8, Section 8.4.

Given this borrowing constraint, the maximum resources available for consumption in period 0 are

$$\frac{(1+r)\,\theta W_0}{1+r+p} + (1 - \theta)\,W_0 \le W_0 \tag{7.4}$$

where the inequality is strict so long as $\theta > 1$.

Figure 7.1 illustrates the budget constraints that the individual faces with and without annuity purchases. The individual can choose to

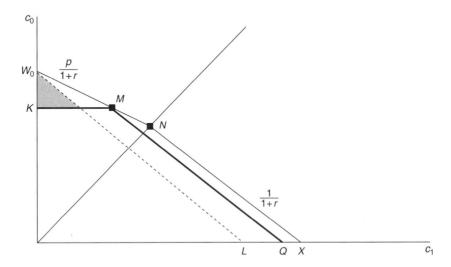

Figure 7.1. Annuitization in a two-period model with conventional annuities and bonds

consume any combination of c_0 and c_1 lying on or to the south-west of the relevant budget constraint: consumption to the north-east of the budget constraint is impossible since it exceeds the individual's wealth.

The first possibility facing the individual is to save wealth from period 0 to period 1 using only bonds. Since bonds receive interest r, £1 saved in period 0 allows increased consumption in period 1 of £$(1+r)$ and hence the budget constraint has a slope of $1/(1+r)$. This budget constraint is shown by the dashed line W_0–L. Alternatively the individual can purchase an annuity as discussed above. Having purchased this annuity, consumption in period 0 cannot be more than the expression in equation (7.4), but it could be less: any additional saving is held in bonds and earns a rate of return r. For a particular size of annuity purchase, this budget constraint is shown by the solid black line: the horizontal section shows the maximum that can be consumed in period 0 and the oblique section shows consumption combinations involving both purchasing an annuity and saving some wealth in bonds.

At point M the individual purchases an annuity and has no savings in bonds at all. This point we refer to as full annuitization since no savings are put into bonds. Notice that this point does not involve the individual putting all of his wealth into an annuity.

When we compare the two budget constraints we see that neither dominates the other. Remember that the individual increases consumption in both periods by moving north-east on the diagram, but it is not the case that the budget constraint obtained with an annuity is always to the north-east of the budget constraint without an annuity since there is the small grey triangle where the bond-only budget constraint is above the annuity budget constraint. This highlights the fact that purchasing an annuity is an irreversible decision: in the simple two-period model this is not very important since the individual chooses his annuity purchase and then consumes immediately so he would never be in a position where he would wish to consume in the grey triangle. But in a many-period model this could be important.

The bold line in Figure 7.1 only shows the budget constraint for a particular annuity purchase (i.e. a particular value of θ). Since the individual can choose to annuitize any amount of his wealth he can achieve any point on the thin black line, which forms an envelope of possible annuity-purchase budget constraints and is thus the relevant constraint for the utility maximizing decision.[2] At point N the individual has used all of his wealth to buy a conventional annuity, so $\theta = 1$, and consumption is equal in both periods: this level of consumption is Friedman's permanent income.

This envelope $W_0 - N - X$ includes a section $N - X$ which is not fully annuitized since some wealth is held in bonds. The reason for this is that so far we have only allowed the individual to purchase either bonds or a conventional annuity making a payment of A in both periods. We now consider what would happen if more sophisticated annuity products were available.

Suppose the individual wished to consume more in period 1 than in period 0 and wished to be fully annuitized. This could be achieved either by purchasing an escalating real annuity or by purchasing a combination of a conventional annuity plus a deferred annuity. The deferred annuity would make at most one payment, which would be in period 1. For £1 purchase price, this payment would be A^{def} and would be paid with probability p (i.e. it would only be paid if the individual were still alive in period 1). The present value in period 0 of this payment would be $p/(1 + r)$, so

$$A^{\text{def}} = \frac{1+r}{p} \tag{7.5}$$

If the individual put all of his wealth into a deferred annuity then he could achieve the consumption bundle at point Z where

$$c_1^{\max} = \frac{1+r}{p} W_0 \tag{7.6}$$

By making appropriate purchases of both a conventional annuity and a deferred annuity the individual could achieve any point along the envelope $N - Z$ in Figure 7.2 and thus the complete annuity budget constraint is $W_0 - Z$. For example, suppose the individual chooses to annuitize at point Q: an appropriate pattern of annuity payments can be achieved with the combination of a conventional and a deferred annuity illustrated in the diagram. Any point on $W_0 - Z$ involves holding no bonds at all and thus the individual is fully annuitized. Importantly, the budget constraint with full annuitization $W_0 - Z$ lies strictly above the budget constraint from using bonds only $W_0 - L$. The difference between the budget constraints $W_0 - N - Z$ in Figure 7.1 and $W_0 - Z$ in Figure 7.2 is that it is only in the latter that there is a full range of annuity products,

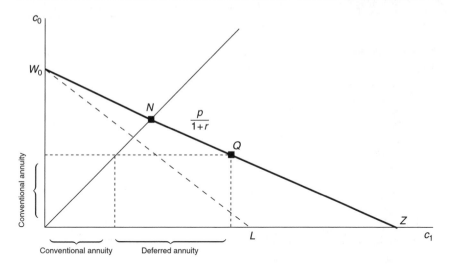

Figure 7.2. Annuitization in a two-period model with conventional and deferred annuities—a perfect annuity market

a situation that we refer to as a perfect annuity market. This is the scenario considered by Yaari (1965).

Yaari's result that full annuitization is optimal in a perfect annuity market follows from the fact that full annuitization results in the budget constraint being as far to the north-east as is possible and does not depend upon the individual's preferences. However, it does rely upon perfect annuity markets being available: in practice there is usually only an extremely limited market for deferred annuities.

We have not yet found the optimal consumption path. Economists assume that an agent has an indifference curve showing the trade-off between certain consumption in period 0 with possible consumption in period 1. Assuming that the indifference curve takes the standard shape, the optimal consumption path is found through a diagram such as Figure 7.3. In this example we show the agent preferring more consumption in period 0 than in period 1, but the converse is also possible. The indifference curve can be derived from an underlying expected utility function, usually of the form

$$V = u(c_0) + p\delta u(c_1) \qquad u'(c) > 0, \quad u''(c) < 0, \quad 0 < \delta \leq 1 \qquad (7.7)$$

where the parameter δ is introduced to allow for agent's impatience: the perceived value today of consumption in the future may be less than

145

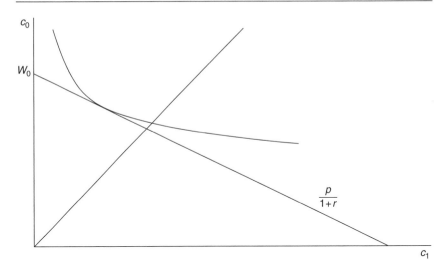

Figure 7.3. Annuitization in a two-period model—finding a solution using utility maximization

that of consumption today ($\delta = 1$ corresponds to an agent who is perfectly patient). This results in a slope of $p\delta$ where the indifference curve crosses the $45°$ line.[3] Equal consumption in both periods would be an optimal solution if $\delta = (1 + r)^{-1}$, in which case the indifference curve will be tangent to the budget constraint on this $45°$ line: it is optimal to put all of one's initial wealth into an annuity only if the interest rate exactly offsets the impatience of the agent to consume today rather than tomorrow.

Having shown that full annuitization (choosing a consumption bundle on $W_0 - Z$) is optimal, we need to find some way of measuring the value of annuitization compared with the alternative. Economists do not believe that the utility function V introduced in equation (7.7) can be used directly for this purpose. This is because any consumption plan that maximizes V will also maximize

$$V^* = \lambda_0 + \lambda_1 V \qquad (7.8)$$

where λ_0 and λ_1 are arbitrary constants subject to $\lambda_1 > 0$: this means that the utility function can take on any value that we like: the value of V has no usable meaning. Instead we may use the concept of Annuity Equivalent Wealth (AEW). We have seen that the ability to buy annuities increases the welfare of the agent: a hypothetical alternative would

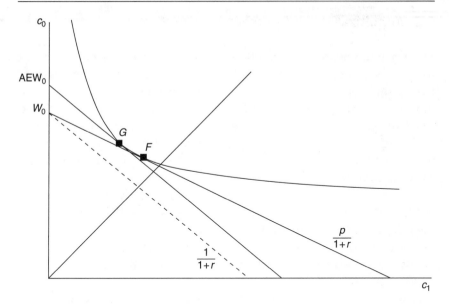

Figure 7.4. Deriving annuity equivalent wealth

be to confine the agent to purchasing bonds and to give him more wealth instead. We now find that level of wealth without annuities which yields the same level of utility to an agent as W_0 with a perfect annuity market.

The diagrammatic solution to this question is illustrated in Figure 7.4: to be indifferent between the two choices the agent must be on the same indifference curve and so we find AEW_0 by finding the lowest possible budget constraint with slope $1/(1 + r)$ which is tangent to this curve. An agent would be indifferent between point F (having wealth W_0 and perfect annuity markets) and point G (having wealth AEW_0 and bonds alone).[4]

This allows us to make an important qualitative point about the effect of p on the utility value of an annuity. If p is low, the budget constraint with annuities $W_0 - Z$ will be relatively flat and far away from the budget constraint without annuities $W_0 - L$, suggesting a large gain to annuitization; whereas if p is high, the budget constraint $W_0 - Z$ will be steep and very close to $W_0 - L$, a small gain to annuitization. Hence the gain to annuitization is higher if the individual has a low life expectancy.

7.2. Annuitization and purchasing annuities

The range of possible consumption patterns in the two-period model of the previous section consumption is very limited since the only possibilities are that consumption rise or fall. In practice agents may prefer much more complicated consumption profiles, but these can only be modelled in a more general multi-period model, to which we now turn.

Throughout this section we shall continue to distinguish perfect annuitization (holding all wealth in life-contingent assets) and purchasing a conventional annuity.

Consider a perfect bond market, where agents can buy bonds of all relevant maturities j, with per-period interest rate r_j: in other words interest rates depend upon maturity and this relationship is summarized by the term structure of interest rates (described in Chapter 4) and agents have access to this entire term structure. In Yaari's model the key distinction is between two sorts of asset:

First, a bond which, in exchange for £1 saved this period yields a total return of $£(1 + r_j)^j$ at a date j periods in the future, regardless of whether the purchaser is alive or dead; and

Second, an annuity which, in exchange for £1 saved this period yields a total return of $£(1 + r_j)^j / s_j$ at a date j periods in the future, if the annuitant is alive at date j, which occurs with survival probability s_j.[5]

Both sorts of asset can be purchased in any quantity with zero transaction costs. In this context, a perfect annuity market refers to the availability of a complete set of assets for every maturity with actuarially fair life-contingent returns; this is the analogue of a perfect bond market where pure discount bonds are available at all maturities.[6] In practice this means that an agent alive for many periods might need a very complicated set of annuity products to achieve his optimal consumption path over time. We can illustrate this using a simple three-period extension of the model: the agent will certainly live in period 0, will be alive in period 1 with probability s_1 and will be alive in period 2 with probability s_2 (obviously $s_2 < s_1 < 1$).

We now consider the following sorts of life annuity products that could be purchased by an agent in a three-period context. Referring back to the annuity types described in Chapter 2, we can envisage the following specific annuities that could be purchased at the beginning of period 0 in exchange for a single premium:[7]

Conventional Annuity. This pays a constant income in all three periods in which the annuitant is alive.

Temporary Annuity. A temporary annuity pays a constant income for a maximum number of years, conditional on the annuitant being alive in that period. In our three-period model the only relevant sort of temporary annuity is one that makes a payment in periods 0 and 1 (a payment for certain in period 0, since the agent definitely lives in that period and a contingent payment in period 1).

Deferred Annuity. A deferred annuity pays a constant real income for all periods that the agent is alive, but beginning at some point in the future (in this case it is possible that no payments will ever be made). In our context there are two possible deferred annuities: deferred one period—this potentially pays an income in both periods 1 and 2; and deferred two periods—this potentially pays an income in period 2 alone.

Temporary Deferred Annuity. This annuity makes a payment in period 1 only, conditional on the annuitant being alive in period 1. It is deferred because it only commences payment in the future (i.e. period 1 rather than period 0) and it is temporary because it ceases payment in period 1 and does not continue to period 2.

We have already noted in Chapter 2 that in practice both temporary and deferred annuities are rare. The final assumption that we make is that the agent is unable to go short in the annuity market—to do this the agent would need to sell a stream of income to an insurance company which would continue until the agent's death.[8]

The agent now has to decide how much to consume in three periods, that is, an optimal consumption path $\{c_0^*, c_1^*, c_2^*\}$ and decide how much of his wealth to hold in bonds and the various annuity products described above. As with the previous model, appropriate combinations of annuity purchases enable the agent to attain a budget constraint which is an envelope of the budget constraints of particular annuity purchase decisions. The precise optimum is determined by the interest rates at different maturities and the agent's indifference curve. If the annuity market is perfect then agents will annuitize fully.

Clearly one possible consumption path to this optimizing problem is that $c_0^* > c_1^* > c_2^*$. We now need to ask what combination of underlying annuities achieves this consumption profile. To obtain consumption of c_2^* the agent can buy a conventional annuity that pays out an income $y = c_2^*$ in each period. There are now two potential ways of ensuring the required level of consumption in periods 0 and 1.

The first solution is to buy the temporary annuity making payments of $c_1^* - y$, the first in period 0 (paid with certainty) and the second in period 1 (paid with probability s_1 if the individual is still alive). In period 0 consumption of c_0^* is then achieved partly by consuming out of the income from two annuities of y and $c_1^* - y$ giving a total of c_1^*: the remainder is funded by a quantity $c_0^* - c_1^*$ from the initial wealth.

The second solution would be to buy an annuity product that was both temporary and deferred: this would make a single payment of $c_1^* - y$ in period 1 (paid with probability s_1 if the individual is still alive). The part of initial wealth used for consumption in period 0 would then be $c_0^* - y$. These two solutions are illustrated in the first two rows of Table 7.1.

The optimal consumption plan of $c_0^* > c_1^* > c_2^*$ is only one possibility. With three periods there are six possible consumption paths. The remaining rows of Table 7.1 illustrate the other five possible consumption paths and how they might be achieved by purchasing different annuity products.

Given the complexity of Table 7.1, which is for a highly stylized three-period model, it seems highly unlikely that the requirements for a perfect annuity market would exist in practice: first, they require annuity products which are not widely available; secondly, such complicated arrangements would be very expensive to implement given the presence of transactions costs; thirdly, determining the correct portfolio of annuities would involve complex calculations—and this is before we take account of risky assets or other complicating factors. For this reason it is unsurprising that we do not observe perfect annuitization in practice. A more relevant question is determining the utility value of a conventional annuity, since these are the products that are widely available. To do this we shall require a more detailed description of agents' utility and corresponding demand for annuities and we consider this in the next section.

7.3. Expected-utility maximization

The simplest way of working out the demand for annuities is to ask how much a potential annuitant would value any given annuity to provide an annuity demand curve and then assume that purchases would be made based on that valuation. This requires some way of measuring the value of an annuity to the annuitant. In Chapter 4 we considered an actuarial measure of the value of an annuity, namely the money's worth, but such an approach fails to take into account the annuitant's attitude to

Table 7.1. Combinations of life annuities needed for three-period model

Possible optimal consumption paths	Consume some initial wealth	Conventional annuity (payments in periods 0, 1, 2)	Temporary annuity (payments in periods 0, 1 only)	Deferred annuity (payments in periods 1, 2 only)	Temporary deferred annuity (payment in period 1 only)	Deferred annuity (payment in period 2 only)
$c_0 > c_1 > c_2$	✓✓	✓✓	✓			
$c_0 > c_2 > c_1$	✓	✓			✓	✓
$c_1 > c_0 > c_2$	✓	✓✓	✓		✓✓	
$c_1 > c_2 > c_0$		✓✓		✓	✓✓	
$c_2 > c_0 > c_1$	✓	✓				✓
$c_2 > c_1 > c_0$		✓✓		✓	✓	✓✓

risk or the value to the annuitant of income payments at different points in time.

Economists resolve this problem with a model of agents' preferences from which can be derived an optimal path of income payments: it is then assumed that agents are capable of finding this optimum and making purchases to achieve it. If economists' characterization of preferences were accurate, then the resulting theory would explain pensioners' actual demand for annuities, resulting in a descriptive (sometimes called positive) theory of annuity demand. However, in practice agents may be unable to calculate the optimum size of annuity purchase and, even if they can calculate it, there may be reasons why they do not purchase it in practice. In this case the theory of annuity demand would not describe actual behaviour, but it would provide a prescriptive (normative) theory of annuity demand which could be used to give advice to pensioners or to policymakers.

The idea that individuals can determine an optimal course of action and that they then choose to follow this course of action is usually referred to as 'economic rationality' or just 'rationality', although it is clear that this does not correspond exactly to rationality as used in everyday language (or in the other social sciences). There is no shortage of popular critiques of economics suggesting that the assumption of economic rationality fundamentally undermines the conclusions of economists.[9] However, in practice economists are much more aware of the problems with 'economic rationality' than is realized and throughout both this and the next chapter we discuss the relevance and meaning of this assumption.

Consider a decision-making unit or agent (in the simplest case an individual pensioner), who will live for at most T periods. The agent is assumed to obtain satisfaction—called utility—from a stream of consumption services, where c_t is consumed in period t. Consumption could be direct consumption of a good which has to be consumed at a point in time (e.g. eating a cake) or it could be consuming services provided by a durable good which will also be available in the future (e.g. using a car). This difference is potentially important because the agent's expenditure is not necessarily the same as the agent's consumption: purchasing a car could involve expenditure at just one point in time but consumption over many subsequent periods. We shall return to this point in Chapter 8. For simplicity we ignore the fact that there are a large number of different goods being consumed by considering only total consumption at different points in time. Assuming that it exists, the mathematical representation of the agent's utility is called the objective function.

The most general objective function that we could use for expected-utility maximization is of the form

$$V_t = E_t [U (c_0, \ldots, c_T)] \tag{7.9}$$

where $E_t [ ]$ is the conventional expectations operator conditional on information available at time t and we write the subscript t on the function V to emphasize that this is the decision taken at time t. However, this is too general to be useful since we have not specified any structure on the function U and so an important part of the expected-utility methodology is determining the form of this function.

We start our discussion with a very common objective function having two particular features called Time Additive Separability (TAS) and Geometric Discounting (GD). With certain lifetime the function is of the following form:

$$V_t = E_t \left[\sum_{j=0}^{T} \delta^j u \left(c_{t+j} \right) \right] \tag{7.10}$$

We start by interpreting this particular functional form. The agent anticipates living for a further T periods and in each period t the agent will directly experience a certain amount of utility dependent upon the per-period utility function (sometimes called the felicity function) which depends only on the amount consumed in that period, c_t. So the utility experienced at a point in time does not depend upon memories of previous consumption or of expected consumption in future periods. Furthermore the objective function is a linear combination of the felicities. These assumptions jointly ensure time additive separability. Since consumption in the future may be uncertain, the felicity is also uncertain and hence the agent cannot maximize utility but maximizes expected utility instead.

The interpretation of the δ^j term is that felicity which is only going to be directly experienced in future periods is subjectively discounted to represent the degree of impatience felt by the agent (since the utility experienced in the initial period 0 is felt contemporaneously it is not discounted). The form of discounting in equation (7.10) is referred to as geometric discounting since this component is a geometric function in j. A more general form of discounting would be to have an objective function

$$V_t = E_t \left[\sum_{j=0}^{T} \delta (j) u \left(c_{t+j} \right) \right] \qquad \delta (j + 1) \leq \delta (j) \tag{7.11}$$

From the point of an agent making an optimizing decision in period 0, utility in two future periods i and j are discounted by $\delta(i)$ and $\delta(j)$, respectively. In period 1, however, the agent could change his plans for future consumption and maximize the new function

$$V_{t+1} = \mathsf{E}_{t+1}\left[\sum_{j=1}^{T}\delta(j)\,u\left(c_{t+j}\right)\right] \tag{7.12}$$

and in so doing would value utility in future periods i and j with new discount factors of $\delta(i-1)$ and $\delta(j-1)$. The relative importance attached to periods i and j when decision-making in period 0 would be different from the relative importance attached to periods i and j when decision-making in period 1 unless the following condition were met:

$$\frac{\delta(i)}{\delta(j)} = \frac{\delta(i-1)}{\delta(j-1)} \tag{7.13}$$

and this will only be true for all values of i and j if the function δ is of the form $\delta(j) = \delta^{j}$ as in equation (7.10).

The assumption of geometric discounting is highly significant for the inter-temporal consistency of decision-making. At time t the agent maximizes the objective function V_t in equation (7.11) and obtains an optimal consumption path of the form

$$\left\{c_0^{(t)}, c_1^{(t)}, \ldots, c_T^{(t)}\right\} \tag{7.14}$$

where we use the superscript (t) to denote that $c_j^{(t)}$ was consumption planned for period j when plans were drawn up in period t. Now consider a world of complete certainty so that all future events can be predicted perfectly, in which case no new information becomes available in the following period and ask what consumption plan will be drawn up in period $t + 1$ to maximize equation (7.12). The agent will not change his plans if

$$\left\{c_1^{(t+1)}, \ldots, c_T^{(t+1)}\right\} = \left\{c_1^{(t)}, \ldots, c_T^{(t)}\right\} \tag{7.15}$$

in which case we say that the objective function will demonstrate inter-temporal consistency. If this is not the case then we are saying that the agent will choose a consumption path in the full knowledge that, even without any new information arriving, he will change his mind in subsequent periods. Of course, it may be the case that in real life some people do behave like this, but it would be difficult to describe this as a sensible way of proceeding: that I make a decision knowing that I will change my mind in the future.

Within the TAS-GD class of objective functions we now need address just two more issues. First, we have assumed so far that lifetime is certain and we now generalize this to uncertain date of death. Clearly an agent cannot consume after death, so the possibility of obtaining felicity from consumption is only relevant while the agent is alive and we can use this to justify the objective function

$$V_t = E_t \left[\sum_{j=0}^{T} I_{t+j} \delta^j u \left(c_{t+j} \right) \right]$$

$$I_{t+j} = \begin{cases} 1 & \text{if the agent is alive in period } t+j \\ 0 & \text{if the agent is not alive in period } t+j. \end{cases}$$

(7.16)

In equation (4.2) we defined the probability of the agent being alive at time $t + j$ as the survival probability s_j where we simplify notation in this chapter by ignoring the current age of the annuitant. Obviously

$$s_j \leq s_{j-1}$$

(7.17)

If this is the only source of uncertainty then equation (7.16) simplifies to

$$V_t = E_t \left[\sum_{j=0}^{T} s_j \delta^j u \left(c_{t+j} \right) \right]$$

(7.18)

where there is uncertainty about the amount of consumption in future periods, but this is independent of the probability of being alive, then we can write

$$V_t = \sum_{j=0}^{T} s_j \delta^j E_t \left[u \left(c_{t+j} \right) \right]$$

(7.19)

The second issue we need to consider is the form of the felicity function. It is common to make the following assumptions:

$$u'(c) > 0, \quad u''(c) < 0, \quad u'''(c) > 0$$

(7.20)

The first condition says that the agent will always prefer to have more consumption to less. This is not a strong assumption, but in the context of a pensioner, especially one in poor health, it may be possible that so long as all medical and care needs were met, then the pensioner might not be capable of consuming more than a given amount.

The second condition says that the agent is risk averse, meaning that given a choice of a certain amount of consumption or an actuarially fair bet, then the agent would always choose certainty. For example, an agent would prefer to receive £100 than to be given the chance of receiving either nothing or £200 on the toss of a fair coin. While a risk-averse agent would always prefer a certain amount to an actuarially fair bet, he might prefer a risky outcome if the odds were sufficiently favourable: continuing the example, he might prefer a 75 per cent chance of £200 (25 per cent chance of nothing) to £100 for certain. It should be noted that if the objective function is not TAS then the conditions for risk aversion are more complicated. The third condition says that the agent is prudent (Carroll and Kimball 1996). In this context the term 'prudence' refers to how an individual responds to increases in risk: prudent agents optimally increase their savings in the face of future uncertainty (a response which is not an automatic corollary of risk aversion).

In a simple atemporal model, it is common to measure an agent's risk aversion using the coefficient of relative risk aversion, defined as

$$\frac{-c\,u''(c)}{u'(c)} \tag{7.21}$$

The problem we are trying to solve in equation (7.16) is a multi-period model and we are also interested in the extent to which an individual is prepared to sacrifice consumption in one period for consumption in another period. In a certain world the usual measure of this is the elasticity of inter-temporal substitution, defined as

$$\frac{-u'(c)}{c\,u''(c)} \tag{7.22}$$

which is just the reciprocal of the coefficient of relative risk aversion.

This allows us to put some economic interpretation on the TAS-GD objective function. We are faced with two conceptually distinct questions: how much does the agent dislike risk and how much consumption is the agent prepared to sacrifice in one period to have more consumption in another period. There is no reason to believe that knowing the answer to one question would enable us to answer the question to another, yet in the TAS-GD framework knowing the answer to one question automatically answers the other. This is both the strength and the weakness of the model: if true it allows us to interpret preferences more easily, but if false it may lead us to erroneous conclusions. Economists commonly solve TAS-GD models by assuming the felicity function to be Hyperbolic Absolute Risk Aversion (HARA), namely

$$u(c) = \frac{(b_0 + b_1 c)^{(b_1-1)/b_1}}{b_1 - 1} \tag{7.23}$$

Special examples of this felicity function which have been widely used in models of annuity demand are:

Constant Relative Risk Aversion (CRRA) $\quad u(c) = \begin{cases} \frac{c^{1-\gamma}}{1-\gamma} & \text{if } \gamma \neq 1 \\ \ln c & \text{if } \gamma = 1 \end{cases}$

$$\tag{7.24}$$

Constant Absolute Risk Aversion (CARA) $u(c) = -be^{-c/b}$.

Because of the peculiar properties of the TAS-GD model more recent analysis has turned to more flexible functional forms. Before we consider this possibility, however, we digress briefly to consider how the riskiness of length of life affects an agent's utility.

7.4. Risk aversion and the form of risk

These felicity functions have been developed primarily to deal with risky consumption: the interpretation of $u(c)$ is the utility from a certain amount of consumption at a certain point in time. With unexpected lifetimes, however, there need be no uncertainty about consumption at all—assuming that the agent is actually alive for the consumption to take place. A feature of models incorporating a role for annuities is that the amount of consumption in each period, conditional on the agent actually being alive, is certain: the only source of uncertainty is whether or not the agent will be alive to experience potential future felicity. Paradoxically this means that the agent continues to face uncertainty even when 'fully insured'. We need to be clear about the form of risk that annuities are designed to insure against.

Contrast two situations where in an atemporal case the agent is faced with risky consumption, with an alternative case where the source of risk is life length and consumption is certain. In the first case an agent faced with risky consumption might receive either $c + \epsilon/\psi$ with probability ψ or $c + \epsilon/(1 - \psi)$ with probability $(1 - \psi)$. The riskiness of the situation is a function of ϵ and ψ. If the agent were to buy full actuarially fair insurance then he would obtain consumption of c for certain and expected utility would be $u(c)$, which is clearly independent of the variance of the payment.

We may contrast this with a situation where an agent is uncertain whether he will live one or two periods. The agent, as described in Section 7.1, will live for one period with probability $(1 - p)$ and for two periods with probability p. Life expectancy is $1 + p$ and the variance of life length is $2p(1 - p)$, which is at its maximum when $p = 1/2$ and equal to zero when $p = 0$ or $p = 1$. For simplicity set $r = 0$, $\delta = 1$ and $W_0 = 1$, so that an actuarially fair annuity payment per period is simply $A = 1/(1 + p)$. Then a fully annuitized agent receives expected utility

$$
\begin{aligned}
V &= u\left(\frac{1}{1+p}\right) + pu\left(\frac{1}{1+p}\right) \\
&= \underbrace{(1+p)}_{\text{Lifetime Effect}} \times \underbrace{u\left(\frac{1}{1+p}\right)}_{\text{Wealth-Spreading Effect}}
\end{aligned}
\tag{7.25}
$$

Thus, even with insurance, expected utility depends upon the variance of life length, since both depend upon p. Let us consider just the effect of p on expected utility: this is ambiguous. People who live longer have more opportunity to experience felicity and therefore tend to have higher expected utility: we refer to this as the lifetime effect and it is represented by the first term of the second line of equation (7.25) which is increasing in p. However, this effect is offset by the fact that they now need to spread their wealth over more periods and can consume less in each period: we refer to this as the wealth-spreading effect and it is represented by the second term of the second line of equation (7.25), which is decreasing in p. So there are two effects of p on expected utility, working in opposite directions. Which effect dominates depends upon the functional form of $u(c)$.[10]

This result is first found in Katz (1979) who concludes with the rather ironic point that individuals would not always prefer to live longer! A more reasonable point that he makes is that the expected utility hypothesis may not be well suited to dealing with risky lifetimes. However, this suggestion is also wrong, since the wealth-spreading effect still exists for agents who have a certain lifetime: the wealth-spreading effect is entirely due to the fact that wealth is fixed.

If the relationship between expected utility and p is complicated, the relationship between the value of insurance and the risk faced by the

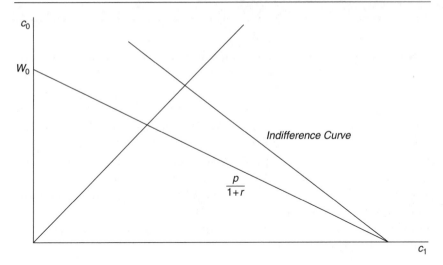

Figure 7.5. Annuitization with risk neutrality

agent is even less intuitive. In the atemporal example above, one way of representing low risk would be to have very small values of ϵ, in which case the value of insurance would be very small. However, in the risky-life length model agents with a very small value of p also face a very small value of risk (obviously if $p \approx 0$ then the risk is negligible). However, counter-intuitively, someone with a very small value of p would have the highest value of annuitizing as measured by annuity equivalent wealth.

This highlights the fact that the real benefit to annuitization lies in the fact that the budget constraint with annuitization is further from the origin than the budget constraint without annuitization. So is it even necessary for the agent to be risk averse? The answer is in fact 'no'. Consider instead the case where the felicity function is linear so that the agent would conventionally be defined as risk neutral: in which case the agent's indifference curves would also be linear. If

$$\frac{p}{1+r} < \delta \tag{7.26}$$

then the optimal consumption is achieved at a 'corner solution' as illustrated in Figure 7.5. In this case the agent puts all of the initial wealth into a deferred annuity and is thus fully annuitized à la Yaari. With appropriate parameters a risk-loving agent might also choose this corner solution.

Given that the agent does not need to be risk averse to benefit from annuitization, it is still interesting to know the extent to which variance in the life length makes an individual better off for a given life expectancy. Counter-intuitively, less variance in life length does not make the agent worse off and ironically this is precisely because the agent is risk averse. Barro and Friedman (1977) contrast an agent with a risky lifetime with the scenario where the agent is told at birth whether he will live for one or two periods (this having been chosen with probabilities $1 - p$ and p respectively). For ease of exposition we continue to use our simplified model where $r = 0$, $\delta = 0$ and $W_0 = 1$. An agent who knew that he would live one period would then consume one unit in that period and an agent who knew that he would live two periods would consume half of a unit in each period, so the maximized utility of the agents who knew their lifetimes would be

$$\text{Agent lives one period} \quad u(1)$$
$$\text{Agent lives two periods} \quad u\left(\frac{1}{2}\right) + u\left(\frac{1}{2}\right) \tag{7.27}$$

Thus if agents lived one period with probability $1 - p$ and two periods with probability p average (expected) utility would be

$$(1 - p)u(1) + 2pu\left(\frac{1}{2}\right) \tag{7.28}$$

We can now compare this to the formula for expected utility in equation (7.25). Since $1/2 < 1/(1 + p) < 1$ and u is concave it follows that for any θ where $0 < \theta < 1$, we have

$$u\left(\frac{1}{1+p}\right) > \theta u(1) + (1 - \theta)u\left(\frac{1}{2}\right) \tag{7.29}$$

Multiplying this expression by $(1 + p)$ and choosing $\theta = (1 - p)/(1 + p)$ we obtain

$$(1 + p)u\left(\frac{1}{1+p}\right) > (1 - p)u(1) + 2pu\left(\frac{1}{2}\right) \tag{7.30}$$

so the agent is better off not knowing how long he is going to live.[11]

For this reason it is not useful to quantify the riskiness of life length since it bears little relationship to the value of insurance and it is also important to be careful in generalizing standard results derived concerning risky consumption to the risky lifetime case.

7.5. Exotic utility functions

Backus, Routledge, and Zin (2004) survey a variety of utility functions which are more general than the TAS-GD forms we have considered hitherto. The primary reason these functions have been developed is to explain the various failings of the TAS-GD models to explain observed behaviour. However, most of these functions have been developed to model consumption or interest-rate risk and we need to bear in mind Katz's (1979) warning that they may be inappropriate to deal with uncertain lifetime. In this section we consider three approaches to relaxing the TAS-GD assumption to test the robustness of Yaari's result when only conventional annuities are available.

The first exotic utility function that we consider retains the TAS specification but drops geometric discounting: this brings us back to the problem mentioned in Section 7.3 that behaviour will be inter-temporally inconsistent. Angeletos et al. (2001) suggest using quasi-hyperbolic discounting, so that equation (7.19) is replaced by

$$V_t = (c_0) + \sum_{j=1}^{T} s_j \beta \delta^j E_t \left[u \left(c_{t+j} \right) \right] \tag{7.31}$$

The relative subjective discounting of felicity in any two adjacent time periods is $\delta^{(s+1)}/\delta^s = \delta$ except for periods 0 and 1, where it is $\beta\delta$. They suggest that to calibrate annual data one could use $\beta = 0.7$ and $\delta = 0.957$ (compared with a calibration in a geometric discounting model of $\delta = 0.944$). Alternatively one could use hyperbolic discounting, so that

$$V_t = (c_0) + \sum_{j=1}^{T} s_j \left\{ \frac{1}{(1 + \eta j)^{-\xi/\eta}} \right\} E_t \left[u \left(c_{t+j} \right) \right] \tag{7.32}$$

(which they calibrate with $\xi = 1$ and $\eta = 4$). In this case the relative subjective discounting of felicity is continually increasing towards unity so that the discounting of two adjacent periods a long way into the future is more or less the same. The effect of these three forms of discounting on the present subjective value of expected utility in future periods is illustrated in Figure 7.6.

Of course, with hyperbolic or quasi-hyperbolic discounting, intertemporal decision-making is inconsistent (Rubinstein 2003). This raises an interesting question: if an agent is rational, to what extent can he form a plan for what he does in the future if he knows that he will wish

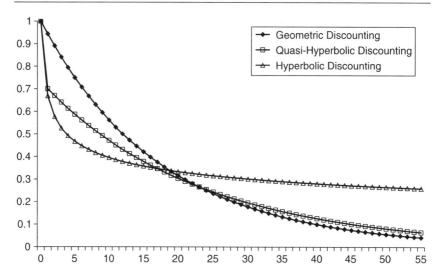

Figure 7.6. Present subjective values of future expected utilities under different forms of subjective discounting

to change the plan later? Economists have used three solutions to this conundrum:

First, agents might realize that in the future they will be unwilling to continue with the consumption plan that appears optimal in the current period. If the only choice variable available to the agent is the current saving rate, then the agent can choose a level of consumption that maximizes this period's objective function given the changes in behaviour that will follow in the future. The modelling strategy is to treat the consumption decision as a game (i.e. as a branch of game theory), where the agents in different periods are playing against each other and the agent this period chooses the sub-game perfect equilibrium strategy. Aside from any other disadvantages with this approach, the resulting consumption path turns out to be the same that would be chosen by an agent with a geometric subjective discount rate of $\beta\delta/(1 - \delta + \beta\delta)$ (see Backus, Routledge, and Zin 2004) and hence it does not provide a resolution to any of the consumption puzzles that the theory of non-geometric discounting was designed to resolve.

The second possibility is that the agent will use a commitment device to ensure that in the future he will have to follow the consumption path which is optimal this period. Examples are savings schemes which automatically deduct money from the agent's bank account, with increasingly large deductions made over time. Angeletos et al. (2001) argue that this is prima facie evidence for non-geometric discounting. Unfortunately this solution does not help very much with the analysis of annuities, since a conventional annuity purchase is an irreversible commitment anyway.

The final solution to modelling non-geometric preferences is to assume that the agents are naive and simply ignore the fact that they will change the plan each period. This would be the first instance of irrationality that we have considered, but at least it is a form of irrationality which may be consistent with the evidence.

The second and third classes of exotic utility functions both retain geometric discounting but drop the TAS assumption. The second class of exotic utility functions does this by considering the possibility that agents have habitual levels of consumption: having gotten used to a high level of consumption in one period an agent needs a relatively high consumption to obtain utility in the next period. One of the motivations for this is to resolve two other consumption puzzles: the equity premium puzzle (rates of return on equity appear higher than is necessary to compensate agents for the risk involved) and the low risk-free rate puzzle (risk-free rates of interest are too low for consumption to be consistent with low inter-temporal elasticity of substitution) (Kocherlakota 1996). Of course, even if these 'exotic' functions do explain the other puzzles, it does not mean that they are well suited to explain the annuity puzzle.

Davidoff, Brown, and Diamond (2005) implement habitual consumption in the context of annuities using

$$U = \sum_{j=0}^{T} \delta^j s_j \frac{\left(c_j/h_j\right)^{1-\varphi}}{1-\varphi}, \qquad h_j = \frac{h_{j-1} + \psi c_{j-1}}{1 + \psi} \tag{7.33}$$

The behaviour of an agent with these sort of preferences depends crucially upon the initial habits h_0 that an individual has and how large these are relative to the individual's level of consumption that could be maintained throughout retirement. The constant level of consumption that could be maintained throughout retirement (sometimes called 'permanent income') is equal to the annuity stream from an actuarially fair annuity, which is just AW_0 where A is the annuity rate and W_0 is initial wealth. If the initial habit level is lower than permanent income, then it is clearly possible to have a consumption path which is growing over time, and this is optimal since utility is higher if current consumption is large relative to previous consumption. A more likely scenario is if the habit level is higher than permanent income, in which case consumption needs to decline throughout retirement. The Pensions Commission (2004) and Hurd and Rohwedder (2005) present evidence for the UK and the USA respectively that consumption expenditure typically falls at the point of retirement and it is usually thought that this fall is larger than can be explained by reductions in work-related costs, increased home production and availability of discounted prices. This suggests that the habit level of income may exceed permanent income for the retired.

The final exotic utility function that we consider uses a more sophisticated approach to decouple the coefficient of relative risk aversion from the inter-temporal elasticity of substitution (again the initial motivation for this approach is to resolve the equity premium and low risk-free rate puzzles mentioned above). Epstein and Zin (1989) suggest the following objective function for an infinitely lived agent

$$V_t = \left\{ c_0^{1-\rho} + \delta \left\{ \mathsf{E}_t \left[V_{t+1}^{1-\alpha} \right] \right\}^{(1-\rho)/(1-\alpha)} \right\}^{1/(1-\rho)} \qquad \delta < 1 \qquad (7.34)$$

and suggest that the incidental conclusions arising from such a model are consistent with observed behaviour of equity returns. The elasticity of inter-temporal substitution is now $1/\rho$ and coefficient of risk aversion is α. An interesting corollary of this function is that agents care not just about the amount of risk they face, but the point of time (in the future) when such uncertainty will be resolved: if $\alpha > \rho$ then the agent would prefer uncertainty to be resolved later rather than sooner.

The original Epstein–Zin model assumes an infinitely lived-agent with uncertain consumption. In our model agents are not infinitely lived and their life length is uncertain. We assume that T is the maximum length of time that an individual could live and that in the last period the value function is just equal to consumption. The value function becomes

$$V_T = c_T$$
$$V_{t+i} = \left\{ c_t^{1-\rho} + \delta \left\{ \mathsf{E}_t \left[I_{t+j+1} V_{t+j+1}^{1-\alpha} \right] \right\}^{(1-\rho)/(1-\alpha)} \right\}^{1/(1-\rho)} \qquad (7.35)$$

Notice that, unlike all the other specifications we have considered, the probabilities enter non-linearly into this objective function. We can now substitute to obtain

$$\mathsf{E}_t \left[I_{j+1} V_{j+1}^{1-\alpha} \right] = p_{j+1} \mathsf{E}_t \left[V_{j+1}^{1-\alpha} \right] = p_{j+1} V_{j+1}^{1-\alpha} \qquad (7.36)$$

where the first equality follows because the probability of survival is independent of any other random components and the second equality follows from the fact that we are assuming that mortality is the only source of uncertainty. Due to the latter assumption we are now in a position to obtain the objective function by backward induction:

$$V_T = c_T$$

$$V_{T-1} = \left\{ c_{T-1}^{1-\rho} + \delta \, (p_{T-1})^{(1-\rho)/(1-\alpha)} \, V_T^{1-\rho} \right\}^{1/(1-\rho)}$$

$$= \left\{ c_{T-1}^{1-\rho} + \delta \, (p_{T-1})^{(1-\rho)/(1-\alpha)} \, c_T^{1-\rho} \right\}^{1/(1-\rho)} \tag{7.37}$$

$$\vdots$$

$$V_0 = \left\{ \sum_{j=0}^{T} \delta^j \prod_{i=0}^{j-1} p_i^{(1-\rho)/(1-\alpha)} c_j^{1-\rho} \right\}^{1/(1-\rho)}$$

$$\equiv \sum_{j=0}^{T} \delta^j s_j^{(1-\rho)/(1-\alpha)} c_j^{1-\rho}$$

where the last equality follows from $s_j \equiv \prod_{i=0}^{j-1} p_i$ (equation 4.2). Note that if $\rho > 1$ then maximizing V_0 is the same as maximizing[12]

$$\sum_{j=0}^{T} \delta^j s_j^{(1-\rho)/(1-\alpha)} c_j^{1-\rho} \tag{7.38}$$

and when $\rho = \alpha$ this reduces to

$$V_0 = \sum_{j=0}^{T} \delta^j s_j c_j^{1-\rho} \tag{7.39}$$

which is the simple expected utility model. However, to explain other aspects of consumption successfully we typically require $\alpha > \rho$. Suggested combinations of parameter values are presented in Kocherlakota (1996: 55), and in nearly all cases these involve $(1-\rho)/(1-\alpha) < 0$, which, when applied to our model, means that $\delta^j s_j^{(1-\rho)/(1-\alpha)}$ is an increasing function of j. This can result in agents, whose objective function is equation (7.38), preferring to consume later rather than sooner, which is unappealing. Kocherlakota does not have this problem since in his model agents do not die, so that $s_j = 1$ and hence $\delta^j s_j^{(1-\rho)/(1-\alpha)} = \delta^j$ which is decreasing in j and means that agents always prefer to consume sooner rather than later. We shall discuss this further in Section 7.6.

7.6. Solving expected utility models

The utility functions described in the previous section provide a series of frameworks within which we can quantify the benefits of buying an annuity. However, before we can generate any numbers we need to provide solutions to the maximization problems. In this section we show how to derive analytical results for the functional forms that we have discussed using the CRRA felicity function as an example.

Throughout all of this we shall assume a perfect bond market so that £1 today can be invested in bonds to yield a certain amount i periods in the future of

$$R_i = \prod_{j=1}^{i} (1 + r_j), \quad R_0 = 1 \tag{7.40}$$

The corollary of this is that £1 at i periods in the future is R_i^{-1}. We consider three possibilities facing the agent:

1. Perfect annuity markets in the sense that there is a complete set of annuity products available as assumed by Yaari (1965) and described in Section 7.2. This means that the relevant budget constraint (the envelope of all budget constraints based on portfolios of different annuities) is

$$W_0 = \sum_{i=0}^{T} s_i c_i R_i^{-1} \tag{7.41}$$

2. Perfect bond markets with no annuities at all. This is the case where agents have to rely entirely on bonds as a means of holding wealth. The relevant budget constraint is

$$W_0 = \sum_{i=0}^{T} c_i R_i^{-1} \tag{7.42}$$

3. Conventional annuities. This is the case where agents have a single opportunity to buy a conventional annuity immediately: having purchased such an annuity their consumption each period is equal to their annuity income.[13] In this case the solution is trivially determined by

$$c_0 = c_1 = \cdots = c_T = \frac{W_0}{\sum_{i=0}^{T} s_i R_i^{-1}} \tag{7.43}$$

In practice agents may face more complicated possibilities, but for simplicity we just consider these three. Some more complicated scenarios will be considered in Chapter 8.

Formally speaking the optimization problem is to maximize the utility function (e.g. equation 7.24) subject to the budget constraint (e.g. equation 7.41). Where an analytical solution is available it can be derived using the Lagrangean method. Details of this method can be found in standard economic textbooks. Here we provide a fully worked out example for the CRRA felicity function and perfect annuitization, that is, the problem

$$\max_{\{c_0,\dots,c_T\}} \sum_{i=0}^{T} \frac{\delta_i s_i c_i^{1-\gamma}}{1-\gamma} \quad \text{s.t.} \quad \sum_{i=0}^{T} s_i c_i R_i^{-1} = W_0 \tag{7.44}$$

We approach this problem using the associated Lagrangean function

$$L = \sum_{i=0}^{T} \frac{\delta_i s_i c_i^{1-\gamma}}{1-\gamma} + \lambda \left[W_0 - \sum_{i=0}^{T} s_i c_i R_i^{-1} \right] \tag{7.45}$$

which we can differentiate with respect to c_i to obtain the $T + 1$ first order conditions:

$$\frac{\partial L}{\partial c_i} = \delta_i s_i c_i^{-\gamma} - \lambda s_i R_i^{-1} = 0, \quad i = 0, \dots, T$$

$$\delta_i c_i^{-\gamma} = \lambda R_i^{-1} \tag{7.46}$$

For $i = 0$ the first order condition simplifies to

$$c_0^{-\gamma} = \lambda \tag{7.47}$$

so

$$c_i = c_0 \left(\delta_i R_i \right)^{1/\gamma}, \quad i = 0, \dots, T. \tag{7.48}$$

We can now substitute this back into the budget constraint to obtain

$$W_0 = \sum_{i=0}^{T} s_i c_i R_i^{-1} = \sum_{i=0}^{T} s_i c_0 \left(\delta_i R_i^{1-\gamma} \right)^{1/\gamma} \tag{7.49}$$

and then rearrange this to obtain the solution for c_0:

$$c_0 = \frac{W_0}{\sum_{i=0}^{T} s_i \left(\delta_i R_i^{1-\gamma} \right)^{1/\gamma}} \tag{7.50}$$

Having obtained the solution for c_0 we can now substitute this back into equation (7.41) to obtain the perfect-annuitization solution for consumption in every other period:

$$c_i = \frac{W_0 \left(\delta_i R_i \right)^{1/\gamma}}{\sum_{j=0}^{T} s_j \left(\delta_j R_j^{1-\gamma} \right)^{1/\gamma}} \tag{7.51}$$

This provides the optimal consumption path when the agent has access to a perfect set of annuity markets. On the basis of this consumption path the optimized value function is

$$\frac{W_0^{1-\gamma}}{(1-\gamma)} \left(\sum_{i=0}^{T} s_j \delta_i^{1/\gamma} R_i^{(1-\gamma)/\gamma} \right)^{\gamma} = \frac{W_0^{1-\gamma}}{(1-\gamma)} \Phi^{PA} \qquad (7.52)$$

where the constant Φ^{PA} is appropriately defined.

This completes the solution of the expected-utility maximization for the CRRA felicity perfect-annuitization scenario (hence the superscript PA). An alternative scenario would be when no annuities are bought at all and the agent has to rely upon bonds alone. In this case the analogous Lagrangean function is

$$\max_{\{c_0,...,c_T\}} \sum_{i=0}^{T} \frac{\delta_i s_i c_i^{1-\gamma}}{1-\gamma} \quad \text{s.t.} \quad \sum_{i=0}^{T} c_i R_i^{-1} = W_0 \qquad (7.53)$$

where the only difference with the previous example is the omission of the p_i term in the constraint. The corresponding optimal consumption path is then described by

$$c_i = \frac{W_0 s_i^{1/\gamma} \delta_i^{1/\gamma} R_i^{1/\gamma}}{\sum_{j=0}^{T} s_j^{1/\gamma} \delta_j^{1/\gamma} R_j^{(1-\gamma)/\gamma}} \qquad (7.54)$$

and the optimized value function is

$$\frac{W_0^{1-\gamma}}{(1-\gamma)} \left(\sum_{i=0}^{T} s_i^{1/\gamma} \delta_i^{1/\gamma} R_i^{(1-\gamma)/\gamma} \right)^{\gamma} = \frac{W_0^{1-\gamma}}{(1-\gamma)} \Phi^{PB} \qquad (7.55)$$

where the constant Φ^{PB} is appropriately defined and PB refers to the fact that there is a perfect bond market.

We can now use equations (7.52) and (7.55) to obtain a measure of the welfare gain from having access to perfect annuity markets. We have already referred to this measure in Section 7.1, namely Annuity Equivalent Wealth, which is the wealth that would give the same level of expected utility in the absence of annuities as can be obtained by W_0 with annuities. We denote the annuity equivalent wealth as AEW_0 and hence it is implicitly defined by

$$\frac{W_0^{1-\gamma}}{(1-\gamma)} \Phi^{PA} \equiv \frac{AEW_0^{1-\gamma}}{(1-\gamma)} \Phi^{PB} \qquad (7.56)$$

Rearranging this we obtain the useful ratio of annuity equivalent wealth to actual wealth as

$$\frac{AEW_0}{W_0} = \left(\frac{\Phi^{PA}}{\Phi^{PB}} \right)^{1/(1-\gamma)} \qquad (7.57)$$

which is a measure of the proportional increase in wealth necessary to compensate individuals for not having access to annuities.

Equation (7.57) is the value of having access to a perfect annuity market. In practice we need to know the value of having access to a conventional annuity as we have previously discussed and described in equation (7.43). This need not be the optimal consumption strategy: an agent may be able to do better by consuming less than the payout of the conventional annuity and by saving the remainder to consume in the following period. To simplify the analysis consider the case where interest rates are constant. If the agent planned to reduce consumption very slightly in period i he would reduce his expected utility by $s_i \delta_i c_i^{-\gamma} dc_i$: investing the money in a bond would enable him to consume $(1+r) dc_i$ next period which would increase his felicity by $s_{i+1} \delta_{i+1} (1+r) c_{i+1}^{-\gamma} dc_i$ so it is optimal to save only if

$$s_i \delta_i c_i^{-\gamma} dc_i < s_{i+1} \delta_{i+1} (1+r) c_{i+1}^{-\gamma} dc_i \tag{7.58}$$

in other words if

$$1 < q_{i+1} \frac{\delta_{i+1}}{\delta_i} (1+r) \tag{7.59}$$

The first two terms on the right-hand side of this equation are less than one and the last term is greater than one. We can see that the agent will want to save out of the annuity payment of a conventional annuity only if first, the mortality is low; secondly, the subjective discounting of period $i + 1$ is not much less than the discounting of period i; thirdly, the interest rate is relatively high.

If we can ignore this situation then the expected utility from a conventional annuity is

$$\frac{W_0^{1-\gamma} \sum_{i=0}^{T} \delta_i s_i}{(1-\gamma) \left(\sum_{j=0}^{T} s_j R_j^{-1} \right)^{1-\gamma}} \equiv \frac{W_0^{1-\gamma}}{(1-\gamma)} \Phi^{CA} \tag{7.60}$$

where Φ^{CA} is appropriately defined and CA refers to the fact that this is a conventional rather than perfect annuitization. Then we define conventional-annuity equivalent wealth or CEW via

$$\frac{W_0^{1-\gamma}}{(1-\gamma)} \Phi^{CA} \equiv \frac{CEW_0^{1-\gamma}}{(1-\gamma)} \Phi^{PB} \tag{7.61}$$

169

and hence the value of a conventional annuity (relative to no annuity at all) as

$$\frac{\text{CEW}_0}{W_0} = \left(\frac{\Phi^{\text{CA}}}{\Phi^{\text{PB}}}\right)^{1/(1-\gamma)} \tag{7.62}$$

Analogous results for Epstein–Zin preferences are

$$\Phi^{\text{PA}}_{\text{EZ}} \equiv \left\{\sum_{i=0}^{T} \delta^{i/\rho} R_i^{(1-\rho)/\rho} s_i^{(1-\rho)/(\rho(1-\alpha))} p_i^{(\rho-1)/\rho}\right\}^{\rho}$$

$$\Phi^{\text{PB}}_{\text{EZ}} \equiv \left\{\sum_{i=0}^{T} \delta^{i/\rho} R_i^{(1-\rho)/\rho} s_i^{(1-\rho)/(\rho(1-\alpha))}\right\}^{\rho} \tag{7.63}$$

$$\Phi^{\text{CA}}_{\text{EZ}} \equiv \frac{\sum_{i=0}^{T} \delta^i s_i^{(1-\rho)/(1-\alpha)}}{\left\{\sum_{i=0}^{T} s_i R_i^{-1}\right\}^{1-\rho}}$$

7.7. Numerical simulations

In this section we report calculations of the value of having either a perfect annuity market or a conventional annuity, compared with a baseline of having no annuities at all. We consider three models of utility maximization: geometric discounting of the future (which is consistent over time), quasi-hyperbolic and hyperbolic discounting (which would result in the agent changing his mind as he goes along). For the second and third cases we only show the agent's plan and expected utility as formulated in period 0. All of our calculations are based upon the mortality of a 65-year-old man in 1992 as projected by the UK's PML92 table of mortality.

It is useful to start by considering what an agent would do in the absence of perfect annuities. Figure 7.7 illustrates the optimal consumption path for an agent who saves entirely in bonds, assuming a constant interest rate of 4 per cent. He starts with relatively high consumption and consumption declines over time. This is to ensure that he does not have too much wealth left when he dies: the consequence of this is that in later years the agent has fewer resources and consumes less. There is little difference in the planned consumption paths of the three forms of discounting except that an agent with quasi-hyperbolic and hyperbolic discounting consumes much more in the first period.

We can contrast this with the consumption path of someone with a conventional annuity, which is shown by the horizontal line in

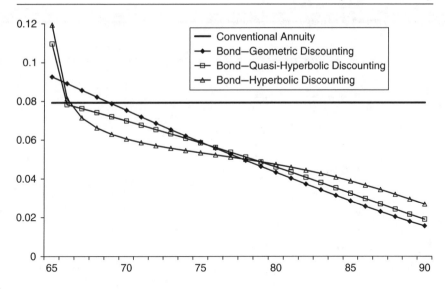

Figure 7.7. Optimal consumption plans without perfect annuities

Figure 7.7. When combined with the PML92 mortality and a money's worth of 100 per cent, an interest rate of 4 per cent implies an annuity rate of 7.92 per cent and the agent could consume this proportion of his wealth in each period.

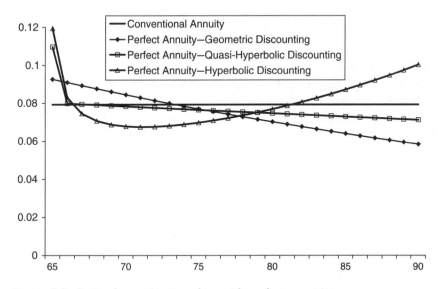

Figure 7.8. Optimal consumption plans with perfect annuities

Table 7.2. Annuity equivalent wealth

Interest rate	Coefficient of relative risk aversion (γ)					
	0.5	1.0	1.5	2	4	8
Panel A: Geometric Discounting						
0%	115.8	131.6	143.8	154.3	184.5	218.1
1%	117.0	131.5	142.1	150.9	174.8	199.9
2%	118.3	131.5	140.6	147.7	166.6	185.3
3%	119.7	131.5	139.1	144.9	159.5	173.4
4%	121.3	131.4	137.6	142.3	153.5	163.6
Panel B: Quasi-Hyperbolic Discounting						
0%	116.9	134.9	147.9	158.7	188.9	221.8
1%	118.5	134.9	146.0	154.8	178.5	202.9
2%	120.1	134.8	144.2	151.3	169.7	187.7
3%	122.0	134.8	142.4	148.2	162.2	175.3
4%	124.1	134.8	140.8	145.3	155.8	165.2
Panel C: Hyperbolic Discounting						
0%	120.4	143.2	157.7	169.1	199.4	230.5
1%	122.9	143.1	155.1	164.2	187.3	209.8
2%	125.7	143.1	152.7	159.7	177.0	193.1
3%	129.0	143.0	150.4	155.7	168.3	179.6
4%	132.6	143.0	148.3	152.0	160.9	168.7

Note: The entries are the percentage in wealth needed to compensate an agent for the absence of a perfect annuity market when only bonds are available.

Source: Authors' calculations based on equation (7.57).

What if the agent had access to perfect annuity markets? Figure 7.8 illustrates that the consumption paths are now rather different. For the geometric and quasi-hyperbolic discounting, agents would always have a preference to consume slightly earlier since the interest rate is insufficient to offset their impatience. This is also true for an agent with hyperbolic preferences for the first seven years of retirement: for periods more than seven years in the future, however, they are currently almost indifferent when they consume and therefore would plan now to have an increasing consumption profile. Unless they were able to commit themselves to this consumption plan they would change their plans as they went along and hence the path plotted would not be observed in practice.

Table 7.2 reports annuity equivalent wealth which is the perceived value in period 0 of having a perfect annuity. In the top left-hand corner of Panel A we report a figure of 115.8 per cent. This means that if the interest rate were 0 per cent and the agent disliked risk, but did not have a strong dislike of risk (since the coefficient of risk aversion is low), then the value of having a perfect annuity would be equivalent to a 15.8 per cent increase in wealth. If the interest rate were as high as 4 per cent then the value of having a perfect annuity market would be equivalent

Table 7.3. Conventional-annuity equivalent wealth

Interest rate	Coefficient of relative risk aversion (γ)					
	0.5	1.0	1.5	2	4	8
Panel A: Geometric Discounting						
0%	98.5	120.0	134.9	146.9	179.8	215.3
1%	104.7	123.7	136.2	146.0	171.9	198.3
2%	110.3	126.6	136.9	144.8	164.9	184.3
3%	115.2	128.8	137.1	143.4	158.7	172.9
4%	119.3	130.3	136.8	141.7	153.1	163.4
Panel B: Quasi-Hyperbolic Discounting						
0%	100.9	125.1	140.5	152.7	185.3	219.6
1%	107.3	128.4	141.2	151.1	176.3	201.7
2%	113.0	131.0	141.4	149.2	168.5	187.0
3%	117.9	132.7	141.0	147.0	161.6	175.0
4%	121.9	133.7	140.1	144.7	155.5	165.0
Panel C: Hyperbolic Discounting						
0%	106.6	135.7	152.3	164.9	197.0	229.1
1%	113.3	138.2	151.7	161.5	185.8	208.9
2%	119.1	139.8	150.4	158.0	176.1	192.6
3%	123.9	140.5	148.7	154.4	167.6	179.3
4%	127.7	140.5	146.6	150.7	160.2	168.3

Note: This shows the percentage of wealth needed to compensate an agent for the absence of a conventional annuity when only bonds are available.

Source: Authors' calculations based on equation (7.62).

to an increase in wealth of 21.3 per cent. Agents who were much more risk averse would attach greater value to the annuity: with a coefficient of risk aversion of eight the annuity equivalent wealth ranges from 218.1 to 163.6 per cent: having access to a perfect annuity market would be equivalent to an increase in wealth of between 118.1 and 63.6 per cent (depending upon the interest rate). The second and third panels show the benefits as perceived in period 0 when the agent's preferences have other forms of discounting. The figures are similar—both qualitatively and quantitatively—so it is clear that irrational discounting of the future has little impact on the perceived value of a perfect annuity.

Conventional-annuity equivalent wealth is reported in Table 7.3. Here we have an example of a figure less than 100 per cent: with an interest rate of 0 per cent an individual with very low risk aversion would have a conventional-annuity equivalent wealth of 98.5, implying that purchasing an annuity would be equivalent to losing 1.5 per cent of his wealth. However this figure is for levels of risk aversion and interest rates that are implausibly low. For more risk-averse agents and for higher interest rates the conventional-annuity equivalent wealth figures are substantially above one. Of course, this assumes a money's worth of 100 per cent: with

Table 7.4. Expected unconsumed wealth

Interest rate	Coefficient of relative risk aversion (γ)					
	0.5	1.0	1.5	2	4	8
Panel A: Geometric Discounting						
0%	11.0	20.0	26.2	31.0	42.5	52.0
1%	11.6	20.0	25.6	29.8	39.7	48.0
2%	12.2	20.0	24.9	28.6	37.2	44.2
3%	12.9	20.0	24.3	27.5	34.8	40.7
4%	13.6	20.0	23.7	26.4	32.5	37.4
Panel B: Quasi-Hyperbolic Discounting						
0%	11.1	21.3	27.7	32.5	43.6	52.8
1%	11.8	21.2	27.0	31.2	40.8	48.7
2%	12.6	21.2	26.3	29.9	38.2	44.9
3%	13.4	21.2	25.6	28.7	35.7	41.3
4%	14.2	21.2	25.0	27.6	33.4	38.0
Panel C: Hyperbolic Discounting						
0%	11.6	23.8	30.7	35.5	46.1	54.4
1%	12.5	23.8	29.8	34.0	43.1	50.2
2%	13.5	23.7	29.0	32.6	40.3	46.3
3%	14.6	23.7	28.2	31.2	37.6	42.6
4%	15.7	23.7	27.5	30.0	35.2	39.1

Note: This shows the expected percentage of wealth that would not be consumed if the agent only saved using the bond market.

Source: Authors' calculations.

a money's worth of 80 per cent (which we know from Chapter 6 to be relatively low) the agent would need a conventional-annuity equivalent wealth of 125 per cent or more to be better off with a conventional annuity. But most of the entries in Table 7.3 are above this figure.

Comparing the corresponding entries in Tables 7.2 and 7.3 we see that conventional-annuity equivalent wealth is frequently only a little less than annuity equivalent wealth. The reason for this is simple: purchasing a conventional annuity shifts out the budget constraint a long way and yields a big improvement in welfare; having such an annuity forces consumption to be constant. Moving from a conventional annuity to a perfect annuity market does not shift out the budget constraint, but allows the agent to have a non-constant consumption profile. However, as illustrated in Figure 7.8 the optimal consumption profile is to have consumption almost constant over time anyway, so the benefit of this flexibility is small.

Table 7.4 provides a measure of the disadvantage of having no access to annuities: it reports the expected amount of wealth that would be left unconsumed if the agent had had to rely upon bonds alone and had

Table 7.5. Optimal annuitization with habitual preferences

$h_0/(AW_0)$	δ	Percentage of wealth annuitized
1	0.97	100%
0.5	0.97	100%
2	0.97	90%
2	0.90	75%

Note: This table illustrates optimal annuitization decisions when an agent has a single opportunity to purchase a conventional annuity and preferences are represented by equation (7.33).

Source: Davidoff, Brown, and Diamond (2005: 29).

chosen the optimal consumption paths, some of which were illustrated in Figure 7.7. The amounts of wealth which would be left are large—up to a half if the agent is very risk averse. Thus it is not surprising that even a conventional annuity provides a large increase in welfare. Mitchell et al. (1999) perform similar calculations for US mortalities and find similar results.

We now turn to the conclusions that we would reach with expected utility functions that were not TAS. Davidoff, Brown, and Diamond (2005) derive results for the habitual preferences in equation (7.33). Rather than reporting the annuity equivalent wealth, they tabulate the proportion of wealth that one would use to purchase a conventional annuity. Their results are reproduced in Table 7.5. If the initial level of consumption is not too high relative to permanent income, then it is optimal to put all of one's wealth into an annuity. Even if the initial level of consumption is twice as high as the sustainable level of consumption, it is still possible to annuitize 90 per cent of wealth. Low annuitization rates are only possible if the agent is very impatient. Davidoff, Brown, and Diamond (2005) conclude that habitual agents would still rationally annuitize a high proportion of their wealth.

We finish this section with a brief discussion of the results we obtain from using an Epstein–Zin utility function. In this specification there are two parameters of interest, representing risk aversion and willingness to transfer consumption from one period to another, which are sometimes summarized by

$$\varphi \equiv \frac{1-\rho}{1-\alpha} \qquad (7.64)$$

When $\varphi = 1$ we have the TAS-GD model discussed above. Clearly there is a wide variety of values that φ can take, but many of these yield

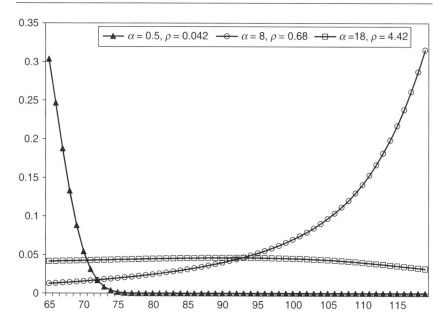

Figure 7.9. Planned consumption paths without annuities and Epstein–Zin preferences taken from Kocherlakota (1996)

nonsensical results. If $\varphi < 0$ then agents will typically plan to have consumption paths which are rising over time, while if $\varphi > 0$ they will be falling over time. There is nothing wrong with either of these solutions in principle: the problem is that for values of φ which are not too close to one, the optimal path can consist of near-zero consumption for most periods and then high consumption either very early on or very late.

Kocherlakota (1996) provides combinations of these parameters which can explain other well-known consumption puzzles. Figure 7.9 illustrates the optimal consumption paths for three of Kocherlakota's parameter combinations when no annuities are available and the interest rate on bonds is 4 per cent. In one case the agent plans to consume virtually everything by the age of 79, whereas in another the agent plans to consume only about 1.3 per cent of wealth early on so that he can consume more than 20 times as much if he lives to age 120. Neither of these descriptions of preferences are plausible. However if both α and ρ are high there is a relatively flat path of consumption. Figure 7.10 contrasts this with other Epstein–Zin parameterizations and the TAS-GD model when $\gamma = 2$ and Table 7.6 reports the corresponding values of AEW and CEW. Arguably the Epstein–Zin models look more reasonable: after all the TAS-GD model suggests that someone would rationally choose to have

Table 7.6. The value of annuities when agents have Epstein–Zin preferences

ρ	0.95	1.5	2	4.42
α	0.9	2	1.5	18
Interest rate				
Panel A: Annuity Equivalent Wealth				
0%	199.6	210.4	146.3	288.4
1%	200.5	203.9	144.0	257.3
2%	201.4	198.0	141.7	232.4
3%	202.4	192.6	139.7	212.3
4%	203.3	187.6	137.8	196.1
Panel B: Conventional Annuity Equivalent Wealth				
0%	187.9	203.9	138.1	275.6
1%	183.6	194.7	138.4	244.0
2%	178.2	185.6	138.1	218.6
3%	171.9	176.7	137.5	197.9
4%	164.8	167.9	136.6	181.1

Note: This shows the expected percentage of wealth needed to compensate the agent for a lack of annuities when the alternative would be bonds.
Source: Authors' calculations.

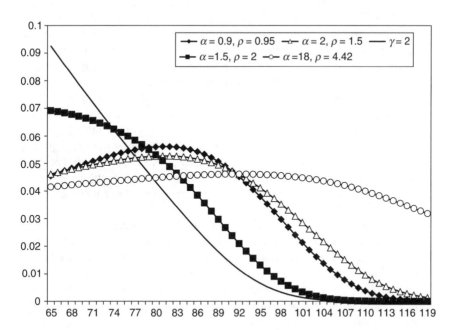

Figure 7.10. Optimal consumption paths without annuities contrasting various Epstein–Zin preferences with TAS-GD preferences

consumption at age 95 only about one-tenth of consumption at age 65 and it is not clear that people really have preferences of that sort. Another interesting feature of these Epstein–Zin consumption paths is that they can explain a desire to having consumption rising (albeit gently) for some period throughout retirement.

Notes

1. A more technical theoretical treatment is provided by Sheshinski (2008).
2. For a fuller discussion of this issue, see Moffet (1978).
3. Strictly speaking the slope is $-p\delta$ rather than $p\delta$ but we are ignoring the minus sign of a downward sloping curve. We obtain the slope by implicit differentiation: the slope of the indifference curve is $-p\delta u'(c_1)/u'(c_0)$ and on the 45° line $c_1 = c_0$.
4. To measure the magnitude of the effect we consider $\text{AEW}_0/W_0 > 1$. Some authors use the reciprocal of this, namely $W_0/\text{AEW}_0 < 1$.
5. The survival probability s_j is defined in equation (4.2).
6. In fact, Yaari's model (1965) is even less restrictive than our current characterization, because it also assumes that individuals are able to borrow money which will only be repaid if they are still alive in the future. This is because Yaari assumes that agents are making their decisions at a time when they are still expecting to receive future labour income. This raises the possibility that agents might wish to bring forward consumption and hence borrow against the future. Financial institutions recognize that agents may die and thus the future labour income is risky: they require borrowers to pay the higher interest rate of $(1+r_j)^j/s_j$, which is higher than would be available to agents who were certain of being alive, who would borrow at an interest rate of $(1+r_j)^j$. In practice something similar to this may be achieved by lenders requiring borrowers to take out life assurance to ensure the loan can be repaid regardless of whether the borrower is alive or not. Throughout most of this book we are assuming that agents are retired and have no future labour income, so the possibility of borrowing does not arise.
7. Here we re-emphasize that these are all life annuities and not term-certain annuities. Real income is constant in each period: we are ignoring inflation.
8. We prefer the term 'to go short on an annuity' instead of 'to sell an annuity' since it makes explicit that the agent is selling an income stream conditional on his (the seller's) survival, whereas the sale of an annuity by an insurance company involves selling an income stream conditional on the buyer's survival. Confusingly, the two terms are frequently used interchangeably in the literature on annuities. In principle, an individual could achieve the same objective by taking out a conventional loan against future (life-contingent)

income in conjunction with life insurance to ensure that the loan could be repaid if the individual died and the future income were not actually received. In practice life insurance markets are not usually available for this sort of transaction and most analysis assumes that individuals are unable to follow this strategy.

9. Rabin (1998) provides a survey of more sophisticated critiques of economic rationality. A counter-critique of behavioural economics is that of Rubinstein (2006).

10. The important feature is $\lim_{c \to 0} u'(c)$. If this is sufficiently large—and in many of the models we have considered it is actually infinite—then by living a little bit longer an agent can always increase utility by reducing consumption in an earlier period where the marginal utility of consumption is low and consuming just a little at the end of life where marginal utility will be high. A counter-argument is provided by Pelzman and Rousslang (1982), who attempt to generalize the objective function to include utility from consumption when the agent is not alive, but we do not find their specification plausible.

11. This result is general to any number of periods, since the proof is a simple application of Jensen's inequality. The key assumption is that the felicity function is concave, i.e., that the agent is risk averse.

12. The move from equation (7.37) to equation (7.38) involves a strictly increasing non-linear function, namely $x \mapsto x^{1-\rho}$. With von Neumann–Morgenstern utility functions it is only valid to take strictly increasing *linear* functions. However, equation (7.37) is not a von Neumann–Morgenstern utility function since we have already substituted explicitly for the random variation. Hence in this case it is appropriate to use a non-linear function.

13. We ignore the possibility that such an agent might defer consumption using bonds.

8

Reasons for the annuity puzzle

The theoretical analysis of the previous chapter suggests that an annuity is the best way for an individual with uncertain lifetime to obtain a secure income, since it maximizes the individual's consumption. But empirical work suggests that annuity markets are actually quite small. This failure of the economic theory to match the evidence constitutes the 'annuity puzzle'. In this chapter we consider possible reasons for this.

It is important to note at the outset that the annuity puzzle is only one of a series of phenomena which are not fully consistent with the canonical economic theory of the previous chapter. Zeldes (1989) observes a series of 'consumption puzzles' of which two are highly relevant in our context. First, the elderly do not dis-save during retirement. In part this is a corollary of the fact that they do not purchase annuities, since it is very difficult to run down wealth without running considerable risks of consuming all of one's income before dying. However, there is some evidence that the elderly keep their wealth constant or even increase it, which cannot be fully optimal. Secondly, consumption expenditure falls discontinuously at the point of retirement, which is inconsistent with consumption smoothing.[1] Poterba's (1994) collection of articles contains savings evidence which demonstrates that these puzzles are an international phenomenon. Thus the annuity puzzle is not a unique problem but part of a general issue in understanding savings behaviour.

If low annuity demand is consistent with rational behaviour and well-functioning markets then there would not be much more to be said. So we start by considering more complicated models than those of the previous chapter to see if additional detail is sufficient to explain low rates of annuitization. There are several issues here: first, we can consider the possibility that there may be specific reasons for consuming earlier in retirement; secondly, we need to consider the fact that annuities are backed by bonds and earn low rates of return compared with equity; thirdly we need to recognize that the state provides a basic state pension (which is itself a form of annuity). These explanations for low annuity demand are all consistent with optimal behaviour and would suggest that low annuity demand is not really a problem.

An alternative possibility is that low annuity demand is due to market failure in the annuity market. This would then make the whole issue one for public policy since the government or regulatory authorities might be able to reduce or eliminate imperfections in the annuity market. We need to ask what form this market failure might take. The evidence we presented in Chapter 4 showed that the money's worth on annuities is typically close to one: prima facie evidence that the market failure is not monopoly power. Instead we consider the possibility that there is adverse selection. This is a situation where different individuals have different life expectancies and, most importantly, the individuals are better informed about their individual life expectancy than the life insurer. Since Akerlof (1970) economists have increasingly stressed that such asymmetries in information can have serious effects on markets and we consider how this can be applied to the annuity market.

The final possibility is that the low demand for annuities is not fully rational: agents would be better off by buying annuities but they do not understand this. At its simplest this could be due merely to a lack of financial education—in which case increased education would be the obvious remedy. However, the UK experience suggests that there is a deeper problem—individuals who join pension schemes which automatically pay a pension are usually happy with that pension while those who pay into a pension fund which they are then required to use to buy an annuity frequently complain about the requirement. Since the two scenarios may be formally identical, it appears that agents' behaviour is determined by the way in which the details of pension are presented: a phenomenon known to economic psychologists as a framing effect. Empirical evidence suggests that framing effects are ubiquitous in explaining people's behaviour and in our final section we discuss these and other psychological determinants of annuity demand.

8.1. Social welfare payments and pre-annuitized wealth

In the previous chapter, we assumed that the optimization problem at retirement was the allocation of a stock of wealth to finance consumption over several periods. In practice, virtually nobody faces this choice, since most elderly people receive some form of income, often in the form of state pensions or welfare payments (and some individuals have occupational pensions). For example, as we have seen in Chapter 3, nearly everyone in the UK receives the Basic State Pension or some other welfare payments.

Whether described as pensions or not, any welfare provision is itself a form of annuity since it is paid while the agent is alive and hence insures against longevity risk. So the choice facing most individuals is how much additional lump sum wealth to annuitize given the value of their pre-annuitized wealth. Under most reasonable assumptions—in fact for any of the utility functions considered in the previous chapter—the marginal utility from annuitizing each extra pound of wealth is diminishing. This means that the gains from purchasing an additional annuity might be relatively small (recall that the simulations in the previous chapter compared the polar cases of annuitizing everything or annuitizing nothing). Quantitatively, the amount of pre-annuitized wealth is important: in the UK, the Pensions Commission (2004: 182) reports that only those individuals whose labour income exceeds about £25,000 have a significant amount of their total wealth in assets other than their state pension.[2]

To illustrate this in the context of our simple two-period model, consider an individual who has wealth W_0 and will receive a welfare payment of S in each period of life. We continue to assume that it is impossible to borrow against future income payments, which means that the budget constraint must be redrawn with a kink as shown in Figure 8.1. In this figure the individual can consume any amount on or to the southwest of the area bounded by $W_0 + S$, X, and Z. This does not mean that the agent will never purchase an annuity: depending on his preferences he may choose a point on the XZ part of the budget constraint which would involve buying an annuity in addition to the existing pension.

As we saw in the previous chapter, however, for some preferences the agent might wish to have much higher consumption in the first period of retirement relative to the last period. This would mean that the indifference curve would be relatively shallow and hence the optimal point might be to consume at the kink marked X on the diagram.

While this two-period example demonstrates why an agent may choose not to buy an annuity, it does not explain why he would save money in conventional bonds rather than a life-contingent product. If bonds were

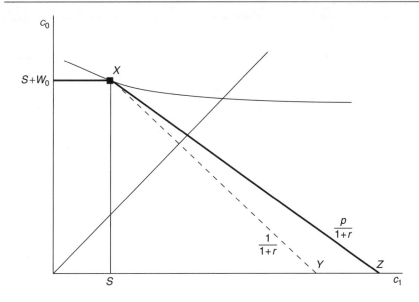

Figure 8.1. Annuitizing when there is a pre-existing pension of S

used instead of an annuity, the budget constraint would be the region bounded by $W_0 + S$, X, and Y (i.e. the dotted line), which is dominated by the region $W_0 + S$, X, and Z representing an annuity purchase and thus it would be better to buy an annuity than to buy a bond.

As we have already seen in Chapter 7, the situation is more complicated when there are many periods and a full range of temporary and deferred annuities are unavailable. In this case the presence of a pension or welfare payments is likely to interact with imperfections in the annuity market and reduce—but not eliminate—the benefits from annuitization.

Even in the two-period scenario, the likely magnitude of pre-annuitized wealth means that the benefits of annuitization will be small as we illustrate in Figure 8.2. If the pre-annuitized wealth is a large proportion of total wealth then S will be large relative to W_0 and the kink in the budget constraint will be close to the 45° line. With perfect annuity markets the relevant part of the budget constraint would then be XTZ. However, with imperfect annuity markets (in particular an absence of deferred annuities), the agent would only have access to bonds if he wished to defer consumption into period 1 and so the relevant budget constraint would have a further kink and be XTY, which can be achieved by a combination of bond and annuity saving. If the agent used bonds alone and did not buy an additional annuity then the budget constraint

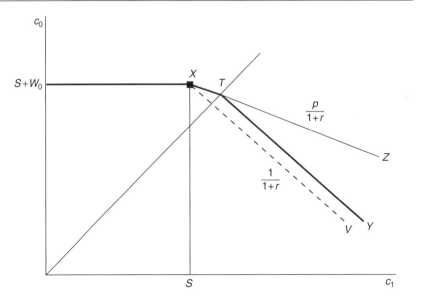

Figure 8.2. The budget constraint with a high degree of pre-annuitization and imperfect annuity markets

would be XV, which is little different from XTY. Therefore, even in the two-period case it is possible that the combination of pre-annuitized wealth and imperfect annuity markets could result in very small benefits to purchasing an additional annuity and these benefits would easily be offset by small transaction costs or other disadvantages to annuitization that we shall discuss below.

8.2. Investing in alternative assets or deferring annuitization

An important assumption that we have made up until now is that there is a single riskless interest rate: this is the underlying framework of the Yaari (1965) model where the savings choice was between a bond and an annuity. In reality there are a variety of interest rates, some of which are risky (such as the return on equity). This means that the optimization decision involves choosing between a portfolio of different assets. In this section we consider the effect of having to choose between bonds, annuities, and equity. We also include the possibility that the individual can choose the timing of the annuity purchase and is not constrained to annuitize at the point of retirement.

Milevsky and Young (2002) suggest that the availability of equity and the option to defer annuity purchase will result in deferral being optimal. The intuition for this rests on two simple observations:

First, the mortality risk for people who have just retired is quite low: typically little more than 1 per cent (this can be seen in both the population and annuitant mortality tables in the UK). So, if a one-year actuarial note were available for someone aged 65, the rate of return on it would only be $(1 + r)/0.99$, which is little better than the rate of return on a conventional bond of $(1 + r)$.

Secondly, the expected rate of return on equity appears to be much higher than can be explained by risk aversion alone: this phenomenon of the 'equity premium puzzle' is well documented both internationally and historically by Dimson, Marsh, and Staunton (2002).

Taken together these two observations mean that the expected return on holding equity at the age of 65 must be quite a lot higher than the expected return on an actuarial note (which is in turn slightly better than the return on a bond). Since the equity premium is much larger than is necessary to compensate for the additional riskiness of equity over bonds, it follows that the expected return on equity must be larger than the return necessary to compensate for the riskiness of equity over annuities. The same logic will follow for any individual with a relatively low mortality rate and therefore it is worth delaying annuitization until one is relatively elderly.

A numerical example may help here: suppose that the equity return is 7 per cent, the bond return 2 per cent (so the equity premium is 5 per cent). Suppose also that agents' attitudes to risk are such that, absent considerations of mortality, they would only require an equity premium of 3 per cent to be indifferent between equity and bonds. Then it would only be optimal to annuitize when the rate of return on annuities were 4 per cent, which would happen when

$$1.04 = \frac{1.02}{p} \Rightarrow p \approx 0.98 \text{ and mortality } \approx 0.02.$$

Using this method one can find the level of mortality and corresponding age at which it is optimal to buy an annuity. Based on US life tables, Milevsky and Young (2002) report the optimal age to be 78 for women and 73 for men with option values (at age 65) of waiting to be 15.3 per cent and 8.9 per cent of total wealth, respectively.[3]

Investing in equity and deferring annuitization is not without risk and Milevsky and Young find that the probabilities of doing worse by following this strategy to be 0.27 for women and 0.32 for men. If there were a significant chance that the fall in wealth would be so high that the annuitant might then be eligible for welfare payments, there would be a moral hazard problem, since agents would rationally gamble, knowing that they would be insured from doing too badly. Prima facie this would provide a role for government intervention: in fact it is unlikely that individuals likely to receive welfare payments would have easy access to equity.

One solution would be for agents to buy investment-linked annuities where annuity payments depend on equity returns, which we described in Chapter 2. Blake, Cairns, and Dowd (2003) consider three types of decumulation distribution programmes: a purchased life annuity (PLA) at 65, an equity-linked annuity (ELA) with a level annuity purchased at 75, and an equity-linked income drawdown product (ELID) with a level annuity purchased at 75.[4] They use simulations to compare the welfare of a 65-year-old male who retires with a pension fund of £100,000 in terms of the discounted lifetime utility from each of the three programmes, when he can either annuitize at 65 (the base case of PLA) or use one of the deferred annuitization options (ELA or ELID) by putting his pension fund into a combination of equities and bonds. They find that for relative risk aversion coefficients of less than 1.25 the best programme is ELA with 100 per cent in equities. For higher risk aversion coefficients the ELA still dominates, but with a greater proportion of the pension fund invested in bonds, until it eventually approaches the PLA. Importantly, the ELA always dominates the drawdown option ELID, but the size of the benefit of the ELA depends on the equity–bond mix. Blake, Cairns, and Dowd (2003) compute equivalent wealth for the dominance of ELA over ELID: a plan member with an RRA of 3.96 would require an extra 25 per cent of wealth in the pension fund for a 75 per cent equities ELID to match the welfare from an ELA.

What is the best age to annuitize? They compare annuitizing immediately (PLA), with delaying annuitization and using the ELA/ELID between age 65 and the point of annuitization. Annuitization after age 85 was not allowed.

Comparing ELA and PLA programmes, they find that it is optimal either to annuitize immediately or to wait until age 85 (when annuitization would be obligatory), but never to annuitize at some intermediate age, consistent with Merton (1983). Comparing ELID and PLA programmes, they find that the optimal age to annuitize is very sensitive to the degree of risk aversion. At low levels of risk aversion the optimal age to annuitize is 79, close to the Milevsky (1998) rule (switching at the point where the mortality drag equals the equity premium). Higher levels of risk aversion result in the plan member annuitizing earlier.

They also compute the cost of a regulation compelling plan members to annuitize at age 75. A plan member with a low RRA of 0.25 would require an extra 1.6 per cent of his retirement fund to compensate for annuitizing at 75 rather than 85, implying that when there is no bequest motive the cost of compulsory annuitization is small. Introducing a bequest motive increases the optimal age of annuitization.

Finally, Blake, Cairns, and Dowd (2003) consider a dynamic stochastic annuitization optimization decision, in which the decision to annuitize depends on the historical performance of the pension fund. They find that a plan member is more likely to defer annuitization, if his investments have been performing well, and to bring forward the annuitization, if his investments have been underperforming. In Table 8.1 we reproduce their summary of results from a number of past studies.

Blake, Cairns, and Dowd (2003) suggest that at higher levels of risk aversion, individuals annuitize earlier. An interesting question is how risk aversion changes along the life cycle. In the standard expected utility model with CRRA preferences, Samuelson (1969, 1989) finds that it is optimal to invest a fraction of wealth in risky assets that is independent of age. This is a counter-intuitive result and many pension products have a 'lifestyle' asset allocation (Byrne et al. 2007). There are many situations where a lifestyle allocation may be optimal, including endogenous labour supply, mean reversion in equity returns, or changing preferences. In experimental work, Barsky et al. (1997) find for a sample of over 50s that the relation between relative risk aversion and age has an inverse U shape, whereas Guiso and Paiella (2001) find a positive relation between risk aversion and age, so the assumption of CRRA preferences may be inappropriate.

Powell and Ansic (1997), Jianakoplos and Bernasek (1998), and Schubert et al. (1999) all find that women are more risk averse than men in a number of financial decision-making contexts. Halek and Eisenhauer (2001) find greater relative risk aversion for women and the elderly. In addition, Barker and Odean (2001) find that men are more over-confident than women in investment decisions. An alternative but indirect approach is to examine the share of wealth held in risky assets, and see how it changes along the life cycle. Riley and Chow (1992) find that relative risk aversion decreases up to age 65 but increases for the elderly. On the other hand, Ameriks and Zeldes (2001) conclude that, after controlling for cohort

Table 8.1. Summary of optimal annuitization decision models with stochastic returns

Article	Model Features				
	Attitude to risk	Type of programme[a]	Bequests	Asset mix	Results
Merton (1983)	Neutral	ELID/ELA	No	Fixed	Purchase a conventional annuity immediately
Milevsky (1998)	Averse	ELID	No	Fixed	Purchase a conventional annuity when mortality drag exceeds the equity risk premium
Kapur and Orszag (1999)	Neutral	ELID[b]	No	Dynamic	Gradual purchases of conventional annuities with full annuitization when mortality drag exceeds the equity risk premium
Milevsky and Young (2002)	Neutral	ELID	No	Dynamic	Switch to conventional annuity at deterministic time T. ELID before T includes optimized dynamic asset mix. T depends on risk aversion and model parameters
Blake et al. (2003: section 4.6)	Neutral	ELID	Yes	Fixed	Switch to conventional annuity at stochastic time T. ELID before T includes optimized static asset mix. T depends on risk aversion and bequest utility

[a] Definitions of acronyms are provided in the text.
[b] In this model the agent receives survival credits before annuitizing.
Source: Blake, Cairns, and Dowd (2003: table 4).

effects, there is a positive relation between the share of financial portfolios held in risky assets and age. But these studies note that education, income, wealth, and age are all correlated, and the relationship may be a function of one of these other variables.

As we conclude this section it is important to note that that one of the underlying ideas in it is that agents do better to hold equity than a conventional annuity when mortality drag exceeds the equity premium. This follows from the fact that the equity premium appears larger than is necessary to compensate agents for risk—which is why it is often referred to as the equity premium 'puzzle'. However, the equity premium puzzle applies not just to the elderly but to everyone and suggests that no one should ever hold bond-like products. In practice, people of all ages do hold bonds, suggesting either a high degree of irrationality in practice or that the underlying theory is wrong.

Since we know that the equity premium puzzle is primarily an artefact of the combination of rational expected utility maximization and TAS-GD preferences, there is no reason to believe that agents are irrational and it may be better to use more exotic utility functions as discussed in Chapter 7, Section 7.5. To the extent that such models suggest that the equity premium is not too high, we conjecture that these models might also suggest that it would not be rational for the elderly to hold their wealth in annuities rather than equity.

8.3. The pattern of expenditure in retirement

In Chapter 7 we saw that the optimal pattern of consumption in retirement might involve consumption rising or falling over time. In all of the cases we considered, these patterns were due to the interaction of rates of return and the extent to which agents wanted to smooth their consumption. However, this approach ignores three important possibilities that we now consider.

First, as already noted, consumption need not be the same as expenditure. Much expenditure of the elderly could be on non-durable consumer goods (so that the expenditure is really a form of investment) and this form of expenditure is typically lumpy even if the consumption services that it provides are smooth. Such investments could include age-specific investments in a house (such as installing a stair-lift) or health expenditure (such as having a hip replacement).[5] In the absence of perfect credit markets, the elderly need to have fungible wealth if they are to be able to make these investments.

Secondly, agents' preferences could change over time: this becomes especially apparent if we recall that preferences can include people's needs for certain sorts of consumption good. More elderly people would attach greater value to health and personal care.

Thirdly, both necessary expenditures and changes in tastes are not certain, since they are likely to arise with changes in health, which is itself difficult to predict. Furthermore, even if an individual is certain of suffering ill health, the timing remains uncertain.

To model these considerations would require a precise knowledge of why agents' expenditures might need to vary over retirement and we do not wish to go into a detailed discussion of all of the possibilities. A simple way of modelling changing preferences is to modify the expected utility function from the previous chapter to

$$V_t = \mathsf{E}_t \left[\sum_{i=0}^{T} p_{t+i} \delta^{-i} u \left(c_{t+i} - e_i \right) \right], \qquad e_i \geq 0 \tag{8.1}$$

where $c_{t+i} \geq e_i$ and e_i is referred to as necessary expenditure.[6] There is no reason for e_i to be known at time t as it may be random. Davidoff, Brown, and Diamond (2005) note that the effect on annuity demand depends crucially on the relative sizes of the different values of the necessary expenditures e_i.

If large expenditures are likely to be needed early in retirement, then agents will wish to have easy access to their wealth, rather than having it tied up in an annuity which will only make payments in the future (and we continue to assume it is impossible to borrow against future payments). So agents will prefer fungible assets, which give the agents the option of making expenditures early on. The value of the option depends upon the size and uncertainty of necessary expenditure, the agent's preferences, and external factors such as the lack of credit availability and interest rates. Since bonds are more fungible than annuities, they have an option value which must be set against the higher consumption possible with an annuity. So full annuitization is unlikely to be optimal unless the option value is small, if there is the possibility of necessary expenditures early in retirement.

On the other hand, if necessary expenditures occur late in retirement, the problem now facing the agent is how to defer consumption. In the three-period example we considered in Chapter 7, this would be represented by planning to have $C_2 > C_1 > C_0$. But from Table 7.1 we know that complete annuitization would only be possible if there were a perfect annuity market: since this is not the case, the best plan would be to put a high proportion of wealth into a conventional annuity, consume less than the annuity payments in periods 0 and 1, and save for high expected expenditures in period 2 using conventional bonds. So this means that full annuitization is unlikely to be observed when there is the possibility of necessary expenditures late in retirement.

We now have reasons for believing that a rational agent might avoid full annuitization when necessary expenditures have to be made either early or late in retirement, especially when then there is some uncertainty involved. The obvious solution would be the purchase of appropriate insurance products to remove this uncertainty, but such insurance is expensive. One of the largest sources of risk will be health costs, but subsidized health care may be provided by the state so most individuals will be adequately insured against health shocks. Hence this cannot be a reason for most people avoiding annuitization.

Richer people may prefer to supplement state health provision with private health insurance, but it is an empirical question whether their demand for such insurance is really a major barrier to buying an annuity.

Murtaugh, Spillman, and Warshawsky (2001) raise the possibility that sophisticated products combining both an annuity and health or care insurance could overcome such problems. Long-term care needs can be based upon measurable activities of daily living and insurance products certainly exist for individuals who are unable to undertake these activities without assistance. Unfortunately such markets are very thin and the costs are very high: this may be because of adverse selection problems.[7] We shall discuss adverse selection in the context of annuity markets in the next section: at this point we note that Murtaugh, Spillman, and Warshawsky (2001) propose a possible solution to problems in both the annuity market and the long-term care insurance market by having products which combine both. This suggestion is based upon the empirical observation that individuals who need care usually have shorter life expectancy. If insurance companies simultaneously sold both an annuity and long-term care insurance they would be selling two insurance products whose risks were off-setting (so the two products are a natural hedge).

This would have two important effects. First, in the UK context there are effectively no products providing an adequate hedge against mortality risk, because life insurance is rarely sold to people of pension age (the situation is different in some other countries). If care insurance provides some sort of hedge then it could buttress the annuity market either for annuity providers or in the re-insurance market by providing some insurance in aggregate annuity risk. Secondly, at the individual level, sales of a combined product would remove adverse selection problems and make both markets more efficient. Webb (2006) analyses an asymmetric information model in which individuals differ in their risk aversion and can take preventative action to reduce mortality risk (such as exercising regularly). He shows that individuals who take preventative actions will be low risk in the long-term care market but high risk to an annuity provider.

He demonstrates that an equilibrium with bundling of annuity and long-term care contracts dominates selling the two products separately. Based on empirical mortality and care experiences in the USA, Spillman, Murtaugh, and Warshawsky (2003) provide quantitative estimates of the cost of providing long-term care insurance and an annuity simultaneously: this would be 3–5 per cent less than selling the two products apart from each other and would result in more purchases overall. However, given the typical pension fund sizes reported by Stark (2003) it is difficult to believe that there would be a substantial market for care insurance, because most elderly people would have insufficient wealth to afford care insurance.

8.4. Theory of adverse selection in annuity markets

It is well known to actuaries that there are selection effects in annuities markets. In discussing the Millard Tucker Report into the UK annuity market, *The Economist* (20 February 1954: 554) notes that 'the purchase of an ordinary life annuity has become highly imprudent to anyone . . . unless he rates his expectation of life very highly'. In summarizing the Finance Act of 1956, the Institute of Actuaries recognized that 'in the case of self-employed contracts one favourable factor was that there should be less self-selection than in the case of immediate annuity purchases' (*Journal of Institute of Actuaries*, LXXXIII, 1957: 19).

Within economic theory the importance of adverse selection has been known since the 1970s within the more general context of the effects of asymmetric information. However, while there is widespread agreement that adverse selection is likely to be present in the annuities market, two different models have been suggested. The difference between the models hinges on whether firms are able to specify different annuity prices for purchases of annuities of different sizes: in particular whether annuity providers can offer lower annuity rates to larger annuity purchases.

We now briefly present the two different models of adverse selection in annuity markets.[7] In each case we shall build upon the simple models presented above, where agents live for one period with complete certainty and for a second period with some probability p_i, which varies between individuals and is known to the individual alone (neither the insurance company nor any government regulator knows any individual's p_i). The distribution of the p_i is common knowledge. An important consideration is whether agents differ in any other respect: typically it is assumed that they do not. A more natural assumption might be that agents with higher life expectancy (higher p_i) would also be richer and have a larger sum of money (larger W) to annuitize. We shall discuss the relevance of this later.

8.4.1. The Eckstein–Eichenbaum–Peled approach

Eckstein, Eichenbaum, and Peled (1985) assume that there are just two types of agent who are identical except for different survival probabilities. The first group of individuals has a low probability p_l of surviving into period 2 and thus has low life expectancy. From the point of view of the life insurer these are low-risk individuals. The second group of individuals has a high probability $p_h > p_l$ of surviving into period 2 and from the point of view of the life insurer they are high-risk individuals. As noted in Chapter 7, the slope of an individual's indifference curve depends upon the survival probability, so low-risk individuals will tend to have flatter indifference curves than high-risk individuals. Note that high-risk individuals have high life expectancy and low-risk individuals have low life expectancy.

If there were perfect information so that high- and low-risk individuals could be offered different contracts, then the situation that we should expect to see is that illustrated in Figure 8.3. Life insurance companies

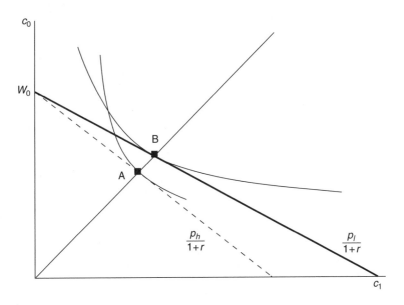

Figure 8.3. A perfect information separating equilibrium

would be able to sell contracts on the solid line to low-risk individuals: contracts offered above this line would be unprofitable for the life insurer while competition would ensure that no company could offer contracts beneath this line: the line itself is actuarially fair (transactions costs of the life insurer are assumed to be minimal and therefore ignored). There is a similar situation for high-risk individuals: life insurance companies would be able to sell such people less generous—but still actuarially fair—contracts on the dashed line. For simplicity we assume that agents' preferences result in them preferring equal consumption in both periods and therefore the optimal solutions to both types are B and A, respectively.

However, if the annuity provider cannot distinguish the high-risk individuals from the low-risk individuals it is not possible to have this form of separation between low-risk and high-risk individuals. If the life insurer offered both contracts then everyone would choose the more generous contract, in which case the annuity company would make a loss.

The solution proposed by Eckstein, Eichenbaum, and Peled (1985) is that life insurers offer two very specific annuity contracts, at points A and C in Figure 8.4. The key assumption made here is that life insurance companies not only set the price of annuities but also the total size of the annuity purchase: we shall discuss this assumption later. High-risk

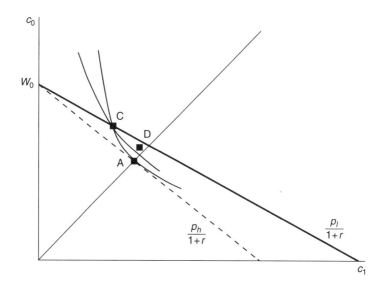

Figure 8.4. An adverse selection separating equilibrium

individuals are indifferent between points A and C and so can choose contract A, which means that annuity providers will break even on these contracts. Low-risk individuals have flatter indifference curves and therefore strictly prefer point C at which point the insurance company is also breaking even.[9] This potential solution is called a separating equilibrium—but it may fail to be an equilibrium.

If contracts A and C were being provided, and a new annuity provider offered a contract at point D, it would be purchased by everyone in the market, since it is preferable to A for high-risk and C for low-risk individuals, respectively. A contract which is purchased by both types is a pooling contract. The question then is whether any new annuity provider would offer such a contract.

A necessary condition is that such a contract at least breaks even. Writing the proportions of high- and low-risk individuals as ψ_h and $\psi_l = 1 - \psi_h$, then the firm will break even so long as it offers an annuity rate

$$z \le \frac{\psi_h p_h + (1 - \psi_h) p_l}{1 + r} \tag{8.2}$$

If ψ_h is relatively high, then points such as D will never make a profit, so such contracts will not be offered. But if ψ_h is relatively low, then a point such as D would make a profit, so it might be offered and thus it might be impossible to have a separating equilibrium.

However, it can be shown that a pooling equilibrium never exists. To see why this is, consider the potential pooling contract at point D in the Figure 8.5.

It is now possible for another annuity provider to offer a contract at a point such as E, which has the property that high-risk individuals prefer D to E, while low-risk individuals prefer E to D: in addition to this, it is clear that the contract at point E makes a profit if only low-risk individuals purchase it. Since all of the low-risk individuals would purchase E in preference to D, the annuity provider offering D would make a loss and hence such a contract could not be offered. It follows that a pooling equilibrium cannot exist.[10]

The conclusion from this analysis is that adverse selection will lead to under-insurance and a less efficient outcome than would be the case if there were perfect information. All individuals will put some of their wealth in an annuity product but some (low-risk) individuals may choose to put some more of their wealth in a conventional bond (thus resulting in less than full annuitization).

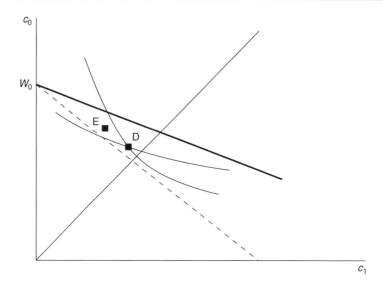

Figure 8.5. Non-existence of a pooling equilibrium

The problem with this approach is that it assumes that insurance companies specify contracts such as A, B, or C. This means that different prices are related to different size of purchase, that larger purchases are offered poorer annuity rates, and that only certain purchase sizes are allowed. However, this does not appear to be an appropriate characterization of the annuity market, because the evidence reviewed in Chapter 2, Section 2.2.1, suggests that most annuity providers do not use size of purchase to separate high- and low-risk types in this way. Furthermore, note that annuity companies cannot observe whether individuals are purchasing multiple annuities from different companies and so cannot observe the total amount of wealth being annuitized, which is crucial to the analysis of Eckstein, Eichenbaum, and Peled (1985). We now turn to a model where annuity providers quote a price and allow individuals to choose any size of annuity purchase.

8.4.2. *The adverse selection models of Abel and Walliser*

This type of model was first suggested by Abel (1986) and has been extended by Walliser (2000). The latter also makes a further change in the model: so far we have assumed that high-risk and low-risk individuals are the same in all respects, but Walliser notes that high-risk (i.e. long

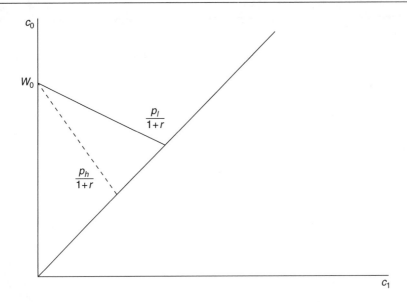

Figure 8.6. Potential annuity contracts in the Abel–Walliser model

life expectancy) individuals will also tend to be richer and hence have a higher W.[11]

Suppose that annuity providers offer an annuity rate at which anyone can purchase any quantity of an annuity. Two extreme cases are that the annuity rate offered would be those at which the annuity provider breaks even if either everyone were high risk or everyone were low risk. We shall also assume that no individual can sell annuities. Then the two possibilities are illustrated in Figure 8.6 in the solid and dashed lines respectively.

With the annuity rate set to be appropriate for low-risk individuals (on the dashed line) the annuity provider would get a mixture of high- and low-risk individuals purchasing annuities and hence make a profit; with the annuity rate set to be appropriate for high-risk individuals (on the solid line) the annuity provider would definitely make a loss. With fairly weak assumptions about preferences, there will be at least one annuity rate somewhere between these two annuity rates where the annuity provider will break even.[12] Writing the equilibrium annuity rate as z, we can say that

$$1 + r < \frac{1+r}{p_h} < z < \frac{1+r}{p_l} \tag{8.3}$$

and that the annuity rate is determined by the break-even condition

$$\frac{\psi_h p_h a(z, W_h, p_h) + \psi_l p_l a(z, W_l, p_l)}{1+r} = z \tag{8.4}$$

where, as defined above, ψ_h and ψ_l are the proportions of high- and low-risk individuals in the population and $a(z, W_i, p_i)$ is the demand for annuities by someone facing annuity rate z who has wealth W_i and survival probability p_i. The average population survival probability is then

$$\bar{p} = \psi_h p_h + \psi_l p_l \tag{8.5}$$

and Abel (1986) shows that[13]

$$\frac{1+r}{p_h} < z < \frac{1+r}{\bar{p}}, \tag{8.6}$$

which follows because high-risk individuals will tend to make larger annuity purchases than low-risk individuals, as shown in Figure 8.7. A consequence of this is that the mortality of annuitants by amounts will be less than that by lives and we have seen in Chapter 4 that this is indeed the case. If high-risk individuals also have more wealth then this effect will be reinforced.

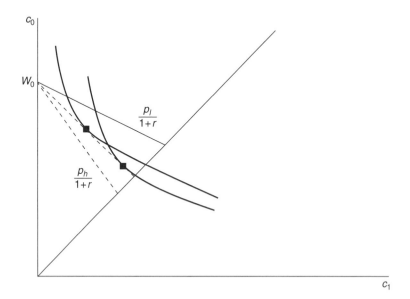

Figure 8.7. Pooling equilibrium and adverse selection in Abel's model

Finkelstein and Poterba (2002) suggest that in fact there may be some separation rather than complete pooling because of the ability to purchase different types of annuities: individuals with low life expectancy would prefer front-loaded (such as level nominal annuities) or guaranteed annuities, while individuals with high life expectancy would prefer real or escalating annuities.

The conclusion from this model is that all agents would choose to buy an annuity and all would be fully annuitized (none would choose to purchase bonds). So it might appear that this model provides no more realistic conclusions than the Eckstein–Eichenbaum–Peled model, even if the assumptions are more realistic. But a further very important extension would also explain why some agents would buy no annuity at all: consider the model of the previous section (where there was a state pension) and combine this with adverse selection. The budget constraint now has a kink as in Figure 8.2, but the different types of agents have distinct indifference curves as shown in Figure 8.8.

In this example, high-risk individuals would prefer to annuitize their financial wealth, but low-risk individuals would prefer not to do so—the latter would rely entirely upon the state pension for an annuity-type income. The reason for this is that, as we have already seen, low-risk individuals would prefer to purchase a smaller annuity than high-risk

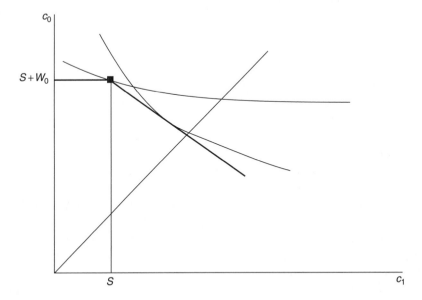

Figure 8.8. Adverse selection and welfare payments

individuals. Because low-risk individuals have flatter indifference curves, they would prefer to consume more in period 0 and less in period 1 than is provided for by the state pension. As they are unable to sell annuities, they are forced to choose to consume on the kink of the budget constraint. Hence annuities are only sold to high-risk individuals (resulting in z being based on the mortality experience of only a subset of the population).

The conclusions of this extended adverse selection model can then be summarized as follows: first, in the presence of a state pension, individuals with low life expectancy may choose not to purchase any annuities because their wealth (predominantly the state pension) is already in annuity form. This would mean that annuitants would have longer life expectancy than non-annuitants.

Secondly, among individuals who do choose to annuitize, the lowest risk individuals will tend to make smaller purchases, so that the actual annuity rate will be lower than one based on the average life expectancy of all annuitants.[14] A corollary of this is that life expectancy of amounts will exceed that of lives, so money's worth of amounts will exceed that of lives, as is observed in the data.

Thirdly, these effects will be reinforced if high-risk individuals tend to be richer (have more wealth to annuitize). In practice this will make it hard to identify whether the features observed in the data are due to adverse selection or wealth effects.

8.5. Behavioural factors

Our discussion so far has assumed that agents are rational utility-maximizing agents with risk-averse preferences. These are very standard assumptions which have been used widely within the economics literature for much of the post-war period. More recently economists have become aware that these assumptions may be inadequate descriptions of actual behaviour and current research is more devoted to the insights that can be learned from economic psychology (Rabin 1998). Much of this research suggests that actual behaviour is frequently irrational and that departures from rationality are both consistent across a range of behaviours and reliably correlated with other factors. Some recent work on behavioural economics and pension provision has been collected in Mitchell and Utkus (2004).

In Chapter 7 we have already begun to consider these behavioural issues. One important issue treated there was the nature of the utility function, with extensions from the Time-Additive-Separable function to Epstein–Zin preferences and habit formation. This extension did not involve irrationality. Alternatively one could consider using non-Geometric Discounting, which, in the version used by us, did involve irrationality. In this section, we consider several further models which have begun to be used by economists to explain behaviour.

8.5.1. Cumulative prospect theory and loss aversion

There is a considerable body of evidence suggesting flaws in the expected utility hypothesis with risk aversion.[15] One well-known problem is that risk-averse individuals would always purchase fair insurance and avoid fair gambles, but it is frequently observed that agents do purchase unfair gambles: that they simultaneously purchase insurance suggests that they cannot be risk-loving. Kahneman and Tversky (1979) have suggested that agents' behaviour is modelled better by *loss aversion* than *risk aversion*. In this theoretical framework, there is a reference or endowment point, which can often be understood as the initial position, and utility depends upon whether the agent's position improves or worsens in comparison with this reference point.

Gains over the reference point yield increased utility at a diminishing rate, consistent with standard risk aversion. Losses compared with the reference point yield lower utility, but there are two important differences with risk aversion: first, there is diminishing disutility to losses, resulting in the utility function being risk-loving for outcomes lower than the reference point; secondly, the marginal disutility to a very small loss is strictly greater than the marginal utility gain to a very small gain, resulting in a kink at the reference point. These preferences are illustrated in Figure 8.9.

A simple example of these preferences is as follows: an agent who initially has £110 and then loses £10 will be less happy than an agent who initially has £90 and then receives an extra £10, even though both end up with the same sum of £100.

The replacement of risk aversion with loss aversion need not suggest a departure from rationality, since there is no necessary inconsistency with these preferences. However, it does raise the question of what is to be taken as the reference point, how the reference point is determined, and how it changes over time. But Tversky and Kahneman (1992) also include a component of explicit irrationality by making an additional (and completely independent) assumption that individuals falsely

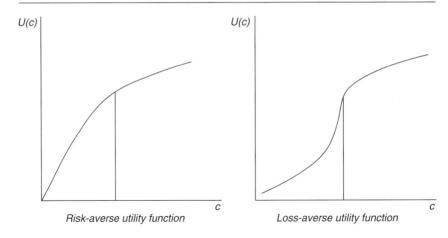

Figure 8.9. Contrasting risk aversion and loss aversion

perceive probabilities, noting that empirically individuals tend to over-estimate the probability of low-probability events and underestimate the probability of high-probability events. Therefore instead of calculating the mathematical expected utility, they calculate a weighted utility metric, where the weights are functions of the probabilities but with these biases built in.

To put this in context, we show how this could be applied to the two-period scenario that we have previously discussed. Consider an individual whose reference point is to consume without purchasing an annuity: this is clearly appropriate in the voluntary purchase market, if less so in the compulsory purchase market. For simplicity we also assume that $\delta = (1+r)^{-1}$, so that the individual prefers to divide his consumption equally between the two periods. In this case the reference level of consumption would be $W_0/2$. Furthermore assume that p, the probability of living into period 1, is relatively high and thus $1-p$ is small. To emphasize the disparity between the magnitudes of the two probabilities, we write

$$p >> 1 - p \tag{8.7}$$

Then the optimization problem with standard preferences would be

$$\max \{u(C_0) + pu(C_1)\} \quad u' > 0; u'' < 0 \tag{8.8}$$

where $u(C)$ is a conventional risk-averse utility function.

We can contrast this with the solution to the problem posed by Tversky and Kahneman (1992). Since $p >> 1 - p$ and agents underestimate the probability of high-probability events, we know that the weights will have the property

$$\xi < p \quad \text{and} \quad 1 - \xi > 1 - p \quad \text{where } 0 < \xi < 1 \qquad (8.9)$$

Given the reference level of consumption the problem that the agent will actually solve will be

$$
\max \{v(C_0) + \xi v(C_1)\}
$$

$$
C > W_0/2 \Rightarrow \begin{cases} v'(C) > 0 & v \text{ concave to the right} \\ v''(C) < 0 & \text{of the reference point} \end{cases}
$$

$$
C < W_0/2 \Rightarrow \begin{cases} v'(C) > 0 & v \text{ convex to the right} \\ v''(C) > 0 & \text{of the reference point} \end{cases}
$$

$$
\lim_{C \searrow W_0/2} v'(C) < \lim_{C \nearrow W_0/2} v'(C) \quad v \text{ kinked at the reference point}
$$

(8.10)

The utility maximization is subject to the relevant budget constraint in both cases. The indifference curve now has a kink where it crosses the 45° line and this characterization violates the assumptions made by Davidoff, Brown, and Diamond (2005), but this does not ensure that the individual would not prefer to be fully annuitized: indeed the presence of the kink would appear to make it more likely that the optimal solution would be to put all of his wealth into an annuity.

Holmer (2003) applies loss aversion to the annuity market and contrasts his results with those in an earlier version of Davidoff, Brown, and Diamond (2005). However, Holmer's analysis concentrates on the effects of stochastic interest rates and his paper is thus more easily compared to that of Milevsky and Young (2002). Unlike Milevsky, who calculates the optimal time to annuitize (given 100 per cent annuitization), Holmer calculates the optimal annuitization given that this is done immediately (at the point of retirement). His results are summarized in Table 8.2, which show the percentage of wealth that should be put into a joint-life annuity for a married couple. The parameterization of the loss-aversion model is

Table 8.2. Comparison of demand for annuities under conventional model and prospect theory

Money's worth of annuity	Expected utility model (risk aversion), CRRA, $\gamma = 2$	Cumulative prospect theory (loss aversion)
100%	71%	16%
85%	30%	0%

Source: Holmer (2003).

taken from Tversky and Kahneman (1992), whereas that for the risk-averse model is based on a reasonable measure of risk aversion (usually thought to be a bit greater than unity).

These results suggest that individuals whose behaviour is characterized by loss aversion are less likely to annuitize, although it is clear that all of the results in the above table rely upon the existence of an excessive equity premium, which may be inappropriate, as we have discussed in Section 8.2.

This area is one for further research. However, one important consideration is whether Holmer's characterization of the reference point is correct: since one of the concerns that many people voice over annuitizing is the possibility that they might die before receiving back their capital, perhaps the reference point is not the continuous stream of consumption that forms the reference point but instead the capital sum. The presence of guaranteed or value-protected annuities is prima facie evidence for this. In the context of the Tversky and Kahneman (1992) approach sketched above, two things are worth noting: first, the probability of dying very soon after purchasing an annuity (and hence getting very little apparent benefit) is very low, but this probability is likely to be overestimated; conversely the significant probability of outliving one's means if one does not annuitize is underestimated; secondly, the gain to annuitizing compared with holding bonds will give a small utility benefit, while the 'loss' of dying early (or worrying about dying early when annuitized) may have a large utility loss. This suggests low annuitization is consistent with cumulative prospect theory.

Interestingly, Chen (2003) suggests that the psychological barriers due to loss aversion to buying long-term care insurance might be partially overcome through bundling the insurance with an annuity, thus providing a psychological rationale to complement the same suggestion by Spillman, Murtaugh, and Warshawsky (2003).

8.5.2. Framing effects

Framing effects occur when individuals' behaviour depends not upon the choices available but upon the way in which they are presented. Plott and Zeiler (2005) present evidence that framing effects may be the cause of many of the other apparent phenomena discovered in economic psychology and suggest that framing is very important. The Pensions Commission (2004) notes that in the USA employees are much more likely to be a member of a 401(k) scheme if they have to opt out than they are if they have to opt in, although this is not a pure framing effect, since employees have to exert different amounts of effort in the different cases.

A UK example is the difference between DB and DC schemes. Casual observations suggests that members of DB schemes who receive a pension and a tax-free lump sum are relatively happy with this arrangement, while members of DC schemes who are required to annuitize their pension fund appear to resent the annuitization requirement. In the USA, the proportion of individuals who opted to take an annuity option from employer-sponsored retirement plans depended strongly on the type of plan, with DB schemes apparently promoting annuity purchase: 22 per cent of individuals with a combined DB–DC scheme took an annuity, whereas only 10 per cent of those with a pure DC scheme (Drinkwater and Sondergeld 2004).

The Pension Research Forum (2004) finds evidence of a pure framing effect when it comes to purchasing different types of annuity. Their research is based on a sample of about 5,000 workers in large corporations (the latter being customers of Watson-Wyatt). Respondents were asked whether at age 65 they would prefer an annuity that paid a constant £7,000 per year or one that was initially £4,900, but rose in line with inflation (in both cases the annuity was actuarially fair). The sample was split into two parts: both groups received exactly the same textual question, but one group was shown a table of numbers and the other a graph: approximate copies are shown in Figure 8.10. Of the group that was shown the table, 65 per cent chose the level annuity and 26 per cent the inflation-linked, whereas of those shown the graph the figures were 48 per cent and 41 per cent, respectively. These discrepancies are due to visual impact that the different forms of presentation have.

Other framing effects occur when the range of options is increased. For example, the choice between two options, A and B, may be affected by whether a third option C is also available. The Pensions Commission (2004) cites a result in Benartzi and Thaler (2001) that the percentage of their wealth that people invest in equity is determined by the proportion of equity funds in the choice set. Another possibility is that people prefer to avoid extremes: while agents may choose A over B (and A may be objectively superior to B), if an alternative C is added so that B is intermediate between A and C, then the most likely choice is B, because it appears more 'average'. The number of choices also matters: greater variety leads to more confusion, potential worry, and greater likelihood of avoiding any decision at all.[16]

Table of annuity payments shown to group A

Age	Level annuity	Inflation-linked annuity
65	7,000	4,900
70	7,000	5,500
75	7,000	6,300
80	7,000	7,100
85	7,000	8,000
90	7,000	9,000
95	7,000	10,300
100	7,000	11,600

Graph of annuity payments shown to group B

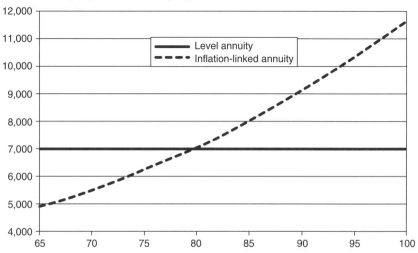

Figure 8.10. Different presentations of annuity options

Source: Pension Research Forum

8.5.3. *Poor financial education*

A final issue that we consider is whether many individuals are really capable of understanding annuity purchases at all. The usual understanding
of rationality in economics is based upon the idea that agents behave in
a fashion which is approximately optimal because they learn to do so
through repeated actions which allow them to learn. So most agents are
quite capable of buying a banana from their local shop, because repeatedly
buying bananas has resulted in them having a good idea of the taste and
quality of bananas and knowing whether to trust their local shopkeeper:
in such situations framing effects may be relatively unimportant as the
quantity and quality of information is high.

For nearly all individuals, the purchase of an annuity is a once-in-a-lifetime decision and so there is no opportunity to learn the optimal strategy through repeat purchases. Without experience agents may be unduly influenced by framing effects as noted above. But another important factor determining their behaviour is their understanding of financial products.

Research published by the Financial Services Authority (2003a) provides little encouragement for the idea that potential annuitants fully understand what they are buying. In two telephone surveys of individuals with a personal pension who were on the verge of having to buy an annuity (i.e. to buy an annuity in the UK compulsory purchase market), only 65 and 71 per cent of respondents felt that they had at least 'some understanding' of what an annuity was. A series of questions was asked to these individuals and based upon their answers the researchers provided their own evaluation of respondents' understanding, resulting in figures of 46 and 55 per cent. Men tended to have a better understanding than women and those with a larger fund value had a better understanding than those with a smaller fund value. Some solace is provided by the fact that those individuals who had read a letter and fact sheet from the FSA (sent to them shortly before the telephone survey) seemed to be better informed than those who had not read them.

In concluding this chapter, the theoretical literature has been able to find scenarios where less than full annuitization is optimal, but the underlying intuition that annuitization expands the budget set still stands. Perhaps the most convincing cases for not annuitizing are

- the fact that better returns can be earned on equity than on bonds, which can be resolved by allowing people to buy equity-based annuities;
- the possibility of adverse selection, which may be alleviated by bundling annuities with long-term care.

In both cases there is a potential solution based on more sophisticated annuity products, but these might only be appropriate for relatively wealthy individuals and might be difficult for many consumers to understand.

Instead it appears likely that psychological explanations, many of which could be characterized as irrational behaviour, may underlie much of the unwillingness to annuitize. Combined with a general ignorance about how annuity products work, this creates major challenges to designing appropriate policy—it is not clear how to maximize welfare

if people's happiness is determined as much by psychological considerations as by financial well-being.

Notes

1. Some of the fall in consumers' expenditure can be explained by the reduction
   in costs faced by the elderly, including an absence of work-related costs and
   implicit and explicit price discounting. The Pensions Commission (2004: 134–
   41) provides evidence on this.
2. These figures are confirmed by Banks et al. (2005); Banks, Blundell, and Smith
   (2003) provide a US–UK comparison. Attanasio and Emmerson (2003: 827)
   report that 60 per cent or people in the British Retirement Survey have
   financial wealth less than £3,000. Of course many individuals hold additional
   wealth in their house, which is not annuitized wealth, but does insure against
   other forms of risk (such as inflation).
3. These figures are based on a constant relative risk aversion parameter of 2, and
   the assumption that the average return on risky assets is 12 per cent (and a
   20 per cent standard deviation), compared with an implied 6 per cent internal
   rate of return on annuities.
4. Income drawdown is the alternative to compulsory annuitization allowed by
   HMRC in the UK (Chapter 3).
5. In the UK health care is provided largely through the NHS, so the availability and quality of this care depends upon the commitment of current and
   future governments to state health provision. Since such commitment is rarely
   completely credible, some elderly people might wish to have the option to
   augment state health care with private care. Similar considerations may apply
   in other countries.
6. The term 'necessary' is being used fairly loosely here: we mean simply that
   without these expenditures the well-being of the individual will be severely
   reduced. More formally, utility is not defined if expenditure falls below the
   minimum.
7. Brown and Finkelstein (2007) provide evidence on supply side failures and
   demand side factors that limit the Market for long-term care in the US.
8. Brugiavini (1993) shows that individuals would prefer to purchase annuities
   when young, before they have acquired private information about their own
   mortality, and we would expect such deferred annuities to exhibit less adverse
   selection than immediate annuities. If we interpret occupational pensions as
   a form of deferred annuity then UK mortality data are consistent with this
   (see Figure 9.1 and related discussion). Sheshinski (2007) questions whether
   it is possible for individuals to pre-commit to a pension when young, since
   individuals who learn that their life expectancy is low in middle age would
   always wish to re-negotiate their pension to obtain better terms. The UK's
   Open Market Option and the A-day reforms explicitly allow this. Palmon and

Spivak (2007) provide simulations showing that the welfare loss of having to buy immediate annuities instead of deferred annuities is small.

9. Low-risk individuals may also be able to increase their utility by saving some of their wealth in a conventional bond, but they would be less well off than if they could annuitize fully since they still cannot attain point B in the previous figure.

10. This also suggests that if there were originally a separating equilibrium then no firm would offer the contract at D, since they would rationally anticipate that it would not be sustainable. Further analysis on this point requires a more sophisticated discussion of game-theoretic equilibrium concepts than we attempt here: for details see Eckstein, Eichenbaum, and Peled (1985). The key conclusions are unaltered: a pooling equilibrium is never possible and a separating equilibrium can exist under some circumstances.

11. A further complication arises if such individuals also have different tastes: for example, inherently prudent individuals might have longer life expectancy, more patience (lower subjective discount rate), and be more risk averse.

12. Continuity of preferences would be sufficient for existence of an equilibrium. It is possible for there to be multiple annuity rates that would break even. Presumably in this case competition would force annuity providers to offer the highest of these multiple alternatives, although this is not discussed fully by either Abel or Walliser (although see Abel, n. 12).

13. Note that in Abel's notation p is the probability of dying, whereas in our notation it is the probability of living: the equation here is in *our* notation.

14. In the models presented in the text, we have only considered the possibility that there are two types of individual. In a model with many types, the lowest risk types will purchase no annuities and among the types that do purchase annuities, the size of annuity purchase will depend positively upon life expectancy.

15. The Kahneman–Tversky approach assumes that loss aversion is a better characterization of behaviour than risk aversion. Plott and Zeiler (2005) argue that these results are due to faulty experiment design and that with appropriate design behaviour appears to be better characterized by risk aversion. Of course, this provides incidental support that framing effects are important: we discuss these effects in Section 8.5.2.

16. Schwartz (2004) argues that agents would be happier at the point of decision if they had fewer choices and attempted merely to satisfice (i.e. aim for some easily achievable target level of utility) rather than maximize (i.e. aim for the maximum possible level of utility); in addition the presence of fewer choices would lead to less delay in decision-making. Delaying decision-making, or procrastination, is consistent with the non-geometric discounting discussed in Chapter 7.

9

Evidence on the workings of annuity markets

9.1. Evidence on selection effects

Warshawsky (1988) suggests that differences in the money's worth calculation from using population life tables and annuitant life tables is a measure of adverse selection in annuity markets. Individuals who expect to live for a long time are more likely to purchase annuities, and the annuity providers recognize these incentives, and price annuities to incorporate these adverse selection problems, but in doing so, annuities are priced relatively highly and may exclude from the annuities market some low-risk (short-lived) individuals. Finkelstein and Poterba (2002) note that differences in the money's worth are not necessarily a measure of adverse selection, since adverse selection involves active selection by the annuitant, and the difference in money's worth may also be measuring passive selection. The difference between active and passive selection is that active selection occurs when annuitants purchase annuities because they have private information not available to the insurance company (i.e. that their life expectancy is longer than the population average). In contrast, passive selection reflects the fact that the characteristics of people who purchase annuities are different from the general population and long life expectancy may be correlated with the underlying characteristics. For example, people who purchase annuities tend to be relatively wealthy and Attanasio and Hoynes (2000) and Attanasio and Emmerson (2003) find that wealth is correlated with life expectancy.

Taking account of Finkelstein and Poterba's distinction between active and passive selection, we simply refer to these effects as selection effects. In Chapter 6 we discussed at length the money's worth of annuities both in the UK and in international markets. Referring back to Table 6.1, and focusing first on the UK, the earlier reported results on money's worth for a 65-year-old male with a level single annuity guaranteed for five years averaged over all years from 1972 to 2002 is 97.9 per cent of the purchase price using the life tables of annuitants. Instead we may calculate the money's worth using the survival probabilities of the general population, which will tend to be lower than for annuitants. For the period 1972–2002, Cannon and Tonks (2004a) calculated the average of the money's worth series based upon population mortality. The population life tables are obtained from English Life Tables no. 15 (published in 1997, based on the 1991 Census). The mean value of the money's worth calculated using population life tables has a value of 95.6 per cent. The difference in means of money's worth over the period 1972–2002 using annuitants and population life tables, representing a selection effect, is 2.3 per cent.[1]

This means that the financial value of annuity for an actual annuitant would have been about 2 per cent more than it would have been for an 'average' member of the general population, the difference arising through the higher life expectancy of the annuitant. Of course, the fact that annuitants live longer than the general population is evidence for selection—although whether this is primarily adverse selection or passive selection is less certain.

The figure of 2.3 per cent is low relative to the evidence in Finkelstein and Poterba (2002) who find that a 65-year-old male annuitant who faces the annuitants' life tables receives a 14.2 per cent increase in the money's worth over an annuitant who faces the population life table. The Finkelstein and Poterba (2002) results are for a particular point in time in 1998, and the Cannon and Tonks results are an average over a much longer time period. On the other hand, Cannon and Tonks' selection effects may not be as pronounced as Finkelstein and Poterba (2002), possibly because (a) the population life projections in Cannon and Tonks (2004a) were too generous in projecting reductions in mortality; and (b) Cannon and Tonks (2004a) are actually using *ex post* mortality for some of the period. The evidence of only a small degree of adverse selection over the time series is consistent with their earlier findings that the money's worth over the whole period is only slightly less than unity.

As discussed in Chapter 3, Section 3.3, the UK is unusual in having both a voluntary and a compulsory annuities market. Finkelstein and Poterba (2002) note that selection effects are likely to be more important in the former than the latter. Only individuals who expect to live for a long time are likely to purchase a voluntary annuity, whereas compulsory annuities are purchased as part of the terms of the pension contract, though there

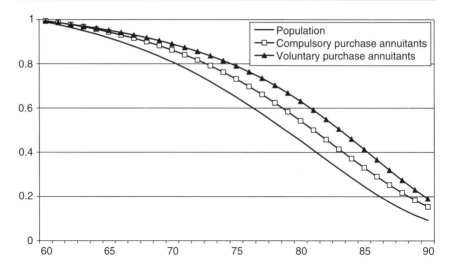

Figure 9.1. Cumulative survival probabilities for 65-year-old male cohort 2000

Source: Population mortality from ONS (2002) Mortality Statistics, DH1, no.33; annuitant mortality from CMI (2006*b*) Working Paper 22 PNML00 and IML00.

could be selection effects in terms of the types of people that subscribe to a personal pension. Finkelstein and Poterba (2002) compare life expectancy of the UK general population, with those who purchase voluntary annuitants, and those who purchase compulsory annuities. They argue that selection effects would result in voluntary annuitants living longer than compulsory annuitants, who in turn would live longer than the general population. Using the actuarial notation introduced in Chapter 4 (where q_x is the death rate and l_x is the life expectancy), we can express this as:

$$q_x^{\text{Voluntary}} < q_x^{\text{Compulsory}} < q_x^{\text{Population}}$$
$$l_x^{\text{Voluntary}} > l_x^{\text{Compulsory}} > l_x^{\text{Population}}$$

(9.1)

Figure 9.1 uses the most recent UK data available to show that this is currently the case for 65-year-old men. Using data from 1998, Finkelstein and Poterba report that for the average 65-year-old man the probability of surviving to 82 is 41 per cent, whereas it is 48 per cent for an average 65-year-old male compulsory annuitant and 56 per cent for an average 65-year-old voluntary annuitant. Figure 9.2 illustrates that the survival probabilities conditioned by the size of the annuity (amounts) are higher than when conditioned by lives: an illustration of another selection effect.

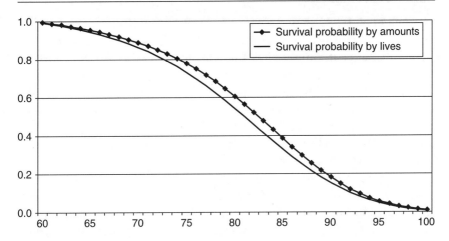

Figure 9.2. Cumulative survival probabilities for 65-year-old male cohort in 2000

Source: CMI (2006*b*) Working Paper 22 PNML00 and PNMA00.

Figure 9.3 illustrates the same picture for males aged 65 in the USA taken from Mitchell (2002), and mortality rates for women show a similar pattern.

The international evidence on money's worth and the degree of selection effects in various annuity markets around the developed world was presented in Table 6.6, summarizing the results in James and Song (2001).

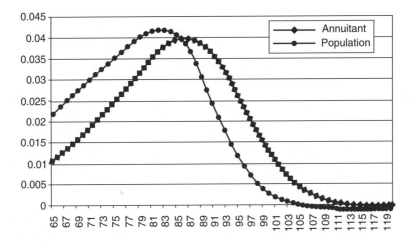

Figure 9.3. Distribution of US male population versus annuitant age at death conditional on survival to age 65

Source: Mitchell (2002).

213

Mitchell et al. (1999) report a trend towards lower selection effects in US annuity market, since in 1985 the selection effects for 65-year-old males were 10.1 per cent, but by 1995 these had decreased to 6.1 per cent and the money's worth for both annuitants and the general population had increased. The international comparison made by James and Song (2001), updating earlier work by James and Vittas (2000), found higher money's worth in general, and smaller selection effects than the earlier US studies, and in fact the selection effects for the UK are much closer to the Cannon and Tonks (2004*a*) numbers.

Finkelstein and Poterba (2002, 2004) emphasize that selection effects are also important in terms of the type of annuity purchased, since persons with long life expectancy are more likely to purchase back-loaded annuities such as escalating annuities, and real annuities; and further, persons with shorter life expectancy are more likely to buy guaranteed annuities, which pay an income into the annuitant's estate even after death.

Furthermore, as we found in Chapter 6 (illustrated in Figure 6.7 and Table 6.5) and as reported in Finkelstein and Poterba (2002), the money's worth of escalating or indexed annuities are particularly poor value. There are several possible reasons for this. On the supply side, provision of escalating or indexed annuities may be more costly to life insurers, due to an absence of matching index-linked assets for the annuity provider to purchase, and if these extra costs are not accounted for in money's worth calculations then they will result in low money's worths. On the demand side, short-lived individuals may rationally anticipate that they are unlikely to benefit from inflation protection and thus choose level annuities; conversely long-lived individuals will choose real annuities. This will result in life expectancy varying systematically with annuity type and life insurers pricing their annuities accordingly. This is active (adverse) selection. Lopes (2003) uses this low money's worth of real annuities (74.9 per cent in Finkelstein and Poterba 2002), to show that in an empirically parameterized dynamic optimization model, risk-averse individuals will not wish to purchase real annuities, because of their unfair prices. Alternatively, individuals who purchase annuities may be inherently 'careful' (presumably because they are both more risk averse and more patient) and such individuals may tend to live longer. This would be a form of passive selection. Finally, we have seen in Chapter 8, Section 8.5, that annuity purchasers are neither well informed nor fully rational and it may be that better educated individuals (who happen to have longer life expectancy) understand more about inflation and choose to purchase. This would be an alternative form of passive selection.

The evidence on the differential money's worth between annuitant and population mortalities reported in Table 6.6 confirms these effects. Level annuities in the UK for a 65-year-old male in 1999 had a differential money's worth of 7.1 per cent, whereas 10-year guaranteed annuities had a money's worth differential of 4.9 per cent. Escalating and real annuities had money's worth differentials of 8.8 per cent and 7.7 per cent, respectively. Panels C and D of Table 6.6 show the similar money's worth differentials for 65-year-old women and, as with the men, the MW using annuitants survival probabilities is typically between 90 and 100 per cent, with selection biases apparent to some degree.

On the other hand, there is some evidence that adverse selection may have been less important in the earlier time periods. Finkelstein and Poterba (2002, 46: table 5) find in their cross-section sample for 1998 (using population life tables) that the money's worth is *lower* for the non-guaranteed annuity than guaranteed which is consistent with the presence of adverse selection in the non-guaranteed annuities market. In Cannon and Tonks' data sample for 1972 and 1973 there is information on annuity rates for both 5-year guaranteed and non-guaranteed annuities, and as can be seen from Figure 5.2, the data suggests that the money's worth of non-guaranteed is *higher* than for the 5-year guaranteed for the two overlapping years 1972 and 1973. This suggests that in 1972 and 1973 there was no evidence of adverse selection in the annuities markets. However, they are not quite comparing like-for-like, since the annuity rates are for different samples of firms and the data for 5-year guaranteed is a relatively small sample. So there is no strong evidence that the money's worths are 'wrong', but conversely there is no evidence at all for adverse selection from looking at these data points.

Finkelstein and Poterba also suggest that under adverse selection, long-lived individuals will purchase larger amounts of annuities (see Figure 9.2), and there will be an inverse relation between size of premium and money's worth. In fact they find that the money's worth of larger amounts of annuities is bigger than the money's worth of smaller amounts of annuities, implying that there is no adverse selection in the larger amounts market. However, they note that this finding is also consistent with fixed costs in the provision of insurance, which might dominate the selection effects. We have already seen that for smaller purchases there is evidence that annuity rates increase with purchase price, which would be consistent with fixed costs but not adverse selection.

In further work using data on a single UK insurance company from 1981 to 1998, Finkelstein and Poterba (2004) examine selection along three features of annuity policies that affect the effective quantity of insurance provided:

First, the initial annual annuity payment. This is the analogue of the payment in the event of a claim, or 'quantity' in most stylized theoretical models and in previous empirical studies. It is straightforward to see that the amount of insurance is increasing in the initial amount of annuity payment.

Secondly, the annuity's degree of back-loading. A more back-loaded annuity is one with a payment profile that provides a greater share of payments in later years. Payments from real annuities and from escalating annuities are both back-loaded relative to those from nominal annuities. An annuitant with a longer life expectancy is more likely to be alive in later periods when the back-loaded annuity pays out more than the flat annuity.

Thirdly, the extent to which payments are not contingent on life (because there is either a guarantee period or a capital protection). The resulting payments to the estate decrease the effective amount of insurance in a given annuity contract and are more valuable to a short-lived than to a long-lived individual.

All three of these features thus satisfy the single-crossing property: at a given price, the marginal value of each annuity product feature varies monotonically with risk type. Theoretical models of equilibrium with adverse selection therefore make clear predictions about the relative mortality patterns of individuals whose annuities differ along these features. Those who buy back-loaded annuities should be longer-lived, conditional on observables, than other annuitants. Similarly, those who buy annuities that make payments to the estate should be shorter-lived, and those who buy annuities with larger initial annual payments should be longer-lived, conditional on what the insurance company observes about the insured, than other annuitants.

The methodology in Finkelstein and Poterba (2004) is to estimate a hazard function, the probability that an annuitant with specific characteristics dies t periods after purchasing the annuity, conditional on living until t. The characteristics include (a) initial payments, (b) whether escalating, and (c) whether guaranteed. They estimate the hazard model for both compulsory and voluntary markets. They expect adverse selection problems to be more acute in the voluntary market.

Their results support these theoretical predictions of asymmetric information. Back-loaded annuities are associated with longer lived individuals; guaranteed annuities are purchased by short-lived individuals. However, with respect to initial payment there is evidence of adverse selection in the compulsory market (individuals with larger initial payments live longer) but not in the voluntary market. They then compute money's worth (using population life tables) to get the 'price of an annuity' (one minus the money's worth), and regress this 'price' on various characteristics.

Finkelstein and Poterba (2004: 31) recognize the limitations of their analysis, in that 'the results are an artefact of the particular firm whose annuity sales we have analysed. This small sample concern is difficult to address without detailed data from other insurance firms, and we do not have such data.'

In summary they find: first, no evidence of selection in the initial payments for voluntary markets; secondly, evidence of selection in back-loading and guaranteed annuities. But caveats are that the selection effects could be a result of moral hazard or passive selection rather than adverse selection. Also the equilibria that they identify could be the outcome of a non-competitive equilibrium with symmetric information (Chiappori et al. 2002). A final caveat is that individuals may have different preferences as well as different risk types (Walliser 2000).

Within the context of the UK compulsory purchase annuity market, Einav, Finkelstein, and Schrimpf (2007) suggest a method to determine the relative importance of individuals' private information (adverse selection) and heterogeneous preferences in determining annuity purchase: the latter is likely to be because the individual attaches value to leaving a bequest, although Einav, Finkelstein, and Schrimpf are agnostic on this point. In the discrete-time notation that we have used throughout the book, the utility function that individual j wishes to maximize is a generalization of equation (7.19) to

$$V_t = \sum_{x=0} s_{j,x} \delta^x \mathrm{E}\left[u\left(c_x\right)\right] + \beta_j B \qquad (9.2)$$

where $s_{j,x}$ is the individual-specific survival probability, β_j is an individual-specific preference parameter, and B is the wealth remaining at death.

Individuals with either lower survival probability or higher values of β_j would prefer a guaranteed annuity to a simple annuity. Einav, Finkelstein, and Schrimpf examine the choice of annuity contracts for an anonymous large UK annuity provider using data on 9,364 individual annuities sold between 1988 and 1994, and the subsequent death rate of some of these annuitants between 1998 and 2005. They make the assumption that mortality for annuitant j is determined by the Gompertz function, which can be rewritten here as[2]

$$\mu_j(x) = GM_j^{0,2}(x) = a_j \exp\left\{\lambda(x - 65)\right\} \qquad (9.3)$$

There are effectively two assumptions being made here: first, that log-mortality is a linear function of age; second, that, although each individual's log-mortality function can have a different intercept (represented by the parameter a_j), all of the log-mortality functions have the same slope (represented by the parameter λ). In fact, the observed aggregate death rate is non-linear: if each individual's mortality function is linear then non-linearity in aggregate is due to heterogeneity in the a_j and the extent of this heterogeneity can be observed by the extent of the curvature. This is a very clever identification strategy since it allows joint estimation of the individual-specific mortality rates and preference parameters even if a_j and β_j are themselves correlated. Einav, Finkelstein, and Schrimpf find that there is a negative relationship between mortality and preference for bequests. That is, people who live longer care more about bequests, which they note could be due to socio-economic variables, such as wealth.

Einav, Finkelstein, and Schrimpf (2007) point out that these results have important policy implications. If annuity markets suffer from adverse selection, then making annuity purchases compulsory can potentially overcome adverse selection problems. However, if individuals differ in their preferences for bequests, as well as information on their own mortality, then making annuitization mandatory is not necessarily welfare improving.

A similar test can be conducted without calculating money's worths: since any differences in money's worth are due entirely to differences in mortality, one can also test for selection by comparing directly the mortalities in different life tables. Mitchell and McCarthy (2002) compute the A/E population metric, which expresses the number of deaths anticipated in a given population using one mortality table, compared with the expected number of deaths in a population using a second mortality table, which acts as a benchmark. Using the US male population period table as the benchmark, they then regress the A/E metrics against gender, type of mortality table (for voluntary or compulsory annuity markets), and country effects. They find that voluntary annuitants have a 32 per cent lower mortality rate, and compulsory annuitants a 26 per cent lower mortality rate than the general US male population. They conclude that this indicates adverse selection, though as we noted earlier it would better be described as evidence of either active or passive selection effects.[3]

9.2. Evidence on the demand for annuities

Having considered the pricing of annuities and the extent of adverse selection in the market we now examine patterns in the demand for annuities, and ask the question: who buys annuities? The answer is that not many people do buy annuities voluntarily. The private immediate annuity market in the USA is small: 'In 1999 premiums for individual immediate annuities totalled $7 billion. By comparison individual life insurance premiums were $94 billion' (Brown et al. 2001: 7). This lack of annuitization is not confined to the USA and the same limited demand in voluntary annuity purchases has been observed in international markets: UK (Blake 1999), Canada (Kim and Sharp 1999), Australia (Knox 2000), Latin America (Callund 1999), and Israel (Spivak 1999). It is only in the markets for compulsory annuities (or pension annuities where annuities are a compulsory part of the pension system) such as the UK, Switzerland, and Singapore that annuities markets are large. Stark (2003) provides a summary of Watson-Wyatt (2003) examining trends in the demand for compulsory annuities in the UK, which we illustrated in Figure 1.7.

We have already discussed Finkelstein and Poterba's (2004) tests for adverse selection. Their analysis was based on a set of both compulsory and voluntary immediate annuities sold by an anonymous large UK annuity company from 1981 to 1998. At the end of the sample period, the firm was among the 10 largest sellers of new compulsory annuities in the United Kingdom. The sample includes a total of 42,054 annuity policies sold by this insurance company over the 17-year period, which Finkelstein and Poterba argue are representative of the UK annuity industry in general.

Table 9.1 shows that the vast majority of annuities sold are in the compulsory market, reflecting the characteristics of the market already alluded to: that the voluntary annuity market is small, and that the future

Table 9.1. Overview of the compulsory and voluntary annuities in the UK sold by the sample firm over the period 1981–98

	Compulsory market	Voluntary market
Number of policies	38,362	3,692
Number of annuitants who are deceased	6,311	1,944
	16%	*53%*
Number of annuitants who are male	29,681	1,272
	77%	*34%*
Average age at purchase	63.2	76.4
Back-Loaded Annuities		
Number of policies that are index-linked	428	66
	1%	*2%*
Number of policies that are escalating in nominal terms	1,492	175
	4%	*5%*
Payments to Estate		
Number of policies that are guaranteed	28,424	872
	74%	*24%*
Number of policies that are capital-protected	0	843
		23%
Initial Annual Annuity Payments (£)		
Average initial payment	1,151	4,773
Median initial payment	627	3,136
Standard deviation of initial payment	1,929	5,229
Average premium	10,523	25,603

Note: All monetary figures in the paper are in December 1998 pounds. The first index-linked policy was sold in February 1985; therefore, percentage of policies index-linked refers to percentage of policies sold since that date.

Source: Finkelstein and Poterba (2004).

growth in the annuities market will continue to be in the compulsory sector. Most annuity purchasers in the voluntary market are women, and at a much older age than in the compulsory market, when the majority of purchasers are men. This follows from the men being more likely to have taken out a personal pension.

Most annuities purchased are flat rate, paying the same nominal sum over the annuitant's life, though a small percentage in both markets are back-loaded, meaning that the payments are increasing over time (real and escalating). Three-quarters of the annuities purchased in the compulsory annuity market have some guarantees, meaning that even on death, some annuity payments will still be paid into the annuitant's estate. But in the voluntary market, guarantees are less common, though this may reflect the fact that in the voluntary market the purchasers are characterized as more elderly women. Finally, the table shows that the average size of the amount annuitized in the compulsory market is just over £10,500 and in the voluntary market is £25,603, yielding annual initial annual annuity payments of £1,151 and £4,773, respectively. These figures are consistent with the evidence in Stark (2002), that the average size of the pension fund that is annuitized is relatively small at £24,357 in 2001, that we discussed in Chapter 3 (Figure 3.2).

Stark (2003) also reports the results of a telephone survey with 500 annuitants aged between 60 and 74 who had purchased a compulsory pensions annuity between 1999 and 2002, and 101 interviews with retired persons aged between 60 and 74 who had not yet annuitized their pension fund. Almost 70 per cent of the sample had retired before 65 with women retiring earlier than men. Of the sample who had purchased an annuity, two-thirds had purchased an annuity immediately on retirement, and one-third had deferred. The 'deferrers' were more likely to have retired before the age of 60, and the main reason given for deferring an annuity purchase was that the retired person had other income so that they did not need the annuity income yet. Interestingly only 1 per cent stated 'inheritance reasons' as the reason for deferring. For 44 per cent of the sample the state pension was the main source of income, implying that the annuity income for this group would be small, with 26 per cent of the sample stating that the pension annuity was their main source of income.

Over 30 per cent of the sample had purchased more than one annuity, with 57 per cent of the sample choosing a level single annuity (either not guaranteed, 42 per cent, or guaranteed, 15 per cent). Only 5 per cent chose an index-linked annuity. Only 12 per cent of the sample purchased a joint annuity, with men being slightly more likely than women to purchase a joint annuity. Two-thirds of the sample had taken advice before purchasing the annuity, either from a financial advisor (40 per cent), or a provider (20 per cent), with a third of the sample exercising their open market option to purchase their annuity from a provider other than their pension provider, and 15 per cent had considered the open market option, but had remained with the pension provider.[4]

Gardner and Wadsworth (2004) undertook a survey of 3,511 individuals aged between 50 and 64 to determine their attitudes to annuitizing a hypothetical sum of £100,000. In the sample 55 per cent were working, 33 per cent were retired, and 11 per cent were out of work. With regard to pension provision, 20 per cent had no private pension and were reliant on the state pension, 45 per cent had one private pension, and 35 per cent had more than one private pension. For those with a private pension 50 per cent were reliant on a DB pension, and 30 per cent on a DC as their main source of income.

They found that almost 60 per cent of the sample would prefer not to annuitize this hypothetical £100,000 sum, if they had the option not to do so. Of the sample that had DC pensions (and would therefore have to annuitize their pension fund), 53 per cent would prefer not to annuitize a hypothetical lump sum. Reasons given for annuitization-aversion included flexibility (74 per cent), self-investment preferred (45 per cent), annuity income too low (45 per cent), bequests (38 per cent), and low life expectancy (37 per cent). Of those who were willing to annuitize there was a preference for annuitizing at earlier ages. In subsequent regression analysis, Gardner and Wadsworth (2004) found that the willingness to annuitize was positively related to perceived health status, positively related to education-status achieved, positively related to the degree of patience of the individual, but negatively related to household size, presumably because the family unit can serve as insurance against longevity risk (Kotlikoff and Spivak 1981).

In order to identify the determinants of annuity demand through an individual's utility maximizing framework, Brown (2001) analyses the relationship between the value of an annuity and the probability of annuity purchase. He does this using a sample of 869 households in 1992 in the US Health and Retirement Study (HRS), where the head of the household is aged between 51 and 61 years. The utility value of the annuity is measured by the concept of Annuity Equivalent Wealth (AEW) introduced in Chapter 7. AEW depends upon the individual's degree of risk aversion (since this determines the value of the insurance), and also upon how much wealth is already held in annuity form (e.g. social insurance) and this differs between the individuals in Brown's data. Formally, AEW is the value of φ in the equation

$$V(y + AW, 0) = V(y, \varphi W) \tag{9.4}$$

where V is the utility function expressed here in terms first of income received until death (annuitized income) and second of wealth at the beginning of retirement; y is pre-annuitized income; A is the annuity rate; and W is wealth available at the beginning of retirement. The left-hand side of equation (9.4) is the utility from being fully annuitized and the right-hand side is the utility from being partially annuitized.

The HRS asks the individuals in the sample the form in which they intend to take their DC pension benefits, and identifies those individuals who will take their benefits as a monthly pension: half of the sample reports that they will annuitize their DC plan. The average household has over half of their wealth pre-annuitized by Social Security and private DB pension plans. Another 10 per cent of wealth is in DC plans which average $60,000 in the sample. The average age in the sample was 55 years old, with an average expected retirement age of 63, and 84 per cent of households consisting of a couple. Using this information, Brown (2001) calibrates the AEW for each individual household, and compares the likelihood of the household annuitizing their wealth as a function of four basic characteristics: mortality risk (proxied by gender), risk aversion (from a series of questions), fraction of total wealth that is pre-annuitized, and marital status. Brown (2001) finds that differences in annuity equivalent wealth can partly explain the probability of annuitizing balances in defined contribution pension plans. The calibrated AEW variable in the probit regression has a mean value of 0.6089 and is highly significant. This value means that a 1 per cent increase in AEW increases the probability of the household annuitizing their wealth by 0.6089 percentage points. Further, Brown adds other explanatory variables (race, education, industry, and occupation) into the probit estimation, but finds that they are not significant and do not alter the basic AEW coefficient. These results give some comfort to the basic life-cycle model of savings/consumption behaviour.

The HRS asks a series of questions concerning the time horizon of the individual which is related to their health and likely survival, but the results are slightly contradictory. For example, one question concerns whether the time horizon for financial planning is one year or less. Brown finds that myopic individuals are much less likely to annuitize. Another HRS question asks about self-reported health status, and individuals with excellent, very good or good health were more likely to annuitize than those in fair or poor health. However, the HRS also asks a question about subjective survival probabilities, but these were found to have no effect on the annuitization decision.

Inkmann, Lopes, and Michaelides (2007) examine the determinants of voluntary annuity demand in the UK, using a sample of 5,233 retired persons from English Longitudinal Study of Ageing (ELSA) panel data-set for two waves: 2002/03 and 2004/05. They find that only 4 per cent of initial sample voluntarily purchases annuities (5.9 per cent in 2004/05), which is confirmation of the annuity puzzle. They find that the annuity purchase is positively related to stock ownership, subjective survival probabilities, education, being single and male, and wealth. They calibrate a life-cycle model of portfolio choice and annuity demand, and in this model can generate the low annuity demand observed in the data.

There is contradictory evidence in the literature concerning the relevance of bequests. Research by Bernheim (1991), Laitner and Juster (1996), and Wilhelm (1996) argue that individuals consciously leave wealth to their heirs, whereas Hurd (1987, 1989) and Brown (1999) suggest that the bequest motive is unimportant.

Brown (2001) assesses the importance of the bequest motive by examining whether the decision to annuitize is affected by whether the household in the HRS sample has any children. If the bequest motive is important, then we would expect to see the decision to annuitize would be negatively related to the number of children. In fact, Brown finds there is little relation between the annuitization decision and the number of children, which suggests bequests are unimportant. In contrast the Inkmann, Lopes, and Michaelides (2007) paper suggests that being single increases the probability of purchasing a voluntary annuity, which is consistent with bequest motives being relevant.

Rowlingson and McKay (2005) have undertaken a survey of attitudes to inheritance in Britain using a nationally representative sample of 2,000 people. They find that 46 per cent of adults have inherited something, but most inheritances are small, with only 5 per cent of their sample inheriting more than £50,000. It appears that people like the idea of leaving a bequest, but do not think that older persons should be careful with their money just so that they have something to bequeath. They report that 90 per cent of the sample is likely to have the potential to bequeath, but two-thirds of those with the potential to bequeath intend to enjoy life, and will not restrict their spending to ensure that they are able to leave a bequest. A quarter of those with the potential to bequeath report that they intend to be careful with their spending to ensure they can bequeath. Rowlingson and McKay conclude that although inheritance is important to most people, it has not become entrenched either as an expectation or a duty. Most people are willing and intend to use their assets for themselves, and the bequests are a residual at the time of death.

Overall there is conflicting evidence on whether bequests are important or not to individuals. To the extent that bequests are regarded as important, this would be an explanation for the unpopularity of annuities. On the other hand, if bequests are unimportant, then the explanation for the unpopularity of annuities must lie elsewhere.

Notes

1. This difference is statistically significant: the t-statistic on the difference is 2.13.
2. This is a special case of the Gompertz–Makeham formula referred to in Chapter 4: in this case it is a $GM^{0,2}(x)$ function.
3. Finkelstein and Poterba (2006) suggest it is possible to distinguish between active and passive selection by examining an annuitant's area of residence, which is correlated with wealth, and the health status of people in that local area. In a further study of UK annuitants they find that an annuitant's socio-characteristics are correlated both with the quantity of annuity insurance purchased and subsequent survival probabilities. This is suggestive of active selection, since the local area's measure of long-term illness is also related to the quantity of insurance purchased, and it is unlikely that an individual's risk preferences are related to health.
4. HMRC rules required that individuals must purchase a real joint annuity with unisex rates with respect to the value of their 'protected rights' in their personal pension fund. Protected rights are the requirement that contracted-out rebates must provide equivalent pension provision to the Second State Pension. From April 2005 the requirement for a real annuity was dropped.

10

Supply of annuities

The Pensions Commission (2005) and Stark (2003) suggest that the projected demand for annuities in the UK may be constrained by the capacity of the annuity supply. The purpose of this chapter is to identify the factors that determine the supply of annuities. Current annuities are almost invariably bond-backed products: life insurers use bonds (government bonds, corporate bonds, and mortgages) as an 'input' and produce annuities as an 'output': the value-added provided by the life insurers is the conversion of these financial instruments into mortality-contingent income streams for individuals.

Wadsworth (2005) claims that the two important issues in the supply of annuities are the development of markets to pool longevity risk and constraints on the supply of long-term government bonds which relates to interest rate risk. Another important issue is the small number of annuity providers, potentially leading to abuse of monopoly power, but also meaning that the failure of any individual annuity provider would have an impact on a very large number of pensioners.

Increased demand for long-dated government debt by insurance companies which have issued annuities and wish to match the duration of their assets and liabilities coincides with a reduction in the size of the UK's national debt through a series of budget surpluses or small deficits. This has led to very high prices of long-dated government debt and relatively low yields, to the point where since the mid-1990s the yield curve has been downward sloping at the long end. According to this 'preferred-habitat' view of the term structure, there is a major distortion of all long-term interest rates that has a corresponding effect on annuity prices. The preferred habitat theories rely on there being poor substitute assets in which to invest. We will assess this feature of the annuities market by considering the substitutes for long-term UK government bonds such as

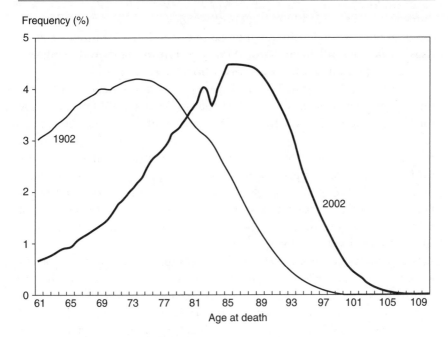

Figure 10.1. Female mortality after age 60, England and Wales, 1902 and 2002

Source: King (2004) from *GAD*.

high-quality corporate bonds, international bonds, and mortgages and the effects of the Debt Management Office's (DMO) issue of ultra-long 4¹/₄ per cent Treasury Gilt 2055, auctioned on 26 May 2005.[1]

Turning to longevity risk, Figure 10.1 shows the distribution of female survival probabilities by age at two points in time. Clearly there has been a huge shift in the distribution between 1902 and 2002, which would have been difficult to predict in 1902.

The Pensions Commission (2004) distinguishes between different types of longevity risk. First, 'specific longevity risk post-retirement' relates to individuals at retirement who do not know their exact length of life. Second, 'average cohort longevity risk post-retirement' relates to the uncertainty as to the length of life of the cohort of persons retiring. These first two risks are typically absorbed by the pension provider, whether a DB pension scheme or an annuity provider for DC schemes. Insurance companies efficiently insure individuals against this first type of idiosyncratic risk, but also bear the average cohort risk of mis-predicting the overall position of the distribution. The Continuous Mortality Investigation

227

Bureau analyses the mortality experience of pensioners and produces quadrennial reports and less frequent tables of predictions of future mortality. As we have seen in Chapter 4, predicting cohort mortality is difficult. An important question is who bears this cohort longevity risk.

A third type of longevity risk is 'long-term average longevity risks pre-retirement', which relates to the fact that projections of life expectancy for the current employed who will retire in the future are very uncertain. In the case of DB schemes, this risk is borne by the DB providers and by the government when they agree to a pension contract which will apply to the current working population. However, in DC schemes individuals bear this risk, through changing annuity rates. The Pensions Commission Final report (2005: 174) emphasizes that pre-retirement longevity risk of a particular cohort should be borne by that generation of individuals through longer working lives.

The regulatory framework for insurance companies has changed considerably from January 2005 as the Financial Services Authority has implemented risk-based measures for company solvency standards. These new regulations, in part influenced by the Equitable Life debacle discussed in Chapter 3, Section 3.4, anticipate likely EU-wide regulations under Solvency 2. We shall consider the implications of the new regulatory framework for annuity markets.

Cannon and Tonks (2004*b*) have documented the declining number of annuity providers over the last 50 years, although the money's worth calculations of Cannon and Tonks (2004*a*) discussed in Chapter 6 suggest that this has had no impact on prices. We now turn to recent evidence on the market shares of life insurers writing annuity contracts.

10.1. Market shares of annuity business in the UK

The risks faced by an annuity provider depend upon the number of annuities written. For example, if the known survival probability in a given period for a cohort of annuitants is s, and n annuities of equal size are sold, the expected payout in that period is $n \times s$, and the standard deviation of the payout is $\sqrt{ns(1-s)}$. Therefore the relative risk declines with the number of annuities sold, and for a sufficiently large company the risks are negligible (for a numerical example and discussion of this point, see Booth et al., 2005: 211). This implies that the annuity industry is naturally oligopolistic, due to efficient pooling of risk. However, this result assumes that s is known: in practice the greater risk is predicting the survival probabilities, which actuaries refer to as parameter error. We address the problems from s being unknown in Section 10.4.

Annuities in the UK are provided by insurance companies and are a heavily regulated industry. From the annual returns submitted by insurance companies to the FSA, we can obtain information on the market share of the main companies.[2] According to the FSA life insurance returns 62 insurance companies sold compulsory annuities in 2005, and in Figure 10.2 we reproduce the distribution of non-profit compulsory annuity sales in 2005 across the largest 23 of the 39 parent companies that sell annuities (since a parent company may submit more than one insurance return for its subsidiary companies). These 23 companies sold £7,398 million of CPA non-profit annuities in 2005 out of a total of £7,433 million for this category.

There were a small number of other categories of compulsory annuities sold in 2005: with-profit annuities (£229 million), index-linked (£510 million), impaired-life (£387 million), but these are not included in Figure 10.2. It can be seen that the CPA market is dominated by a small number of insurance companies: the five-firm concentration ratio is 72 per cent for these annuity sales, with the Prudential the largest supplier of compulsory annuities with over 23 per cent of new business in 2005. In order to examine the pattern in the concentration ratio over time, in Figure 10.3 we plot the six-firm concentration ratio from 1985 to 2005 of CPA sales.

This figure is based on the CPA annuity sales of all the individual company FSA returns, rather than aggregate sales across the parent companies, since insurance company mergers make it difficult to extract the parent information in a particular year. Hence Figure 10.3 is likely to understate the effective degree of concentration. In 2005, Figure 10.3 reveals that the six-firm concentration ratio was 68 per cent compared to the five-firm concentration ratio of 72 per cent in Figure 10.2. The other major players in the market are Legal and General, Aviva, Canada Life, and Lloyds TSB.

Another measure of the size and structure of the annuity market is the amount and share of annuity payments. The annual payments made on existing annuity contracts is a measure of existing business, or more correctly obligations that relate to business conducted historically, as distinct from new business. There are 71 insurance companies making annuity payments totalling £11.2 billion in 2005, and this includes payments in the voluntary and the compulsory markets. In Figure 10.4 we plot the distribution across the largest 21 parent companies.

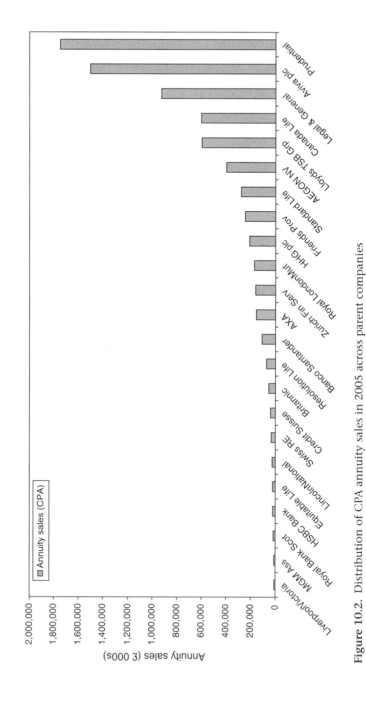

Figure 10.2. Distribution of CPA annuity sales in 2005 across parent companies

Source: Synthesis 2005, FSA Life Returns, Forum 47 line 400.

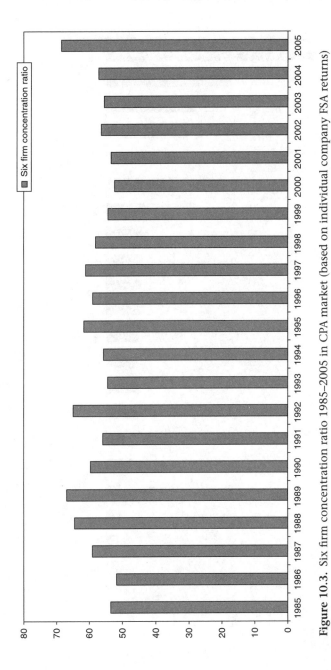

Figure 10.3. Six firm concentration ratio 1985–2005 in CPA market (based on individual company FSA returns)

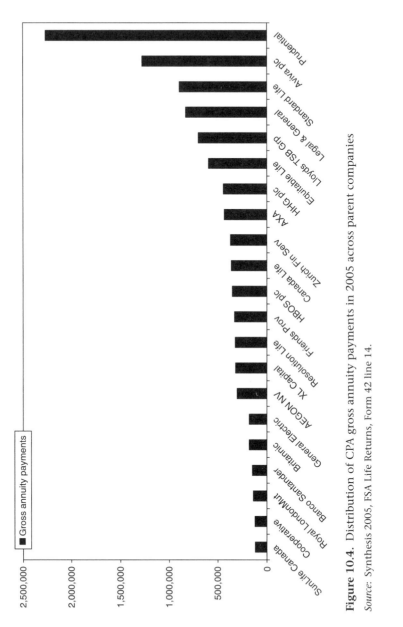

Figure 10.4. Distribution of CPA gross annuity payments in 2005 across parent companies

Source: Synthesis 2005, FSA Life Returns, Form 42 line 14.

It can be seen that Prudential dominates the annuities market just as much in existing payments (20 per cent of the market), as in new business (23 per cent). However, the share of the largest five firms is only 53 per cent, so that it appears that the market for annuity payments is less concentrated than the market for new business. This is probably because some companies who have sold annuities in the past are no longer seeking to increase their market share. The most notable example of this trend is Equitable Life, which has been closed to new business since 2000.

Cannon and Tonks (2004*b*) report that the number of annuity providers quoting annuity prices has fallen substantially over the last 40 years: as recently as 1970 almost 100 companies' annuity rates were quoted in the trade magazine *The Policy*, while the current number of companies quoting annuity rates on the FSA website is about 20 and some of these are specialist providers.[3]

Given this high degree of market concentration particularly with respect to new business, it is perhaps surprising that the money's worth calculations in Chapter 6 suggested no evidence of monopoly profits in the voluntary annuities market.

There have been two new entrants to the market in recent years, suggesting that there are no significant barriers to entry: The Pension Annuity Friendly Society started business in 1995, demutualizing to become Partnership Assurance in 2005; Just Retirement started business in 2004. Although these two annuity providers are small, they are backed with capital from larger companies.[4] In addition, although writing a small amount of new business, Resolution Group specializes in the consolidation of closed life funds (Britannic, Phoenix, Royal & Sun Alliance, Sun Alliance & London, Swiss Life). There have also been a number of new companies established, such as Paternoster and Synesis, backed by funds from financial institutions specializing in the bulk buy-out market.

The small number of active annuity providers in the UK could benefit from potential advantages of economies of scale, especially through more effective risk-pooling, but the near constancy of the money's worth over a period of increased concentration suggests that this consideration is also unimportant. Our comparison of money's worth across the globe suggests that money's worth is high just about everywhere. In the countries surveyed annuity providers are typically life insurers, though in some European countries these are part of the larger bancassurance groups. Cardinale, Findlater, and Orszag (2002) note that Australian and German annuity markets are less concentrated than those in France and the UK, though they note that in every country there has been a trend towards greater consolidation over time in the life insurance industry.

10.2. Regulation of annuity providers

Standard welfare economics suggests that industries are candidates for regulation under several circumstances: first, if there is abuse of market power; second, if there are externalities in the market; third, if there is asymmetric information; and fourth, if consumers are not fully rational. As Davis (2004) notes, the supply of annuities is heavily regulated, because in annuity markets around the world all of these situations are likely to apply.

As Figure 10.2 shows for the UK, and as reported in Cardinale, Findlater, and Orszag (2002) for other countries, the annuity industry is highly concentrated, with a declining number of annuity providers writing annuity business, so that abuse of market power is a possibility. The Equitable Life case illustrates that assumptions made by one annuity supplier can impact on the rest of the industry. We have already discussed in Chapter 9 how selection effects and the problems of information asymmetries pervade the annuity market. As discussed in Chapter 8, annuities are complex financial products, the characteristics of which are not easily understood by consumers, so that like 'treatment goods', it is only long after the event of purchase (approximately if the annuitant lives for longer than his or her life expectancy) that annuitants appreciate the benefit of an annuity product. Hence, annuity markets satisfy each and every criterion for regulation.

10.2.1. *EU regulations and Solvency 2*

Providers of annuities in the UK are insurance companies, and are regulated by the UK's Financial Services Authority (FSA), which incorporates the European Union Life Directives for the insurance industry. The basis of insurance regulation are prudential requirements, meaning that the regulations require insurance companies to have sufficient financial resources to provide for its liabilities. The FSA's General Prudential Sourcebook GENPRU 2.1.8 implements the minimum EC standards for the capital resources required to be held by an insurer undertaking business that falls within the scope of the *Consolidated Life Directive* (2002/83/EC), the *Reinsurance Directive* (2005/68/EC), or the *First Non-Life*

Directive (1973/239/EEC) as amended. In 2007, these EU Life Directives set the base capital at €3.2 million, and the percentage of capital that must be set against technical reserves to cover four risk components: death risks (0.3 per cent), expense risks (1 per cent), market risks (3 per cent), and health risks. In the case of annuities, there are no death risks or health risks, and so the amount of capital set aside to cover liabilities is a total of 4 per cent of the mathematical reserves. Booth et al. (2005) provide a summary of the general principles and purposes of the provision of technical reserves (i.e. liabilities) for insurance products.

The FSA makes clear that 'It is widely recognized that the existing capital requirements for insurance companies as set out by the European Directives are inadequate and not sufficiently risk-sensitive' (FSA 2005: 19, paragraph 3.5). Hence, subsequent FSA regulations are more comprehensive than the European Directives, partly anticipating the likely risk-based solvency requirements, in Solvency 2 rules.

The EU's Solvency 2 programme is intended to apply to the insurance industry the risk sensitive regulatory approach adopted in the Basel 2 reforms for the banking industry.[5] Basel 2 is made up of three regulatory pillars. The first pillar consists of risk-responsive capital requirements; the second pillar represents additional capital requirements imposed by the regulator following individual company risk assessments; and Pillar 3 relates to disclosures to ensure market disciplines can operate.

The timetable for Solvency 2 has repeatedly fallen behind schedule. According to Jordon (2006) it was not expected to be implemented until 2010; the Framework Directive was eventually published in Summer 2007, and at the time of writing is expected to come into effect in 2012. In the meantime the FSA has proceeded with its own risk-based solvency requirements, in part anticipating the likely Solvency 2 rules. Muir and Waller (2003: 2) note that the FSA's enthusiasm to implement reforms in advance of the rest of Europe has also been driven by events specific to the UK's insurance industry, including the closure of Equitable Life, the Sandler Review of medium and long-term savings in the UK, a number of high-profile compliance failings, and the fall in equity values after 2000.

10.2.2. *UK annuity regulation*

Annuity providers in the UK are regulated in three ways: first, by solvency regulations of the annuity provider in terms of reserves and capital adequacy (FSA), secondly, by the way information is provided to consumers (also FSA), and thirdly, through the design of products which are acceptable to the HMRC and the DWP. In fact the first two of these regulations are statutory objectives of the UK's Financial Services Authority, under the Financial Services and Markets Act 2000. The first falls within the FSA's obligation to secure an appropriate degree of protection for consumers, and is covered by the FSA's rules on prudential standards. The second relates to the FSA's remit of promoting public understanding of the financial system, and falls under the FSA rules on conduct of business. In addition annuity providers, as with all financial institutions, must satisfy the FSA's requirements on high-level principles.

Annuity holders are protected from insurance company insolvency by reserving and capital adequacy requirements. Daykin (2001, 2004) outlines a number of issues in reserving for annuities, and points out that reserving may be carried out for a number of different reasons: (*a*) to support the sound and prudential management of the insurer; (*b*) to ensure that the insurer's accounts give true and fair picture of its assets and liabilities; and (*c*) to provide information for tax authorities. As we note below, these reasons may not be in conflict: the pillars enshrined in Basel 2, likely to be applied to the insurance industry in Solvency 2, recognize that if an insurer's accounts give an accurate picture of its asset–liability mix, then this should ensure that the market will provide the discipline for the insurer to practise the appropriate level of prudential management.

Prudential Regulation (or solvency rules) applied to insurance companies in the UK is enacted under the Financial Services and Market Act 2000. Under this act, insurance regulation was transferred to the FSA in 2001 from the Department of Trade and Industry, and the FSA inherited the previous regulatory framework enshrined in the Interim Prudential Sourcebook IPRU(INS). Subsequently the FSA has developed a new regulatory framework represented by the General Prudential Sourcebook GENPRU and the Prudential Sourcebook for Insurers INSPRU which came into effect from 1 January 2007. What remains of the Interim Prudential Sourcebook covers the completion of the FSA insurance returns, and the rules covering the distribution of surplus between insurance company shareholders and insurance company policyholders.

The principle behind prudential regulation is stated in the General Prudential Sourcebook: according to GENPRU 1.2.12 the purpose of the prudential regulation is to ensure that a firm has adequate financial resources and adequate systems and controls for the effective management of its prudential risks. In particular concentrating on financial resources,

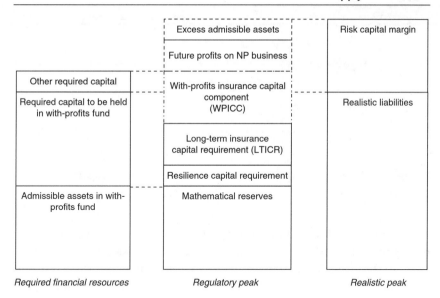

Figure 10.5. The FSA's twin peaks approach to life insurance regulation
Source: FSA Handbook.

GENPRU 1.2.26 requires that firms have sufficient capital resources (the capital resources requirement) that there is no risk that the firm cannot meet its liabilities when they fall due. The major sources of risk identified in GENPRU 1.2.30 are credit risk, market risk, liquidity risk, operational risk, insurance risk, concentration risk, residual risk, securitization risk, business risk, interest rate risk, and pension obligation risk.

The capital requirement reforms for insurance companies outlined in FSA (2005) apply the principles enshrined in the proposed Solvency 2. These are based on a 'twin-peaks approach' risk-sensitive regime for with-profit insurance companies: a regulatory peak and a realistic peak. Firms with significant with-profits liabilities are required to make a realistic assessment of these liabilities to determine whether they need to hold additional capital on top of their regulatory reserves, to cover their expected discretionary bonus payments.[6] Both of these peaks constitute Pillar 1 of the regulatory regime.

Under the twin peaks approach illustrated in Figure 10.5, firms compute the value of the regulatory peak using actuarial methods to calculate mathematical reserves (INSPRU 1.2) and the realistic peak using market values for assets and liabilities; so that in effect the realistic peak is marked-to-market. The realistic peak includes an allowance for the Risk

CRR	Higher of
	(1) MCR; and
	(2) ECR
MCR	Higher of
	(1) Base requirement; and
	(2) Sum of LTICR & resilience capital requirement
ECR	Sum of
	(1) LTICR
	(2) Resilience capital requirement; and
	(3) WPICC

Figure 10.6. Relationship between definitions of capital requirements

Source: FSA Handbook.

Capital Margin which addresses the main business risks faced by a with-profits insurer: market risks (resilience test), credit risks, and persistency risks. If the realistic peak is greater than the regulatory peak, the firm must increase its regulatory capital by the with-profits insurance capital component (WPICC) to bring it up to the level of the realistic peak.

The FSA's General Prudential Sourcebook (GENPRU 2.1) explains the calculation of the Capital Resources Requirement (CRR) for an insurance company, and requires that the firm be able to demonstrate to the FSA at any time the adequacy of its capital resources. According to GENPRU 2.1.18, the company must maintain capital resources no less than the higher of its Minimum Capital Requirement (MCR) and its Enhanced Capital Requirement (ECR). In turn, GENPRU 2.1.24A states that the MCR is the higher of the base capital requirement and the sum of the long-term insurance capital requirement and the resilience capital requirement. The resilience capital requirement arises from market risks for equities, real estate, and fixed income securities held as assets. The MCR follows on directly from the EU Directive and is equal to the higher of the base capital (GENPRU 2.1.30) or the long-term capital requirement set at 4 per cent of mathematical reserves (GENPRU 2.1.36). The MCR represents the regulatory peak of the twin-peaks under Pillar 1. The relationships between CRR, MCR, and ECR are illustrated in Figure 10.6.

The Enhanced Capital Requirement, for a life company with with-profits insurance liabilities above £500 million, is the sum of the long-term capital requirement and the with-profits insurance capital component. The with-profits capital component represents the 'realistic peak' of the twin-peaks regime under Pillar 1, and is specified in INSPRU 1.3. Life firms that have with-profits liabilities in excess of £500 million must make realistic assessments of their risk-based capital to satisfy the realistic peak, ensuring that they have adequate capital to honour the expected terminal bonuses of policyholders. Realistic valuations must allow for the costs of guarantees and the costs of embedded options.

The realistic peak requirements only apply to firms that write significant with-profits business, so that annuities that are written in separate non-profit funds would not be required to comply with the realistic peak, but annuity business written in funds that included significant with-profit business would have to comply.

Under the Pillar 2 rules, according to GENPRU 1.2.42, a firm must carry out annual (or more frequently if needed) individual capital adequacy (ICA) assessments, relating to other types of risk [group, operational, insurance (including longevity), credit, and liquidity risks] based on stress and scenario testing, to determine whether they need to hold additional capital. Guidance on the form of the stress and scenario tests is given in GENPRU 1.2.63–1.2.78. The need to hold additional reserves to satisfy the Pillar 2 requirements depends on the views of the senior management of the company and private discussions with the regulator. Firms and the FSA have been preparing for the new system since 2002. The FSA also intends that a company's realistic balance sheets will be published, to allow the market to discipline companies, in line with Pillar 3. It is appropriate that the risk of annuities be assessed on an individual firm basis, since the risks for insurance companies selling annuities will be offset by the sales of life insurance by the same company that will act as a partial hedge against longevity risk.

The eligible capital resources available for an insurer can be calculated by two approaches. Under Approach 1 available capital is the total of eligible assets less foreseeable liabilities (which is the approach taken in the EU *Insurance Directives*). Approach 2 identifies the components of capital. Both calculations give the same result for the total amount of capital available. Figure 10.7 illustrates the two approaches via a simple example.

Having stated the capital resources requirements for a firm, given its business activities, GENPRU 2 Annexe 1 then describes the tiers of capital that constitute the capital resources available. Tier 1 capital must be permanent, able to absorb losses, junior in the event of winding up, and have no fixed costs attached. The forms of capital that qualify as Tier 1 capital include: share capital, profit and loss account and reserves, and the share premium account. Tier 2 capital includes cumulative preference shares, and Tier 3 capital includes subordinated debt of short maturity. The various tiers of capital resources available differ in the quality of

Liabilities		Assets	
Borrowings	100	Admissible assets	350
Ordinary *shares*	200	Intangible assets	100
Profit and loss account and other reserves	100	Other inadmissible assets	100
Perpetual subordinated debt	150		
Total	<u>550</u>	Total	<u>550</u>

Approach 1: Calculation of *capital resources*: eligible assets less foreseeable liabilities	
Total assets	550
Less intangible assets	(100)
Less inadmissible assets	(100)
Less liabilities (borrowings)	(100)
Capital resources	<u>250</u>

Approach 2: Calculation of *capital resources*: components of capital	
Ordinary *shares*	200
Profit and loss account and other reserves	100
Perpetual subordinated debt	150
Less intangible assets	(100)
Less inadmissible assets	(100)
Capital resources	<u>250</u>

Figure 10.7. Approaches to calculating capital resources

Source: FSA Handbook GENPRU 2.2.22 G.

protection they provide to the firm, and capital resource gearing rules (GENPRU 2.2.24) impose restrictions on the percentages of each tier that can be included as eligible capital. For example GENPRU 2.2.32 states that at least 50 per cent of the MCR must be core Tier 1 capital.

Turning from prudential regulation, to the other types of regulation, the FSA's high-level standards are not controversial and require that a firm 'conducts its business with integrity, . . . due skill, care and diligence' (PRIN 2.1.1). The Conduct of Business rules are more prescriptive and follow on from the general high-level principles; so that when a firm communicates with a customer 'the *firm* must take reasonable steps to communicate in a way which is clear, fair and not misleading' (COB 2.1.3). Other rules under Business Standards cover inducements, disclosures, Chinese walls, financial promotion, past performance, advising, suitability, right-to-cancel, and projections. For example, the assumptions made for projections relating to annuities must be based on lower, intermediate, and higher rate of return assumptions of 5, 7, and 9 per cent (COB 6.6.50). The formula for converting a retirement fund into an annuity is specified in COB 6.6.81. The appropriate mortality tables to be used in annuity projections are specified in COB 6.6.84. The calculation of the value of the retirement fund for a protected rights annuity under an appropriate personal pension scheme is given in COB 6.6.41.

Prudent management of reserves is important, and imprudent management can have catastrophic consequences as illustrated by the Penrose (2004) report into the Equitable Life case, as we discussed in Chapter 3. Equitable Life had offered deferred guaranteed annuities to individuals who saved through an Equitable Life personal pension. However, the company rather recklessly appeared to have made no charge for these guarantees nor made any attempt to set aside reserves to cover the cost of the guarantees. Other companies that had also offered these guaranteed annuities undertook prudential management in a number of ways: reserving, capping, and reinsurance. Equitable Life sought to manage these liabilities by discriminating terminal bonuses on the with-profits personal pensions between those policyholders with guarantees and those without. This discrimination was subsequently ruled illegal, and the fund was closed to new members in December 2000. This case illustrates the importance of sound and prudential financial management and the role of reserving.

10.3. Managing interest rate risk and bond markets

Interest rate risk is the risk that interest rates will change to leave the present value of the assets less than the present value of the liabilities. As we have already mentioned in Figure 10.7, insurance companies may avoid this risk by exactly matching the profile of the assets with the profile of the liabilities. In practice, insurance companies use a combination of existing long-, medium- and short-term government bonds, as well as other financial instruments including swaps and other derivatives, to immunize the portfolio of liabilities against interest rate risk. Figure 10.8 shows that the mixture of government bonds (approved) and corporate bonds (other) has shifted over time: in 1985 life insurance companies held five times as many government bonds as corporates; by 2005 this ratio was almost unity.

Insurance companies would like to hold long-term government bonds to match the long-term nature of their annuity liabilities, and are competing with occupational pension schemes, which have the same problems (Wadsworth 2005). Table 10.1 shows the term structure of government and corporate bonds held by Norwich Union in 2004. It can be seen that 74 per cent of these securities are dated above 15 years.

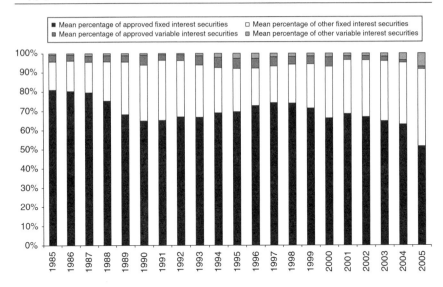

Figure 10.8. Type of debt instrument held by insurance companies

Source: FSA Returns Form 49.

The aggregate figures for all insurance companies by duration of bond assets are plotted in Figure 10.9. It can be seen that there has been an increase in the holdings of bonds with durations greater than 25 years, but this has been at the expense of medium-term bonds rather than short-term bond holdings.

Table 10.1. Analysis of term holdings for Norwich Union

	Fixed interest approved	Variable interest approved	Percentage of total approved securities	Other fixed interest	Percentage of other securities
< 1	10,340		1%	3,524	0%
1–5	43,066	1,026	3%	93,111	3%
5–10	312,033	519	23%	288,525	9%
10–15	194,801	266	14%	443,287	14%
15–20	116,406	1,219	9%	767,403	25%
20–25	131,512		10%	518,015	17%
> 25	468,974	314	35%	717,006	23%
Irredeemable	74,142		5%	272,905	9%
Total	1,351,274	3,344		3,103,776	4,458,394

Figures in £000s unless stated otherwise.

Source: FSA Returns 2004.

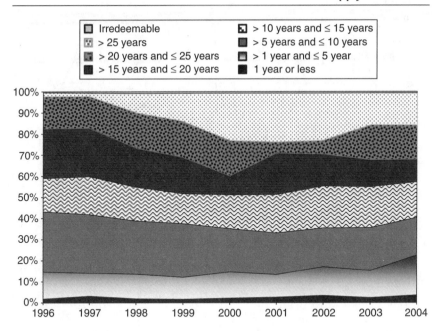

▢ Irredeemable	▣ > 10 years and ≤ 15 years
▦ > 25 years	▩ > 5 years and ≤ 10 years
▤ > 20 years and ≤ 25 years	▢ > 1 year and ≤ 5 year
▆ > 15 years and ≤ 20 years	▆ 1 year or less

Figure 10.9. Life-insurers: Fixed interest approved securities: Bond durations
Source: FSA Returns.

Figure 10.10 shows the monthly yield spread on 10-year minus 1-year government bonds, and 20-year minus 1-year bonds from 1979 to 2007, and it can be seen that since the late 1990s the yield spread has been negative, suggesting that the term structure is 'humped'. Figure 10.11 shows the daily yield spread on 10-year bonds minus 3-month Treasury Bills and again this illustrates that the yield spread is variable, but over the last 5 years has been negative. These data would be consistent with some investors desiring to hold long-term bonds, but there being insufficient supply, resulting in yields on long-term bonds being low.

According to the DMO (2005: 11) the UK Government's debt management policy objective is 'to minimize over the long term, the costs of meeting the Government's financing needs, taking into account risk, whilst ensuring that debt management policy is consistent with the aims of monetary policy'. It achieves this objective and arrives at its issuance plans each year by taking into account: (*a*) the Government's appetite for risk (both nominal and real in each year); (*b*) the shape of the yield curves (nominal and real) and the expected effect of issuance policy; (*c*) investors' demand for gilts; and (*d*) cash management requirement for Treasury Bills and other short-term debt instruments. In 2006/07, planned

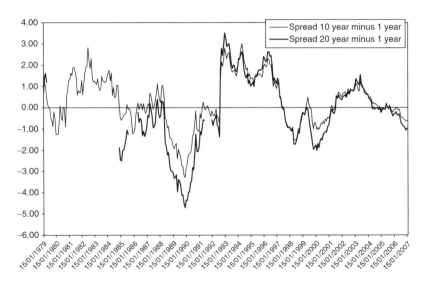

Figure 10.10. Spreads between monthly bond yields of different maturities 1979–2007

Source: Bank of England website.

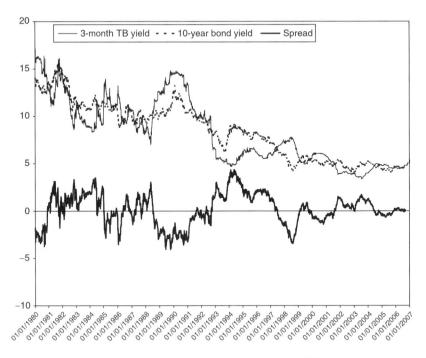

Figure 10.11. Spread between long-term and short-term UK daily government bond yields 1980–2007

Source: Datastream.

	Estimated market values at 30 September 2004 (£ bn)
Gilts (15+)	
– conventional	82
– price indexed	38
Non-gilts (Investment grade/15 years +)	
– conventional	90
– price indexed	8
Mortgages (balances outstanding)	850
Occupational Pension Scheme Assets	750
Annuity reserves (excluding investment linked)	80

Figure 10.12. Summary data on volumes of long bonds and mortgages

Source: Wadsworth (2005).

gilt sales totalled £63 billion, split between short conventional gilts (at least £10 billion), medium conventional gilts (at least £10 billion), long conventional gilts (at least £19.5 billion), and index-linked gilts (at least £16 billion). Following calls from the pensions industry during 2004 for more and longer-dated debt, the DMO via the National Association of Pension Funds consulted with participants in the pensions industry, and in his 2005 Budget speech the Chancellor of the Exchequer announced that the Government would issue conventional gilts with maturities of up to 50 years from May 2005 onwards. A new 50-year maturity conventional gilt was issued in May 2005 and a new 40-year conventional gilt followed in May 2006. The first 50-year index-linked gilt was issued in September 2005.

Wadsworth (2005) argues that there are insufficient long-term government and corporate bonds available to satisfy the potential demand by insurance companies and occupational pension schemes. Figure 10.12 shows that the outstanding quantities of long-term government and corporate bonds are small relative to the potential demand for annuities (based on total pension scheme assets).

There are a number of other alternatives to long-term government bonds: corporate bonds, overseas bonds, and mortgage-backed securities. However, Wadsworth (2005) reports a survey by Watson Wyatt of company treasurers which finds there is no general desire by company treasurers to issue long-term index-linked bonds. However, specific sectors such as the utility industries have issued long-term index-linked bonds. In February 2006 United Utilities Water plc issued £50 million of 40-year index-linked bonds, and predicted that other utility companies would follow suit depending on the regulators' response to utilities taking advantage of low long-term yields.[7]

Overseas bonds carry currency risk and sometimes they are not even available. For example, one of the largest potential issuers, the USA treasury, stopped issuing bonds dated more than 10 years in 2001 (Bank for International Settlements 2001). Elsewhere in the Eurozone government bond issues are also more frequent in the short and medium segment. European governments do issue some long-term issues, but they constitute a limited share of total issuance.

According to Holmans, Karley, and Whitehead (2003) there has been a strong growth in the securitization of mortgages since 1998. Figure 10.12 also shows the quantity of mortgages outstanding in the UK. However, a potential problem with mortgages as an asset for insurance companies is that most UK residential mortgages are variable interest, with the holder of the mortgage suffering the potential of prepayment risk when interest rates fall.

In order to illustrate the portfolio allocation of one UK annuity provider, we reproduce in Table 10.2 the balance sheet of one major annuity provider taken from the FSA returns. It can be seen that most of Norwich Union's assets in 2004 are in Mortgages, Approved and Other Fixed Interest securities: most of these mortgages are fixed rate commercial mortgages rather than residential mortgages. However, we should emphasize that the Norwich Union is relatively unusual among annuity providers in placing such a high proportion of its reserves in mortgages.

10.4. Managing longevity risk

The cash flows in an annuity contract between the insurance companies which supply or write annuities and the annuitants who purchase them are illustrated in Figure 10.13. In return for a single annuity premium, the insurance company agrees to pay the annuitant a series of regular annuity payment until death. The insurance company then has a liability to the annuitant, and may protect or offset this liability in a number of ways. The standard investment would be for the premium received from the annuitant to be invested in an asset that matches the properties of the liabilities: asset–liability management. The trick is to identify assets with the same properties as the liabilities. Insurance companies operate an annuity portfolio, and given the characteristics of the annuitants in

Table 10.2. Assets for insurance business of Norwich Union, 2004

	Value	Percentage of assets	Percentage of yield
Assets: Non-index-linked (Form 48)			
Land and buildings	3,088	0.02%	8.71%
Approved fixed interest	1,351,274	9.62%	4.77%
Other fixed interest	3,103,776	22.10%	5.85%
Approved variable interest	3,344	0.02%	1.65%
Other variable interest		0.00%	
Equity		0.00%	
Loans secured by mortgages	8,062,335	57.40%	6.37%
Other income producing assets	126,169	0.90%	5.5%
Other assets	686,198	4.89%	
Total non-index-linked	13,336,184	94.95%	5.75%
Assets: Index-linked (Form 56/1)			
Corporate index-linked bonds	443,041	3.15%	
Land and buildings	54,064	0.38%	
Derivatives	−5,043	−0.04%	
Government/public index-linked bonds	217,367	1.55%	
Total index-linked	709,429	5.05%	
Total assets	14,045,613		
Liabilities (stock of annuities written) (Form 51)			
UK non-linked net total	11,415,134		
Overseas	361,400		
UK linked	438,773		
Reinsurance	709,429		
Total liabilities	12,924,736		

Figures in £000s unless stated otherwise.

Source: 2004 FSA returns, tables 48, 51, and 56.

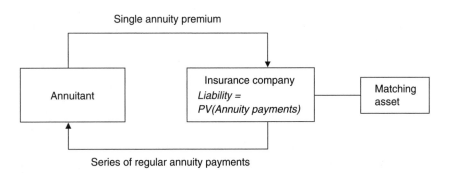

Figure 10.13. Relationship between annuitant and annuity provider

the portfolio are able to estimate the likely future annuity payouts from the portfolio.

Prudential risk management dictates that the insurer will invest the pool of annuity premium proceeds in assets whose payouts and risk profile closely match the pool of expected future annuity payouts in order to minimize the risk to the insurance company that it will not be able to fund the annuity contract. Long-term government bonds are one such asset, as discussed in the previous section, though James and Song (2001) note one possibility for the documented high money's worth of annuities is that annuity providers may have been investing in riskier securities such as corporate bonds. An ideal matching asset would be a longevity bond (Blake 1999; Blake and Burrows 2001; Dowd 2003).

10.4.1. Longevity bonds

A longevity bond is a long-term bond whose coupon payments increase in line with the number of lives surviving from a specified reference population (all of the same age and hence in the same cohort). Since coupon payments increase in line with the number of people surviving, they are negatively related to the realized death rate (mortality). Suppose the reference population is a group of people aged x at time t (i.e. the cohort born in year $t - x$). We write the percentage of people surviving to time $t + i$ as S_{t+i} (this is the realized survival percentage rather than the *ex ante* survival probability s_{t+i}). Then a longevity bond would be a bond making a series of coupon payments £S_{t+1}, £S_{t+2}, £$S_{t+3}, \ldots,$ £S_{t+T} where in practice there might be a maximum duration for payments T and no final payment of principal in the final period.

So in the unlikely event of 100 per cent of the reference population remaining alive in year $t + i$, the coupon payment that year would be £1.

The expected present value of this longevity bond is

$$\text{EPV} = \frac{S_{t+1}}{(1 + y)} + \frac{S_{t+2}}{(1 + y)^2} + \frac{S_{t+3}}{(1 + y)^3} + \cdots + \frac{S_{t+T}}{(1 + y)^T} \tag{10.1}$$

where y is the yield to maturity for this longevity bond, and the bond may repay the principal through a sinking fund provision (a portion each period) or the repayment of the principal may also be related to the survival of the reference population.

An advantage to a pension provider or insurance company from purchasing such a longevity bond is that the bond's cash flows provide a close match to their liabilities. If actual survival rates are high, they receive high coupon payments to pay out the promised pensions; if realized survival rates are low, the bond's coupon payments are reduced, but there are a corresponding lower percentage of pensioners to pay out the pensions to. However, there are potential problems with such a bond. First, the mortality experience of the pool of annuitants held by the insurer may be different from that of the reference population; secondly, although a longevity bond may provide a hedge against interest rate movements, it may not be as liquid as a government bond; and thirdly the credit risk of the issuer of the bond might make it riskier than a government bond.

In November 2004 the European Investment Bank announced its intention to issue a 25-year longevity bond. The annual coupon payments on the bond are determined by the number of lives in the English and Welsh male population reaching age 65 in 2003 and then surviving to each subsequent year. Coupon payments decrease in line with the number of lives surviving, as estimated by the UK's Office of National Statistics.[8] The bond issue of £500 million was arranged by BNP Paribas, and was reinsured with PartnerRE, who assumed the longevity risk. Blake, Cairns, and Dowd (2006) report that this EIB/BNP was only partially subscribed and later withdrawn for redesign. They suggest a number of reasons for the failure of this bond to be fully subscribed: perhaps 25-year maturity was too short; the amount of capital required relative to the risk reduction was too high; the model and parameter uncertainty meant that there was uncertainty as to the appropriate price of the bond; and uncertainty concerning basis risk, reflecting a mismatch between the hedging instrument (the longevity index) and the underlying pool of lives to be hedged.

The DMO (2005: 22) reports that as part of its consultation exercise with the pensions industry in 2004, it had considered the issuance of longevity bonds, however it reports that the consultation exercise displayed 'very limited interest in gilts structured in an annuity format. Concerns were expressed about the potential illiquidity of such instruments and it was felt that annuities would be of interest to particular individual investors rather than of generic widespread interest. The Government therefore decided that it would not issue conventional or index-linked annuity type gilts in 2005–06 or in the near future.'

10.4.2. *Reinsurance and securitization*

As Figure 10.14 illustrates, two alternatives to an insurance company investing the proceeds of the annuity premiums in matching assets would be to sub-underwrite some of the annuity risks through reinsurance, or to

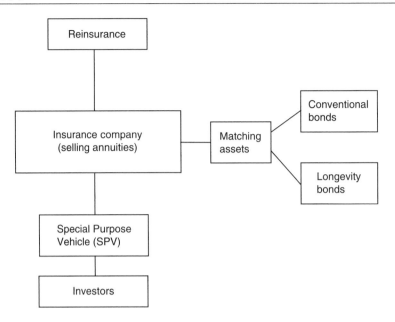

Figure 10.14. Relationship between annuity provider and alternative risk management choices

reinsure through securitization. Under securitization, a Special Purpose Vehicle (SPV) is created to purchase the annuity liabilities from the insurance company, and in turn issues bonds to outside investors. The advantage of setting up an SPV is that through various credit enhancement mechanisms, the credit risk of the SPV is determined by the annuity provider.[9]

The seminal paper on reinsurance is by Borsch (1962), who explains that reinsurance is concerned with the transfer of risk. Companies in the reinsurance market deal with other insurance companies to redistribute risk that each company has accepted by its direct underwriting for the public: companies that gain from these risk transfers pay cash compensation to the companies that take on the risk. The Borsch model starts by assuming that insurers take on insurance contracts with the general public, and that the risks insured by these contracts are *independent* of each other. In the reinsurance market these companies can trade with other insurance companies (reinsurers) to redistribute these insurance claims. The size of the global reinsurance market in 2007 was $153 billion, and the five largest reinsurers in the world are listed in Table 10.3.

Borsch shows that a reinsurance price exists which equates supply and demand for insurance contracts between insurers, but that the resulting

Table 10.3. Largest reinsurers in the world in 2006

Company	Net reinsurance premiums	Country
Munich Re	25,432	Germany
Swiss Re	23,841	Switzerland
Berkshire Hathaway Re	11,576	USA
Hannover Re	9,353	Germany
Lloyd's	8,445	UK

Figures in $ million.

Source: Standard & Poors, Insurance Information Institute http://www.iii.org/.

outcome is not Pareto efficient. He suggests that this division is best characterized by cooperative bargaining, which corresponds to how much reinsurance is conducted. The optimal arrangement is for the insurance companies to place all of their insurance portfolios in a central pool to spread the risks as widely as possible, and then agree on a sharing rule as to how payments of the claims against the pool should be divided up.

Powers and Shubik (2001, 2005) consider a reinsurance market with a non-cooperative bargaining equilibrium and show that if the number of primary insurers is large then the optimal number of reinsurers is approximately the square root of the number of primary insurers. They also note that an analogous 'fourth-root-rule' applies to markets for retrocession (the reinsurance of reinsurance).

An important assumption in Borsch's work is that the individual insurance claims are independent leading to the result that pooling all risks is optimal. This may not be a valid assumption for annuity providers, since the mortality experience of one company is likely to be correlated with that of the others.

An alternative form of reinsurance is securitization. In this case the original insurer purchases reinsurance of the annuity payments from a Special Purpose Vehicle (SPV) which, in return for the reinsurance premium, agrees to make reinsurance payments to the insurer, in the event that the survival of a reference population is higher than expected. The SPV then issues mortality bonds (Lin and Cox 2005) to outside investors, whose coupon payments or terminal face value is a decreasing function of the survival rates of the reference population. The difference between a mortality bond and a longevity bond is that with a mortality bond the coupon payments *decrease* if the survival of the reference population increases, whereas with a longevity bond the coupon payments *increase* with the survival of the reference population. Special Purpose Vehicles are standalone companies that are legally separate from the issuing company, and

251

are used extensively in debt securitization issues. They allow the issuer to remove the debt from its balance sheet, and they ensure that the holders of the bond face a credit risk appropriate to the bond issue.

The SPV will use the proceeds from the mortality bonds to purchase similarly structured government bonds. Because the mortality bonds are risky, the investor will pay less for them than the SPV's government bonds whose payouts are not conditioned on survival probabilities. The SPV will use the proceeds from the reinsurance premiums to offset the difference in the price that it receives for the mortality bond and the price it pays for the government bond. Cox, Pedersen, and Fairchild (2000) note that these arrangements for mortality bonds are very similar to those for catastrophe bonds, for which there is an active market. They argue that catastrophe bonds are popular because catastrophe risks are uncorrelated with stock and traditional bond markets, so that investors who add catastrophe bonds to their portfolios improve their investment opportunities.

Cox and Lin (2007) cite Swiss Re who issued a bond in December 2003 based on the mortality index of the general population of the USA, United Kingdom, France, Italy, and Switzerland. The term of the bond was three years; issued at a price of $400 million; paying LIBOR plus 135 basis points. If the mortality index exceeds 130 per cent of the 2002 level, the principal repayment is reduced. Cox and Lin (2007) note that these payments are increasing in the survival rates (since they are decreasing in mortality rates) since Swiss Re were issuing a bond that insured against rises in mortality (due to famine/plague/disease) which is the opposite of an SPV that wished to issue a mortality bond to insure against longevity risk, but Cox and Lin suggest there will be investors who are willing to bear the risk of increased longevity. One obvious set of investors who would be willing to hold this type of bond are DB pension plans, whose liabilities will reduce as mortality increases. Blake, Cairns, and Dowd (2006) report that the Swiss Re issue was fully subscribed and that investors appeared 'happy' with the issue. Indeed, in April 2005, Swiss Re announced that it had issued a second life catastrophe bond with a principal of $362 million, and maturity date of 2010. This bond was issued in three tranches, with different tranches bearing varying amounts of mortality risk.

10.4.3. *Example of mortality securitization*

To illustrate a mortality bond, and how an annuity provider might use such a bond, consider the following simplification of Lin and Cox (2005).

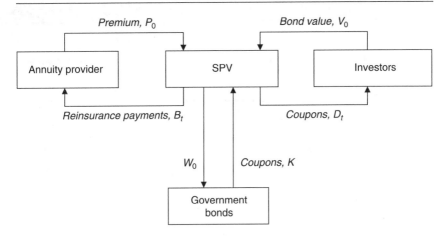

Figure 10.15. Illustration of the securitization of mortality risk

At the outset, $t = 0$ an annuity provider has agreed to pay a pool of annuitants an annuity payment of £1 per year to each annuitant in the pool, and S_t is the percentage of the pool that is still alive at time period t. At $t = 0$ the percentage of the pool which will be alive in period t, $0 \leq S_t \leq 1$ is a random variable, and this exposes the annuity provider to longevity or mortality risk (Figure 10.15).

The annuity provider may reinsure part of the longevity risk in this contract using a Special Purpose Vehicle (SPV) subsidiary. The annuity provider buys reinsurance from the SPV and pays a single premium, P_0, illustrated in Figure 10.15. This reinsurance contract partly insures the annuity provider against the risk in the percentage of the pool that is still alive in period t. In return for the up-front payment P_0, the annuity provider is paid reinsurance payments, B_t, which depends on the realization of the random variable S_t, up to a cap K in each period, where $0 < K \leq 1$:

$$B_t = \begin{cases} K & \text{if } S_t > K \\ S_t & \text{if } S_t \leq K \end{cases} \qquad (10.2)$$

The reinsurance payments as a function of S_t are illustrated in Figure 10.16, and it can be seen that they are capped at K. Since the annuity provider is committed to pay the annuity payments, S_t, the annuity provider's outgoing net cash flows (NCF) are

$$\text{NCF} = S_t - B_t = \begin{cases} S_t - K & \text{if } S_t > K \\ 0 & \text{if } S_t \leq K \end{cases} \qquad (10.3)$$

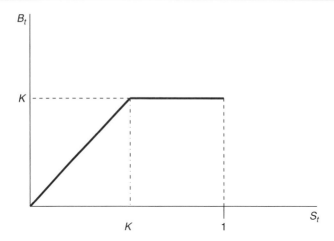

Figure 10.16. Reinsurance cash flows payments as a function of S_t

The annuity provider's net cash flows as a function of S_t are illustrated in Figure 10.17. In this example, the annuity provider has reduced the longevity risk, but not eliminated it (except when $K = 1$, which represents full reinsurance). If $K < 1$, for high survival rates, the annuity provider is not fully reinsured and makes losses.

The annuity provider has passed on some of the longevity risk to the SPV. To offset this risk, the SPV now issues a mortality bond to investors

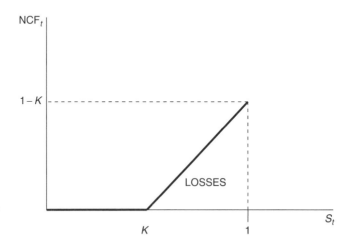

Figure 10.17. Annuity provider's outgoing net cash flows payments as a function of S_t

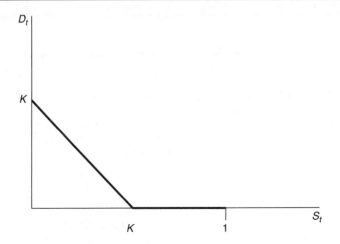

Figure 10.18. Mortality bond coupon payments as a function of S_t

at a price V_0 that has a coupon payment, D_t, where

$$D_t = \begin{cases} 0 & \text{if } S_t > K \\ K - B_t & \text{if } S_t \leq K \end{cases} = \begin{cases} 0 & \text{if } S_t > K \\ K - S_t & \text{if } S_t \leq K \end{cases} \tag{10.4}$$

As shown in Figure 10.18 the coupon payments on the mortality bond are decreasing in the percentage of the annuitants who are alive S_t. Combining equations (10.2) and (10.4), the total cash flows paid out of the SPV are

$$B_t + D_t = K \tag{10.5}$$

which is a constant for all t, and is independent of the actual realization of the percentage of annuitants in any period: the SPV has indeed completely offset the longevity risk. Therefore the SPV can purchase a risk-free bond at a price W_0, which pays coupon payments of K each period, to cover its total cash flow payments:

$$W_0 = P_0 + V_0 \tag{10.6}$$

As illustrated in Figure 10.15, the longevity risk has been passed on by the annuity provider to the SPV, and from the SPV to the capital markets via the mortality bond. Lin and Cox (2005) go on to estimate the values P_0 and V_0 of the mortality bond. This is a non-trivial exercise which depends on appropriate assumptions on the mortality of the pool of annuitants.

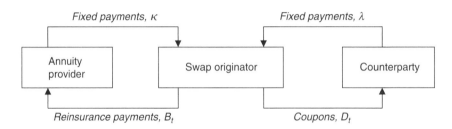

Figure 10.19. Mortality swap payment arrangements

10.4.4. *Mortality swaps*

Lin and Cox (2005) and Blake, Cairns, and Dowd (2006) note that a possible alternative to issuing a mortality bond is a series of swap agreements between the annuity provider and some counterparty which will provide the same cash flows B_t and D_t. A mortality swap is an agreement between two counterparties to exchange cash flows based on the realization of a mortality index.

Under a swap agreement the annuity provider's payment of P_0 in exchange for the reinsurance payments B_t can be replaced with a series of fixed payments κ, where

$$P_0 = \kappa \sum_{t=1}^{T} (1 + y_\kappa)^{-t} \tag{10.7}$$

y_κ is the yield to maturity on these payments, and the swap arrangements are illustrated in Figure 10.19. The swap originator can offset the mortality risk by setting up a series of payments λ with the counterparty in exchange for the coupons D_t such that

$$V_0 = \lambda \sum_{t=1}^{T} (1 + y_\lambda)^{-t} \tag{10.8}$$

and y_λ is the yield to maturity on the fixed payments from the counterparty. Just like the SPV, the swap originator is hedged against the mortality risk, and receives a series of fixed payments $\kappa + \lambda$ to cover its obligations $B_t + D_t$. In practice the fixed payments κ will be netted out against the mortality-dependent payment B_t in each period, and similarly the difference between the fixed payments λ and D_t will also be netted out in each period. As with the mortality bond, the mortality swap passes on some or all of the mortality risk to investors who are willing to bear this risk.

A disadvantage of a mortality swap over the mortality bond is that without any exchange of the principal acting as collateral the swap payments are subject to counterparty risk: the risk that one of the parties to the swap transaction will default on its obligation. The swap originator will need to ensure that this counterparty risk is minimized.

Stark (2003) and Wadsworth (2005) express concern that the insurance and the reinsurance industries do not have the capacity to absorb cohort longevity risk. Wadsworth (2005) suggests that although reinsurance is common in other sectors of the insurance industry, reinsurers seem reluctant to sub-underwrite annuity business, presumably because reinsurers are not able to diversify the 'average cohort longevity risk' between the pool of reinsurers. In addition annuity business, and indeed other forms of life insurance, differs from general insurance, since the insurance company receives up-front premiums which need to be managed for long periods of time. For this reason life insurers have traditionally specialized in fund management, whereas reinsurers have expertise in arbitrage opportunities. Since arbitrage opportunities in the annuities market are difficult to identify (except for regulatory arbitrage) and running an annuity book involves considerable amounts of fund management, there may be few incentives for life insurers to reinsure.

King (2004) notes that for average cohort (or collective) longevity risks, the burden of unexpectedly high longevity for a particular cohort should be spread over as many generations as possible, and this provides a potential role for government to share risks across generations, since the private sector may be unable to provide these risk-sharing contracts. If the government is unwilling to underwrite this cohort longevity risk through issuing longevity bonds, or if neither reinsurers nor individual investors are willing to bear this cohort longevity risk, then the only people who can bear this risk are the pensioners themselves. This could be achieved either by premiums rising to the point where reinsurers or investors are willing to enter the market or by annuity payments being linked to cohort mortality. The latter solution involves pensioners receiving annuity payments that are dependent upon cohort survival rates, so that annuities only insure the annuitants against their idiosyncratic mortality risk and not the cohort mortality risk. This cohort-mortality dependent annuity would be very similar to the tontines discussed in Chapter 3, Section 3.2.

Notes

1. 'Gilt' is the common term for a UK government bond.
2. *Source*: Calculations from FSA Insurance Returns, Form 47 from Synthesis Database.
3. B&CE Insurance Ltd only sells annuities to people who have worked in the construction industry and the NFU only to farmers. Partnership Insurance specializes in impaired lives annuities.
4. Partnership Assurance is backed by Phoenix Equity Partners and HBOS; Just Retirement by Langholm Capital Partners, Hannover Re, and Robeco.
5. These regulatory pillars (Balse/Solvency) should not be confused with the pillars of pension provision classified by the World Bank (1994).
6. With-profit policies are explained in Chapter 3, Section 3.4.
7. Ofwat/Ofgem (2006) issued a consultation paper concerning the financing of UK network utilities.
8. Alternative life indices to the ONS population data for the UK are JPMorgan's LifeMetrics index (JPMorgan 2007) and an index produced by Credit Suisse First Boston (CSFB 2007). Both of these are based on international official data.
9. An SPV is a separate legal entity, and credit enhancement mechanisms include: (*a*) corporate guarantees (though then the credit rating depends on the rating of the guarantor); (*b*) letters of credit from a bank; and (*c*) bond insurance.

11
Conclusions

This book has examined the properties and characteristics of annuity markets. We started by explaining the role of annuities within the context of increased demand around the world, as increasing numbers of people retire, and pension systems shift from pay-as-you-go and defined benefit to defined contribution. Two alternatives to buying an annuity are for pensioners to take their pension wealth as a lump sum or to have a phased withdrawal, under which access to pension wealth in any year is restricted. Neither of these choices offer insurance against longevity risk, which is the major advantage of an annuity.

As we explained in Chapter 5, on the whole annuity market provision around the world is limited, with only a small number of countries having sizeable annuities markets, and these countries do so, as a result of their pension programmes. Why does a country have a pension programme? Pensions are seen as an aspect of public policy, whereby governments ensure that provisions are made for income support in old age. This may be compulsory or encouraged through tax incentives. To ensure that the resulting pension fund is actually used for a pension income, governments may require either annuitization or phased withdrawal. If there are no restrictions on access to pension wealth, there is a risk that pensioners will use their accumulated wealth for non-pension purposes. On the other hand, many pensioners might benefit from having some flexibility in how they spend their pension wealth. The UK's 75 per cent compulsory annuitization requirement is an example of applying this trade-off.

In Chapter 2 we described the many types of annuity products available, and provided examples of annuity prices quoted by providers. We explained the construction of a voluntary and compulsory annuity price series, and derived the movement in annuity prices over time. In

Chapter 4 we considered the methods used by actuaries to predict mortality and price annuities, and described the measurement of life expectancy. We examined the factors that determine annuity prices and showed that the price of annuities depends on interest rates, projections of life expectancy, size of the pension fund, type of annuity, and the annuity providers' markup (which may depend upon the cohort mortality risk). An additional consideration is the extent to which a group of annuitants' mortality has special characteristics. After a decade of underestimating mortality improvements, the UK actuarial profession was criticized in the Morris Report (2005), but recent developments in actuarial practice have sought both to improve the quality of mortality projections and to quantify their uncertainty. It is possible that the pendulum has swung too far, since there is a small amount of evidence that the most recent projections overestimate improvements in mortality.

We predict two likely developments with respect to the types of annuity products available in the future. Annuity providers will become more and more sophisticated in pricing annuity products, and will design annuity products that satisfy the needs of particular clienteles. As we saw in Chapter 2, annuity rates increase with age, and males are quoted higher annuity rates than females of the same age. In both cases this is because there are clear mortality differences between these different groups. It is likely that annuity providers will develop more sophisticated methods for predicting mortality, identifying individual characteristics that are correlated with mortality. It is surprising that to date, annuity providers have used so little information in annuity pricing, since there are other variables that are potentially useful in predicting mortality such as age of a parent at their death, or wealth.

In 2007 Legal & General announced that they were carrying out a pilot study of annuities based on postcodes. Some areas of the UK have higher mortality than others and postcodes also reflect housing wealth, so that by pricing annuities on the basis of postcodes individuals will pay an annuity price that reflects their specific group mortality experience. Insurance companies will be able to separate out those individuals with high mortality from low mortality, and hence there will be a reduction in the cross-subsidy inherent in a large single pool of annuitants. With the advent of increased precision in individual mortality projections using genetic information, this cross-subsidy could be all but eliminated, although the use of genetic information relies upon legal sanction.

Interestingly, the current cross-subsidy is usually from the poor to the wealthy, since it is the poor that have lower life expectancy. As annuity providers identify groups of low-risk individuals (from the insurance company's point of view, the individuals with low life expectancy), they will be able to offer these groups higher annuity rates, with a corresponding reduction in annuity rates to high-risk groups, predominantly the wealthy. Most policymakers would view this redistribution from the wealthy to the poor as socially beneficial.

We commented on the growth of the impaired life market, illustrating how insurance companies can select groups of annuitants with particular mortality characteristics. A further development along these lines in the UK is the expansion of the bulk buy-out market, which has seen an increase in the number of providers. This market had been dominated by Legal & General and Prudential, but as large employers have closed down their defined benefit pension schemes, and switched to defined contribution schemes, there have been a number of new entrants willing to buy out these pension liabilities with bulk annuities. The reason for the influx of new entrants is that these new companies argue that they have better risk management and more accurate mortality models than existing annuity providers (Wood 2006). A particular occupational pension scheme will typically include a pool of pensioners who are relatively homogeneous, and it may be possible to provide a bespoke bulk annuity product that is designed with this group's specific mortality risk clearly identified, leading to more efficient annuity pricing.

There are also developments to link the provision of long-term care with annuities. Johnstone (2005) observes that the market for long-term care insurance has not been successful, and since 2004 the main providers have withdrawn from the market. These products were unpopular because they were seen as complex, expensive, and poor value for money. The only long-term insurance product that has shown positive sales growth has been immediate needs annuities, paid gross to a residential care home when someone needs care. Johnstone (2005) suggests that linking lifetime mortgages to points of need care is a potential funding solution for this provision. Coupling long-term care with annuities is a reversion to corrodies, used in the Middle Ages by the Church to provide real annuities, as we discussed in Chapter 3.

In Chapter 6, we explained the money's worth calculation of annuities, and examined whether annuities are fairly priced, by considering the evidence on money's worth from a number of studies. While there is evidence to suggest that annuities are probably priced slightly higher than would be suggested by pure actuarial considerations, estimated markups (or loadings) in annuity markets around the world do not seem excessive compared with the cost of other financial services, and other insurance products. There is a remarkably consistent body of evidence over time and across countries, that annuities are fairly priced.

However, recent evidence in Chapter 6 is that the money's worth of UK compulsory purchase annuities has fallen slightly over the period 1994–2007. Two possible reasons for this decline are increases in market power of providers or higher costs due to increased regulation, both of which we have discussed in Chapter 10. In our view, neither of these can have explained the money's worth decline on their own. Instead, we suggest three further possibilities: (*a*) the existence of an insurance cycle; (*b*) the pricing of mortality uncertainty; and (*c*) the growth of impaired lives annuities.

There is a wide literature referring to a phenomenon called the 'insurance cycle' (surveyed in Harrington 2004). This refers to the tendency of insurers to increase their premia after periods when negative shocks have resulted in *ex post* losses, resulting in significant reductions in capital. Since it appears that life insurers may have been making *ex post* losses on annuities over some of this period, due to unanticipated reductions in mortality (i.e. when the money's worth was above unity), the observed reductions in annuity rates may be an example of the insurance cycle. This should be a short-term phenomenon because after life insurers recoup their losses, the cycle will restart.

Standard economic theory would suggest that competitive pressures would make the insurance cycle impossible. However, more sophisticated theories suggest that increasing premia may be rational, since the negative shock may have resulted in rational updating of probabilities and hence life insurers reducing their projections of mortality by more than suggested in the CMI reports. This brings us to the second reason why the money's worth may have declined.

We have already discussed in Chapter 4 changes in actuarial methodology and how the most recent developments attempt to include estimates of the uncertainty in mortality projections. Pricing uncertainty into annuity premia would tend to result in lower annuity rates and it is possible that life insurers have been paying more explicit attention to this in the relevant period. Circumstantial evidence for this is the 'Dear CEO' letter sent to annuity providers by the FSA in 2007, reflecting on the debate over future annuitant longevity improvements. The letter recognized that companies would usually make assumptions based on their own mortality experiences,

However, if this is not possible we would expect firms to consider the different industry views in this area and to err on the side of caution.

(FSA Dear CSO letter, April 2007)

This letter could be interpreted as an instruction to annuity providers, from the regulator, to price annuities conservatively to reflect the risk of mortality improvements. The danger of excessive prudence is that while this ensures the sustainability of the annuities payments, it results in poor money's worth for consumers. Where annuities are purchased voluntarily a consequence could be a collapse of the market, as happened in the Netherlands in the mid-nineteenth century (Stamhuis 1988). Where annuitization is compulsory, such excessive prudence is likely to result in high *ex post* profits to life insurers.

The final explanation for the decline in the money's worth follows on from the growth in the impaired lives market. According to Peter Quinton, then of the Annuity Bureau, writing in the June 2003 edition of *Pensions Management*, there was an increase in the impaired life market of 23 per cent between 2001 and 2002. In 2005, the *Synthesis* database reports that of £8.5 billion sales of CPA annuities only £386 million (4.5 per cent) were impaired life. According to Ainslie (2000), the impaired life annuity market needs a market share of 7.5 per cent per annum to be a viable business model, but once it achieves this level, it will have an impact on the profitability of the remaining standard model. Our estimates of money's worth in Chapter 6 make no allowance for any growth in the impaired life market, since the life tables that we use are unable to distinguish between impaired and non-impaired lives. This growth in the impaired life market would have resulted in the remaining annuitants in the conventional market having average lower mortality. If life insurers priced this information into annuities, they would have been assuming lower mortality than in the standard tables: this could have explained a decline in the recent measure of the money's worth.

In Chapter 7 we explained Yaari's (1965) result that a risk-averse individual who is concerned about longevity risk will always purchase actuarially fair annuity contracts, enabling them to smooth consumption in every period of retirement. We observed that Yaari's result depends upon a variety of considerations and does not square with the evidence that actual annuity markets are small. We modelled the demand for annuities in an expected utility framework, and demonstrated the value of annuities under various specifications of preferences.

The theoretical welfare benefits of annuitization sit uncomfortably with the fact that voluntary annuity markets are small. We went on to consider whether this annuity puzzle could be resolved by resorting to habit formation and other more exotic utility functions, in the same way that other consumption puzzles have been so resolved. However, the general point from this section appeared to be that whatever utility function is employed, pensioners who are concerned about longevity risk should annuitize a large percentage of their wealth. So recourse to preference specification does not appear to solve the annuity puzzle.

In Chapter 8 we considered a range of factors that could explain the annuity puzzle. These included bequests; existence of state pension benefits, so that individuals are already heavily annuitized; means testing; selection effects; deferred annuitization; and behavioural aspects. All of these factors may provide reasons why demand for relatively inflexible annuity products is low. If we had to nail our flag to the mast and identify the reason for the annuity puzzle, we believe that the demand for voluntary annuities is low because of a combination of rational reasons (due to the inflexible nature of existing annuity products) and irrational reasons (a misunderstanding of the nature of mortality drag and annuity products). Better financial education and explanation of the advantages of annuity products may reduce this second type of annuity aversion.

In Chapter 9 we presented evidence on the demand for annuities, and discussed the existence of selection effects in annuity markets. Finkelstein and Poterba (2002) observe that selection effects may be active or passive. The distinction between active and passive selection is important for public policies towards annuities. If active selection effects drive annuity demand, then any market failures may be overcome by compulsory annuitization. On the other hand, if passive selection determines annuity demand, compulsory annuitization may not lead to a welfare improvement. As we discussed in Chapter 9, the evidence on the existence of active selection effects is ambiguous.

We examined the supply of annuities in Chapter 10, and noted that annuity markets are highly regulated and highly concentrated. The number of annuity providers in the UK has fallen significantly over the last 50 years and one firm (the Prudential) accounts for 23 per cent of this market. Typically life insurers write annuity contracts, and invest the annuity premiums in matching assets. There are two sets of risks that the annuity providers face with respect to the availability of matching assets: interest rate risk, because the duration of the assets is typically less than the liabilities, and cohort longevity risk. Cohort longevity risk is the risk that future cohorts of individuals will benefit from a significant increase in longevity, and annuity providers will then be required to honour the annuity contracts that have become unprofitable.

The small number of annuity providers means that the cohort longevity risk is highly concentrated in a small number of firms, and there is a question whether these providers have the capacity to absorb the extra risk associated with increased annuity demand. If this limited number of firms were not able to bear the total longevity risk, then mechanisms would need to be found for this risk to be held elsewhere. Possible candidates are (*a*) individual investors or other financial institutions, who would hold mortality bonds (issued by reinsurers) in a diversified portfolio; (*b*) the government, or other bond issuers, by issuing longevity bonds; and (*c*) the annuity holders themselves, by making the annuity payments conditional on cohort survival rates.

Annuity providers would be better able to minimize the risks of an asset–liability mismatch by the availability of more long-term government bonds. The Debt Management Office's new issue of longer term gilts in 2005 and 2006 has partly addressed this problem, and it should be the case that if an increasing number of annuities need to be provided, the cost of the national debt may be minimized by the DMO issuing long-term bonds.

Annuity markets are likely to grow in size in the future as pension policies around the world move to funded defined contribution schemes, raising the question of how the accumulated pension funds should be converted into a pension. There is a diverse body of research into the operation of annuity markets, dispersed across the disciplines of actuarial science, demography, economics, finance, and insurance. In this book we have synthesized these different approaches, to provide what we hope is a coherent treatment of the issues that need to be addressed by practitioners, policymakers, and researchers in the field of annuity markets.

Glossary of the mathematical symbols most commonly used in the book

Symbol	Variable	Defined in equations	Comments
a, $_r a_{\overline{n}\rvert}$, a_x, etc.	Value of an annuity; net present value of income stream of £1 per period	4.1, 4.5, 4.11, 4.12	Actuarial notation
A	Annuity rate; annual payment per £1 premium		$A = 1/a$
b			
c	Consumption		NB: used as a parameter in Chapter 4
d			
E	Expectations operator		
f	Forward rate	4.8	NB: used as a parameter in Chapter 4, Section 4.4
g	Growth rate of annuity payment	4.11	Used for escalating annuity
h	Habitual consumption	7.33	
i, j			Used as indices, often in expressions involving summations. In actuarial notation i is an interest rate, but we never use that notation
I	Indicator function		Takes the value 0 or 1
k			NB: used as a parameter in Chapter 4
K	Upper limit to reinsurance payments	10.2	Used in our discussion of mortality bonds
l_x	Life expectancy	4.4	Actuarial notation
m	Death rate		Actuarial notation. Proportion of a group of lives that die in a given period
p, p_x, etc.	Probability of still being alive one period later		When the period is a year this is actuarial notation $p_x \equiv 1 - q_x$
$p_x^{(j)}$	Probability of living exactly j years	4.3	
q_x	Probability of dying in the next year		Actuarial notation

Symbol	Description	Reference	Notes
r	Interest rate		This is the real or nominal interest rate, depending on context
R_i	Present value based on compounded interest rates	7.40	
s, s_x, etc.	Survival probability; probability of being alive after a defined length of time	4.2	This is the realization of s
S	Welfare payments per period	Chapter 8	
S_t	The proportion of a population that survives t periods	Chapter 10	
t	Time		
T	Final period in finite-period maximization		
u	Per-period utility (felicity)		
V	Utility maximizer's objective function		
W	Wealth		
x	Age of annuitant		
y	Yield to maturity		
z	Equilibrium annuity rate for pooled high- and low-risk individuals	8.3	
α	Chapter 4: set of parameters used in Gompertz–Makeham formulae	4.14, 4.15	
	Chapter 7: coefficient of risk aversion in Epstein–Zin utility function	7.34	
β	In Chapter 4: set of parameters used to model mortality	4.17	
	In Chapter 7: additional discount factor of the future used in quasi-hyperbolic discounting	7.31	
γ	Coefficient of relative risk aversion in CRRA utility function	7.24	γ is a measure of curvature of the function $u(c)$ for certain functional forms
δ	Subjective discount factor	Discussed in Section 7.3	$(1-\delta)^{-1}$ is often referred to as the subjective discount rate. The lower the value of δ, the more impatient the agent (less value attached to the future)
κ	Fixed payment by annuity provider to mortality swap	10.7	
λ	Fixed payment by counterparty to mortality swap	10.8	
μ_x	Mortality		Continuous-time analogue of p_x
ξ	Weights devoted to utility maximization in Tversky–Kahneman model	8.9	ξ is a mis-estimate of the true value p
π	Inflation rate		
ρ	Reciprocal of coefficient of inter-temporal substitution	7.34	
ψ_h, ψ_l	Proportions of high and low-risk types in adverse selection model of annuities	8.2	

Bibliography

Abel, A. B. (1986). 'Capital Accumulation and Uncertain Lifetimes with Adverse Selection', *Econometrica*, 54(5): 1079–98.

Adda, J. and Cornaglia, F. (2006). 'Taxes, Cigarette Consumption and Smoking Intensity', *American Economic Review*, 96(4): 1013–28.

Ainslie, R. (2000). 'Annuity and Insurance Products for Impaired Lives', Paper presented to the Staple Inn Actuarial Society.

Akerlof, G. A. (1970). 'The Market for "Lemons": Quality Uncertainty and the Market Mechanism', *Quarterly Journal of Economics*, 84(3): 353–74.

Alter, G. and Riley, J. C. (1986). 'How to Bet on Lives: A Guide to Life Contingent Contracts in Early Modern Europe', *Research in Economic History*, 10: 1–53.

Ameriks, J. and Zeldes, S. (2001). 'How Do Household Portfolio Shares Vary with Age?', Working Paper 6-120101, TIAA-CREF Institute.

Anderson, N. and Sleath, J. (1999). 'New Estimates of the UK Real and Nominal Yield Curves', *Bank of England Quarterly Bulletin*, 384–92.

Angeletos, G.-M., Laibson, D., Repetto, A., Tobacman, J., and Weinberg, S. (2001). 'The Hyperbolic Consumption Model: Calibration, Simulation, and Empirical Evaluation', *Journal of Economic Perspectives*, 15(3): 47–68.

Annual Abstract of Statistics (2007). Palgrave Macmillan.

Association of British Insurers (2004). *The Pension Annuity Market: Developing a Middle Market.* London: ABI.

Attanasio, O. P. and Emmerson, C. (2003). 'Mortality, Health Status and Wealth', *Journal of the European Economic Association*, 1(4): 821–50.

—— and Hoynes, H. W. (2000). 'Differential Mortality and Wealth Accumulation', *The Journal of Human Resources*, 35(1): 1–29.

Australian Prudential Regulation Authority (1999). Market Statistics, unpublished.

Backus, D., Routledge, B., and Zin, S. (2004). 'Exotic Preferences', NBER Working Paper No. 10597.

Ballotta, L. and Haberman, S. (2004). 'Guaranteed Annuity Conversion Options and their Valuation', Chapter 7 in E. Fornero and E. Luciano (eds.), *Developing an Annuity Market in Europe.* Cheltenham: Edward Elgar.

Bank for International Settlements (2001). 'The Changing Shape of Fixed Income Markets: A Collection of Studies by Central Bank Economists', BIS Papers no. 5, Monetary and Economic Department (October).

Banks, J., Blundell, R., and Tanner, S. (1998). 'Is there a Retirement-Savings Puzzle?', *American Economic Review*, 88(4): 769–88.

————and Smith, J. P. (2003). 'Understanding Differences in Household Financial Wealth Between the United States and Great Britain', *Journal of Human Resources*, 38(2): 241–79.

——Emmerson, C., Oldfield, Z., and Tetlow, G. (2005). *Prepared for Retirement? The Adequacy and Distribution of Retirement Resources in England.* London: IFS.

Barber, B. and Odean, T. (2001). 'Boys will be Boys: Gender, Overconfidence, and Common Stock Investment', *Quarterly Journal of Economics*, 116(1): 261–92.

Barro, R. J. and Friedman, J. W. (1977). 'On Uncertain Lifetimes', *Journal of Political Economy*, 85(4): 843–9.

Barsky, R. B., Juster, F. T., Kimball, M. S., and Shapiro, M. D. (1997). 'Preference Parameters and Behavioral Heterogeneity: An Experimental Approach in the Health and Retirement Study', *Quarterly Journal of Economics*, 112(2): 537–79.

Bateman, H. and Piggott, J. (1997). 'Private Pensions in OECD Countries: Australia', OECD Labour Market and Social Policy Occasional Papers, No. 23, OECD Publishing.

——Kingston, G., and Piggott, J. (2001). *Forced Saving: Mandating Private Retirement Incomes.* Cambridge: Cambridge University Press.

Benartzi, S. and Thaler, R. H. (2001). 'Naive Diversification in Defined Contribution Savings Plans', *American Economics Review*, 91(1): 79–98.

Benjamin, B. and Soliman, A. (1993). *Mortality on the Move: Methods of Mortality Projection.* London: Institute of Actuaries.

Bernheim, D. D. (1991). 'How Strong Are Bequest Motives? Evidence based on Estimates of the Demand for Life Insurance and Annuities', *Journal of Political Economy*, 99: 899–927.

Blake, D. (1999). 'Annuity Markets: Problems and Solutions', *Geneva Papers on Risk and Insurance*, 24(3): 358–75.

——(2003). 'Reply to "Survivor Bonds: A Comment on Blake and Burrows"', *Journal of Risk and Insurance*, 70(2): 349–51.

——and Burrows, W. (2001). 'Survivor Bonds: Helping to Hedge Mortality Risk', *Journal of Risk and Insurance*, 68(2): 339–48.

——Cairns, A. J. G., and Dowd, K. (2003). 'Pensionmetrics 2: Stochastic Pension Plan Design During the Distribution Phase', *Insurance: Mathematics and Economics*, 33: 29–47.

—————(2006). 'Living with Mortality: Longevity Bonds and other Mortality-linked Securities', Cass Business School: Pensions Institute Discussion Paper 06-01 (paper presented to the Faculty of Actuaries, 16 January 2006).

——Dowd, K., and Cairns, A. J. G. (2007). 'Longevity Risk and the Grim Reaper's Tail: The Survivor Fan Charts', Cass Business School: Pensions Institute Discussion Paper 07-05.

Blundell, R. and Stoker, T. M. (1999). 'Consumption and the Timing of Income Risk', *European Economic Review*, 43: 475–507.

Bodie, Z. (1990). 'Pensions as Retirement Income Insurance', *Journal of Economic Literature*, 28: 28–49.

Booth, P., Chadburn, R., Haberman, S., James, D., Khorasanee, Z., Plumb, R. H., and Rickayzen, B. (2005). *Modern Actuarial Theory and Practice*, 2nd edn. Boca Raton, Florida: Chapman & Hall/CRC.

Borella, M., Fornero, E., and Ponzetto, G. (2004). 'The Market for Annuities in Italy: Reality or Chimera?', Chapter 11 in E. Fornero and E. Luciano (eds.), *Developing an Annuities Market in Europe*. Cheltenham: Edward Elgar.

Borsch, K. (1962). 'Equilibrium in a Reinsurance Market', *Econometrica*, 30: 424–44.

Brown, J. R. (1999). 'Are the Elderly Really Over-annuitized? New Evidence on Life Insurance and Bequests', NBER, Working Paper No. 7193.

——(2001). 'Private Pensions, Mortality Risk, and the Decision to Annuitize', *Journal of Public Economics*, 82(1): 29–62.

——and Finkelstein, A. (2007). 'Why is the Market for Long-Term Care Insurance so Small?', *Journal of Public Economics*, 91: 1967–91.

——and Poterba, J. M. (2006). 'Household Ownership of Variable Annuities', National Bureau of Economic Research, Working Paper 11964.

——Mitchell, O. S., Poterba, J. M., and Warshawsky, M. J. (2001). *The Role of Annuity Markets in Financing Retirement*. Cambridge: MIT Press.

Brugiavini, A. (1993). 'Uncertainty Resolution and the Timing of Annuity Purchases', *Journal of Public Economics*, 50(1): 31–62.

——and Galasso, V. (2004). 'The Social Security Reform Process in Italy: Where Do We Stand?', *Journal of Pension Economics and Finance*, 3: 165–95.

Bütler, M. (2004). 'Mandated Annuities in Switzerland', Chapter 10 in E. Fornero and E. Luciano (eds.), *Developing an Annuities Market in Europe*. Cheltenham: Edward Elgar.

——and Ruesch, M. (2007). 'Annuities in Switzerland', World Bank Policy Research Working Paper 4438.

——and Teppa, F. (2005). 'Should You Take a Lump-Sum or Annuitize? Results from Swiss Pension Funds', Working Paper.

Byrne, A., Blake, D., Cairns, A., and Dowd, K. (2007). 'Default Funds in U.K. Defined-Contribution Plans', *Financial Analysts Journal*, 63(4): 40–51.

Cairns, A. J. G., Blake, D., and Dowd, K. (2006). 'A Two-factor Model for Stochastic Mortality with Parameter Uncertainty: Theory and Calibration', Cass Business School: Pensions Institute Discussion Paper 06-11.

——————Coughlan, G. D., Epstein, D., Ong, A., and Balevich, I. (2007). 'A Quantitative Comparison of Stochastic Mortality Models Using Data from England & Wales and the United States', Cass Business School: Pensions Institute Discussion Paper 07-01.

Callund, J. (1999). 'Annuities in Latin America', World Bank, Santiago, Chile, Working Paper.

Cannon, E. and Tonks, I. (2004*a*). 'UK Annuity Rates, Money's Worth and Pension Replacement Ratios 1957–2002', *The Geneva Papers on Risk and Insurance*, 29(3): 394–416.

——— (2004*b*). 'UK Annuity Price Series 1957 to 2002', *Financial History Review*, 11(2): 165–96.

——— (2006). *Survey of Annuity Pricing*, DWP Research Report 318.

Cardinale, M. and Orszag, J. M. (2002). 'Paying Out Private Pensions in Latin America: A Review of Latin American Annuities Markets', *Watson Wyatt Technical Paper* 2002-RU14, December.

—— Findlater, A., and Orszag, J. M. (2002). 'Paying Out Pensions: A Review of International Annuities Markets', (Watson Wyatt).

Carroll, C. D. and Kimball, M. S. (1996). 'On the Concavity of the Consumption Function', *Econometrica*, 64(4): 981–92.

Chen, Y.-P. (2003). 'Funding Long-term Care', *Journal of Aging and Health*, 15(1): 15–44.

Chiappori, P. A., Jullien, B., and Salanie, F. (2002). 'Asymmetric Information in Insurance: Some Testable Implications', mimeo, University of Chicago.

Clark, G. (1999). *Betting on Lives*. Manchester: Manchester University Press.

Clark, G. L. and Monk, A. H. (2006). 'The "Crisis" in Defined Benefit Corporate Pension Liabilities Part I: Scope of the Problem', *Pensions*, 12(1): 43–54.

CMI (1993). 'Inter Office Comparisons', *Continuous Mortality Investigation Report*, 13: 117–21.

—— (2002). 'An Interim Basis for Adjusting the "92" Series Mortality Projections for Cohort Effects', Continuous Mortality Investigation Working Paper No. 1.

—— (2006*a*). 'Stochastic Projection Methodologies: Further Progress and P-Spline Model Features, Example Results and Implication', Continuous Mortality Investigation Working Paper No. 20.

—— (2006*b*). 'The Graduation of the CMI 1999–2002 Mortality Experience: Final "00" Series Mortality Tables', Continuous Mortality Investigation Working Papers Nos. 21 and 22.

Cox, S. H. and Lin, Y. (2007). 'Natural Hedging of Life Insurance and Annuity Mortality Risks', *North American Actuarial Journal*, 11(3): 1–15.

—— Pedersen, H. W., and Fairchild, J. R. (2000). 'Economic Aspects of Securitization of Risk', *ASTIN Bulletin*, 30(1): 157–93.

CSFB (2007). 'Longevity Index', available at: www.csfb.com.

Currie, I. D. (2006). 'Smoothing and Forecasting Mortality Rates with P-Splines', Talk given at the Institute of Actuaries, June 2006.

Daunton, M. J. (1985). *Royal Mail: The Post Office since 1840*. London: The Athlone Press.

Davidoff, T., Brown, J. R., and Diamond, P. A. (2005). 'Annuities and Individual Welfare', *American Economic Review*, 95(5): 1573–90.

Davis, E. P. (1995). *Pension Funds, Retirement-Income Security, and Capital Markets: An International Perspective*. Oxford: Clarendon Press.

—— (2004). 'Issues in the Regulation of Annuities Markets,' Chapter 3 in E. Fornero and E. Luciano (eds.), *Developing an Annuity Market in Europe*. Cheltenham: Edward Elgar.

—— and Steil, B. (2001). *Institutional Investors*. MIT Press.

Daykin, C. D. (2001). 'Reserving for Annuities', Paper presented to the International Social Security Association (ISSA) Seminar for Social Security Actuaries and Statisticians, Montevideo.

—— (2004). 'Annuities and Alternative ways of Providing Retirement Income', Presented to the PBSS Seminar Part of the IACA, PBSS & IAAust Colloquium, 31 October–5 November 2004.

Debt Management Office (2005). 'DMO Annual Review 2004/05', (July).

Department for Social Security (1998). *A New Contract for Welfare: Partnership in Pensions*, Cm. 4179, (The Stationery Office).

Department for Work and Pensions (2002). *Simplicity, Security and Choice: Working and Saving for Retirement*, Cm. 5677, (The Stationery Office).

—— (2006). *Personal Accounts: A New Way to Save*, Cm. 6975, (The Stationery Office).

—— and HMRC (2002). 'Modernising Annuities: A Consultative Document', (The Stationery Office).

Diamond, P. A. (1977). 'A Framework for Social Security Analysis', *Journal of Public Economics*, 8: 275–98.

Dickson, P. G. M. (1967). *The Financial Revolution in England: A Study in the Development of Public Credit, 1688–1756*. London: Macmillan.

Dilnot, A. and Johnson, P. (1993). *The Taxation of Private Pensions*. London: IFS.

Dimson, E., Marsh, P., and Staunton, M. (2002). *Triumph of the Optimists*. Princeton University Press.

Dowd, K. (2003). 'Survivor Bonds: A Comment on Blake and Burrows', *Journal of Risk and Insurance*, 70(2): 339–48.

—— Blake, D., and Cairns, A. J. G. (2007). 'Facing up to the Uncertainty of Life: The Longevity fan Charts', Cass Business School: Pensions Institute Discussion Paper 07-03.

Drinkwater, M. and Sondergeld, E. T. (2004). 'Perceptions of Mortality Risk: Implications for Annuities', in O. P. Mitchell and S. P. Utkus (eds.), *Pension Design and Structure: New Lessons from Behavioral Finance*. Oxford: Oxford University Press.

Dyson, E. J. W. (1969). *The History of Individual Annuity Contracts*. Insurance Institute of London.

Eckstein, Z., Eichenbaum, M. S., and Peled, D. (1985). 'Uncertain Lifetimes and the Welfare Enhancing Properties of Annuity Markets and Social Security', *Journal of Public Economics*, 26: 303–26.

Economic Policy Committee (2001). 'The Budgetary Challenge Posed by Ageing Populations', *European Economy Reports and Studies*, No. 4, European

Commission, Directorate General for Economic and Financial Affairs, available at: http://europa.eu.int/comm/economy_finance/publications/european_economy/2001/eers0401_en.pdf.

——and the European Commission (DG ECFIN) (2006). 'The Impact of Ageing on Public Expenditure: Projections for the EU25 Member States on Pensions, Health Care, Long-term care, Education and Unemployment Transfers (2004–2050)', Special Report 1/2006.

Einav, L., Finkelstein, A., and Schrimpf, P. (2007). 'The Welfare Cost of Asymmetric Information: Evidence from the UK Annuity Market', NBER Working Paper No. 13228.

Epstein, L. G. and Zin, S. E. (1989). 'Substitution, Risk Aversion, and the Temporal Behavior of Consumption and Asset Returns: A Theoretical Framework', *Econometrica*, 57(4): 937–69.

European Commission (2004). *Directive of the European Parliament and of the Council on the Implementation of the Principle of Equal Opportunities and Equal Treatment of Men and Women in Matters of Employment and Occupation*.

Exley, C. J., Mehta, S. J. B., and Smith, A. D. (1997). 'The Financial Theory of Defined Benefit Pension Schemes', *British Actuarial Journal*, 3: 835–938.

Financial Services Authority (2000). 'Endowment Mortgage Complaints', FSA Consultation Paper 75, November.

——(2002). 'FSA on Track to Bring the Pensions Mis-selling Review to a Close', FSA Press Release FSA/PN/010/2002 January.

——(2003a). 'Purchasing Annuities and an Examination of the Impact of the Open Market Option', *Consumer Research*, 22.

——(2003b). 'Enhanced Capital Requirements and Individual Capital Assessments for Life Insurers', FSA Consultation Paper 195, August.

——(2004). *FSA Guide to Annuities and Income Withdrawal*. London: FSA.

——(2005). *Insurance Sector Briefing: Delivering the Tiner Insurance Reforms*. London: FSA.

——(2006). *Mortgage Endowments: Delivering Higher Standards*. London: FSA.

Finkelstein, A. and Poterba, J. M. (2002). 'Selection Effects in the United Kingdom Individual Annuities Market', *Economic Journal*, 112(476): 28–50.

————(2004). 'Adverse Selection in Insurance Markets: Policyholder Evidence from the U.K. Annuity Market', *Journal of Political Economy*, 112(1): 183–208.

————(2006). 'Testing for Adverse Selection with "Unused Observables"', NBER Working Paper No. 12112.

Fong, W. F. (2002). 'On the Cost of Adverse Selection in Individual Annuity Markets: Evidence from Singapore', *Journal of Risk and Insurance*, 69(2): 193–207.

Forfar, D. O., McCutcheon, J. J., and Wilkie, A. D. (1988). 'On Graduation by Mathematical Formula', *Journal of the Institute of Actuaries*, 115: 1–149.

Fornero, E. and Luciano, E. (eds.) (2004). *Developing an Annuity Market in Europe*. Cheltenham: Edward Elgar.

Fornero, E. and Piatti, L. (2007). 'La riforma? Successo ma soltanto a metà', cerp.unito.it.

Franks, J., Mayer, C., and da Silva, L. C. (2003). *Asset Management and Investor Protection: An International Analysis.* Oxford: Oxford University Press.

Franzoni, F. and Marin, J. M. (2006). 'Pension Plan Funding and Stock Market Efficiency', *Journal of Finance*, 61(2): 921–56.

Friedman, B. M. and Warshawsky, M. J. (1988). 'Annuity Prices and Saving Behaviour in the United States', in Z. Bodie, J. Shoven, and D. Wise (eds.), *Pensions in the US Economy.* Chicago University Press.

—————(1990). 'The Cost of Annuities: Implications for Saving Behaviour and Bequests', *Quarterly Journal of Economics*, 105(1): 135–54.

Gardner, J. and Wadsworth, M. (2004). *Who Would Buy an Annuity?* Watson-Wyatt Technical Report.

Gramlich, E. (1996). 'Different Approaches for Dealing with Social Security', *Journal of Economic Perspectives*, 10(3): 55–66.

Greenwood, M. (1940). 'A Statistical Mare's Nest?', *Journal of the Royal Statistical Society*, 103(2): 246–8.

Guiso, L. and Paiella, M. (2001). *Risk Aversion, Wealth and Background Risk.* CEPR Discussion Paper no. 2728. London: Centre for Economic Policy Research.

Haberman, S. and Sibbett, T. A. (eds.) (1995). *The History of Actuarial Science.* London: William Pickering.

Halek, M. and Eisenhauer, J. G. (2001). 'Demography of Risk Aversion', *The Journal of Risk and Insurance*, 68(1): 1–24.

Hannah, L. (1986). *Inventing Retirement.* Cambridge: Cambridge University Press.

Harrington, S. E. (2004). 'Tort Liability, Insurance Rates, and the Insurance Cycle', *Brookings-Wharton Papers on Financial Services*, 97–138.

Heywood, G. (1985). 'Edmond Halley: Astronomer and Actuary', *Journal of the Institute of Actuaries*, 112: 279–301.

HM Treasury (2006). *The Annuities Market*, December. London: HMSO.

Holmans, A., Karley, N. K., and Whitehead, C. (2003). 'The Mortgage Backed Securities Market in the UK: Overview and Prospects', *Council of Mortgage Lenders Research.* London.

Holmer, M. R. (2003). 'Simulation Analysis of the Decision to Annuitize Pension Balances', *Policy Simulation Group*, www.polsim.com.

Holzmann, R. and Hinz, R. (2005). *Old-Age Income Support in the 21st Century.* World Bank.

Howard, R. C. W. (2006). *Canadian Annuitant Mortality Table.* (CIP 2005).

Hurd, M. D. (1989). 'Mortality Risk and Bequests', *Econometrica*, 57(4): 779–813.

——(1987). 'Savings of the Elderly and Desired Bequests', *American Economic Review*, 77(3): 298–312.

Hurd, M. and Rohwedder, S. (2005). 'The Retirement-Consumption Puzzle: Anticipated and Actual Declines in Spending at Retirement', Rand Working Paper, WR-242.

Inkmann, J., Lopes, P., and Michaelides, A. (2007). 'How Deep Is the Annuity Market Participation Puzzle?', FMG Discussion Paper 593 (UBS Paper 044), July.

Institute of Actuaries (1949). 'International Actuarial Notation', *Journal of the Institute of Actuaries*, 75: 121–9.

James, E. (1997). 'New Systems for Old Age Security', World Bank Report, November 1997.

——and Song, X. (2001). 'Annuity Markets Around the World: Money's Worth and Risk Intermediation', CeRP Working Paper 16/01.

——and Vittas, D. (2000). 'Annuity Markets in Comparative Perspective: Do Consumers Get Their Money's Worth?', World Bank Policy Research Working Paper No. 2493.

James, K. R. (2000). 'The Price of Retail Investing in the UK', FSA Occasional Paper, 6.

James, M. (1947). *The Metropolitan Life: A Study in Business Growth*. New York: Viking Press.

Jianakoplos, N. A. and Bernasek, A. (1998). 'Are Women More Risk Averse?', *Economic Enquiry*, 36: 620–30.

Johnson, P. (1985). *Saving and Spending: The Working-class Economy in Britain 1870–1939*. Oxford: Oxford University Press.

Johnstone, S. (2005). *Private Funding Mechanisms for Long-Term Care*. Joseph Rowntree Foundation.

Jordon, K. (2006). 'Prudential Regulation under the Financial Services and Markets Act 2000', Chapter 4 in A. Winckler (ed.), *A Practitioner's Guide to the FSA Handbook*, 4th edn. Surrey: City & Financial Publishing, 133–235.

JPMorgan (2007). 'LifeMetrics: A Toolkit for Measuring and Managing Longevity and Mortality Risks', available at: www.jpmorgan.com.

Kahneman, D. and Tversky, A. (1979). 'Prospect Theory: An Analysis of Decision Under Risk', *Econometrica*, 47(1): 263–91.

Kapur, S. and Orszag, M. (1999). 'A Portfolio Approach to Investment and Annuitization During Retirement', Working Paper. Birkbeck College, London.

Katz, E. (1979). 'A Note on Uncertain Lifetimes', *Journal of Political Economy*, 87(1): 193–5.

Kim, H. T. and Sharp, K. P. (1999). 'Annuities in Canada', Institute of Insurance and Pension Research, University of Waterloo Working Paper, 99-13.

King, M. (2004). 'What Fates Impose: Facing Up to Uncertainty', Paper presented to The British Academy, December.

Knox, D. M. (2000). 'The Australian Annuity Market', World Bank Policy Research, Working Paper No. 2495.

Kocherlakota, N. (1996). 'The Equity Premium: It's Still a Puzzle', *Journal of Economic Literature*, 34(1): 42–71.

Kotlikoff, L. and Spivak, A. (1981). 'The Family as an Incomplete Annuities Market', *Journal of Political Economy*, 89(2): 372–91.

Laitner, J. and Juster, F. T. (1996). 'New Evidence on Altruism: A Study of TIAA-CREF Retirees', *American Economic Review*, 86(4): 893–908.

Lawson, N. (1992). *The View from No.11: Memoirs of a Tory Radical*. London: Bantam Press.

Lee, R. D. and Carter, L. R. (1992). 'Modeling and Forecasting U.S. Mortality', *Journal of the American Statistical Association*, 87: 659–75.

Lewin, C. G. (2003). *Pensions and Insurance before 1800*. East Linton: Tuckwell Press.

LIMRA (2006). 'Substandard Annuities', LIMRA International in collaboration with the Society of Actuaries and Ernst & Young.

Lin, Y. and Cox, S. (2005). 'Securitisation of Mortality Risks in Life Annuities', *Journal of Risk and Insurance*, 72(2): 227–52.

Loh, M. and Gosden, M. (2007). 'Variable Annuities', *The Actuary*, June 24–6.

Lopes, P. (2003). 'Are Annuities Value for Money? Who Can Afford Them?', Financial Markets Group Discussion Paper no. 473.

—— and Michaelides, A. (2005). 'Rare Events and Annuity Market Participation', *Finance Research Letters*, 4: 82–91.

Mays (1979). 'Ulpian's Table', Actuarial Research Clearing House, 2.

McCarthy, D. and Mitchell, O. S. (2004). 'Annuities for an Ageing World', in Chapter 2 E. Fornero and E. Luciano (eds.), *Developing an Annuity Market in Europe*. Edward Elgar.

—— and Neuberger, A. (2003). *Pensions Policy: Evidence on Aspects of Savings Behaviour and Capital Markets*. London: Centre for Economic Policy Research.

MacDonald, A. S. (ed.) (1997). *The Second Actuarial Study of Mortality in Europe, Groupe Consultatif des Associations d'Actuaires des Pays Communautés Européenes*. Oxford.

MacKenzie, G. A. (2006). *Annuity Markets and Pensions Reform*. Cambridge: Cambridge University Press.

Merton, R. C. (1983). 'On Consumption-indexed Public Pension Plans', in Z. Bodie and J. Shoven (eds.), *Financial Aspects of the US Pension Plan System*. Chicago: University of Chicago Press.

Miles, D. and Timmerman, A. (1999). 'Costing Pension Reform: Risk Sharing and Transition Costs in the Reform of Pension Systems in Europe', *Economic Policy*, 14(29): 253–86.

Milevsky, M. R. (1998). 'Optimal Asset Allocation Towards the end of the Life Cycle: To Annuitise or not to Annuitise?', *Journal of Risk and Insurance*, 65(3): 401–26.

—— and Young, V. (2002). 'Optimal Asset Allocation and the Real Option to Delay Annuitization: It's Not Now-or-Never', Individual Finance and Insurance Decisions Centre Working Paper, www.ifid.ca.

Mitchell, C. and Mitchell, C. (2004). 'Wordsworth and the Old Men', *Journal of Legal History*, 25(1): 31–52.

Mitchell, O. S. (2002). 'Developments in Decumulation: The Role of Annuity Products in Financing Retirement', in A. Auerbach and H. Herman (eds.), *Ageing Financial Markets and Monetary Policy*. Berlin: Springer-Verlag, 97–125.

—— and McCarthy, D. (2002). 'Estimating International Adverse Selection in Annuities', *North American Actuarial Journal*, 10(3): 38–54.

———— (2004). 'Annuities for an Ageing World', in Chapter 1 E. Fornero and E. Luciano (eds.), *Developing an Annuity Market in Europe* Cheltenham: Edward Elgar.

—— and Utkus, S. P. (eds.) (2004). *Pension Design and Structure: New Lessons from Behavioral Finance*. Oxford: Oxford University Press.

—— Poterba, J. M., Warshawsky, M. J., and Brown, J. R. (1999). 'New Evidence on the Money's Worth of Individual Annuities', *American Economic Review*, 89(5): 1299–1318. This article is reprinted in Brown et al. (2001).

Moffet, D. (1978). 'A Note on the Yaari Life Cycle Model', *Review of Economic Studies*, 45(2): 385–8.

Morley, J. (1903). *The Life of William Ewart Gladstone. 2, 1859–1880*. London: Macmillan.

Morris, D. (2004). 'Morris Review of the Actuarial Profession: Interim Assessment', HM Treasury, HMSO.

—— (2005). 'Morris Review of the Actuarial Profession: Final Report', HM Treasury, HMSO.

Muir, M. and Waller, R. (2003). 'Twin Peaks: The Enhanced Capital Requirement for Realistic Basis Life Firms', Paper presented to Staple Inn Actuarial Society.

Murphy, R. D. (1939). *Sales of Annuities by Governments*. New York: Association of Life Insurance Presidents.

Murtaugh, C. M., Spillman, B. C., and Warshawsky, C. M. (2001). 'In Sickness and in Health: An Annuity Approach to Financing Long-Term Care and Retirement Income', *The Journal of Risk and Insurance*, 68(2): 225–53.

Murthi, M., Orszag, J. M., and Orszag, P. R. (1999). 'The Value for Money of Annuities in the UK: Theory, Experience and Policy', Birkbeck College, London. Discussion Paper.

Myners, P. (2001). 'Institutional Investment in the United Kingdom: A Review', HM Treasury, HMSO.

Official Journal of the European Communities (2002). *Directive 2002/83/EC of the European Parliament and of the Council of 5 November 2002 concerning life assurance*, Vol. L 345/1, 19 December.

OFWAT/OFGEM (2006). 'Financing Networks: A Discussion Paper', available from http://www.ofwat.gov.uk.

Oliver, Wyman and Company (2001). 'The Future of Regulation of UK Savings and Investment: Targeting the Savings Gap', A Study Commissioned by the Association of British Insurers.

Palacios, R. and Pallares-Miralles, M. (2000). 'The Social Protection Advisory Service', World Bank.

Palme, M., Soderlind, P., and Sunden, A. (2007). 'How Do Individual Accounts Work in the Swedish Pension System?', *Journal of the European Economic Association*, 5(2–3): 636–46.

Palmon, O. and Spivak, A. (2007). 'Adverse Selection and the Market for Annuities', *The Geneva Risk and Insurance Review*, 32(1): 37–59.

Pelzman, J. and Rousslang, D. (1982). 'A Note on Uncertain Lifetimes: A comment', *Journal of Political Economy*, 90(1): 181–3.

Pemberton, H. (2006). 'Politics and Pensions in Post-war Britain', in H. Pemberton, P. Thane, and N. Whiteside (eds.), *Britain's Pension Crisis: History and Policy*. Oxford: Oxford University Press.

Penrose, L. (2004). *Report of the Equitable Life Inquiry*. London: HMSO.

The Pensions Commission (2004). *Pensions: Challenges and Choices: The First Report of the Pensions Commission*. London: HMSO.

—— (2005). *A New Pension Settlement for the Twenty-First Century: The Second Report of the Pensions Commission*. London: HMSO.

—— (2006). *Implementing an Integrated Package of Pension Reforms: The Final Report of the Pensions Commission*. London: HMSO.

Pension Research Forum (2004). 'Effective Member Engagement—Does One Size Fit All?', Watson Wyatt.

Perry, C. R. (1992). *The Victorian Post Office*. The Royal Historical Society.

Plott, C. R. and Zeiler, K. (2005). 'The Willingness to Pay–Willingness to Accept Gap, the "Endowment Effect," Subject Misconceptions, and Experimental Procedures for Eliciting Valuations', *American Economic Review*, 95(3): 530–45.

Poitras, G. (1996). 'From Commercial Arithmetic to Life Annuities: The Early History of Financial Economics, 1478–1776'. mimeo, Simon Fraser University.

Poterba, J. M. (1994). *International Comparisons of Household Saving*. Chicago: University of Chicago Press.

—— (1997). The History of Annuities in the United States, National Bureau of Economic Research, Working Paper 6001.

—— (2001a). 'A Brief History of Annuity Markets' in Brown et al. (2001).

—— (2001b). 'Annuity Markets and Retirement Security', *Fiscal Studies*, 22(3): 249–70.

—— (2005). 'Annuities in Early Modern Europe', in W. N. Goetzmann and K. G. Rouwenhorst (eds.), *The Origins of Value: The Financial Innovations That Created Modern Capital Markets*. Oxford: Oxford University Press.

Powell, M. and Ansic, D. (1997). 'Gender Differences in Risk Behavior in Financial Decision-Making: An Experimental Analysis', *Journal of Economic Psychology*, 18(6): 605–28.

Powers, M. R. and Shubik, M. (2001). 'Toward a Theory of Reinsurance and Retrocession', *Insurance: Mathematics and Economics*, 29(2): 271–90.

—— and Shubik, M. (2005). 'A Note on a "Square-Root Rule" for Reinsurance', Cowles Foundation Discussion Paper, No. 1521, June.

Punter Southall (2006). 'Developments in the Buy-out Market', *Briefing Note*, May (www.puntersouthall.com/UK/tech_bulletins/Brief_Buyout.pdf).

Rabin, M. (1998). 'Psychology and Economics', *Journal of Economic Literature*, 36(1): 11–46.

Reno, V., Graetz, M., Apfel, K., Lavery, J., and Hill, C. (eds.) (2005). *Uncharted Waters: Paying Benefits from Individual Accounts in Federal Retirement Policy, Study Panel Final Report*. Washington, DC: National Academy of Social Insurance.

Renshaw, A. E. and Haberman, S. (2006). 'A Cohort-based Extension to the Lee-Carter Model for Mortality Reduction Factors', *Insurance: Mathematics and Economics*, 38: 556–70.

Riley, W. B., Jr., and Chow, K. V. (1992). 'Asset Allocation and Individual Risk Aversion', *Financial Analysts Journal*, 48(6): 32–7.

Rocha, R. and Thorburn, C. (2006). *Developing Annuity Markets: The Experience of Chile*. The World Bank.

Rogers, J. E. T. (1866). *A History of Agriculture and Prices in England*, Vol. 1. Oxford: Clarendon Press.

Rowlingson, K. and McKay, S. (2005). *Attitudes to Inheritance in Britain*, Joseph Rowntree Foundation (The Policy Press).

Rubinstein, A. (2003). ' "Economics and Psychology"? The Case of Hyperbolic Discounting', *International Economic Review*, 44(4): 1207–16.

——(2006). 'Comments on Behavioral Economics', in R. Blundell, W. K. Newey, and T. Persson (eds.), *Advances in Economic Theory (2005 World Congress of the Econometric Society)*, Vol. 2. Cambridge: Cambridge University Press, 246–54.

Samuelson, P. A. (1969). 'Lifetime Portfolio Selection by Dynamic Stochastic Programming', *Review of Economics and Statistics*, 51: 239–43.

——(1989). 'The Judgment of Economic Science on Rational Portfolio Management: Indexing, Timing, and Long-Horizon Effects', *The Journal of Portfolio Management*, 16: 4–12.

Sandler, R. (2002). '*Medium and Long-Term Retail Savings in the UK: A Review*'. HM Treasury.

Sargent, T. J. and Velde, F. R. (2002). *The Big Problem of Small Change*. Princeton: Princeton University Press.

Schnabel, R. (2004). 'Private Annuities and Public Pensions in Germany', Chapter 9 in E. Fornero and E. Luciano (eds.), *Developing an Annuities Market in Europe*. Cheltenham: Edward Elgar.

Schubert, R., Brown, M., Gysler, M., and Brachinger, H. W. (1999). 'Financial Decision-Making: Are Women Really More Risk Averse?', *American Economic Review, Papers and Proceedings*, 89(2): 381–5.

Schwartz, B. (2004). *The Paradox of Choice: Why More Is Less*. New York: Harper Collins Publishers, Inc.

Sheshinski, E. (2007). 'Optimum and Risk-Class Pricing of Annuities', *Economic Journal*, 117(516): 240–51.

Bibliography

Sheshinski, E. (2008). *The Economic Theory of Annuities*. Princeton: Princeton University Press.

Spillman, B. C., Murtaugh, C. M., and Warshawsky, M. J. (2003). 'Policy Implications of an Annuity Approach to Integrating Long-Term Care Financing and Retirement Income', *Journal of Aging and Health*, 15(1): 45–73.

Spivak, A. (1999). 'Pension Reform in Israel', Ben Gurion University Working Paper.

Stamhuis, I. H. (1988). 'The Mathematician Rehuel Lobatto Advocates Life Insurances in the Netherlands in the Period 1830–1860', *Annals of Science*, 45: 619–41.

Stark, J. (2002). 'Annuities: The Consumer Experience', ABI Research Report.

—— (2003). 'The Future of the Pension Annuity Market—Summary Report' (ABI, London). Summary of Watson Wyatt LLC, 'Pension Annuities; Market Dynamics and Implications for Supply'.

Stewart, F. (2007). 'Policy Issues for Developing Annuities Markets', OECD Working Paper on Insurance and Private Pensions, No. 2.

Sundén, A. (2006). 'The Swedish Experience with Pension Reform', *Oxford Review of Economic Policy*, 22(1): 133–48.

Tonks, I. (2006). 'Pension Fund Management and Investment Performance', Chapter 23 in G. L. Clark, A. H. Munnell, and J. M. Orszag (eds.), *Oxford Handbook of Pensions and Retirement Income*. Oxford: Oxford University Press.

Tversky, A. and Kahneman, D. (1992). 'Advances in Prospect Theory: Cumulative Representation of Uncertainty', *Journal of Risk and Uncertainty*, 5(1): 297–323.

US Congressional Budget Office (2006). 'Measures of the US Government's Fiscal Position under Current Law', CBO Paper, June.

Visco, I. (2005). 'Ageing and Pension System Reform: Implications for Financial Markets and Economic Policies', Report for Deputies of the Group of Ten.

Von Gaudecker, H. and Weber, C. (2004). 'Surprises in a Growing Market Niche: Evaluation of the German Private Life Annuities Market', *The Geneva Papers on Risk and Insurance*, 29(3): 394–416.

Wadsworth, M. (2005). *The Pension Annuity Market*. Association of British Insurers.

—— Findlater, A., and Boardman, T. (2001). 'Reinventing Annuities', Staple Inn Actuarial Society.

Walker, E. (2006). 'Annuity Markets in Chile: Competition, Regulation and Myopia?', World Bank Policy Research Working Paper 3972.

Walliser, J. (2000). 'Adverse Selection in the Annuities Market and the Impact of Privatizing Social Security', *Scandinavian Journal of Economics*, 102(3): 373–93.

Warshawsky, M. J. (1988). 'Private Annuity Markets in the United States: 1919–1984', *Journal of Risk and Insurance*, 55(3): 518–28. This article is reprinted in Brown et al. (2001).

Watson-Wyatt (2003). *Pension Annuities—Market Dynamics and Implications for Supply*. Association of British Insurers.

Webb, D. C. (2006). 'Long-term Care Insurance, Annuities and Asymmetric Information: The Case for Bundling Contracts', FMG Discussion Paper 530 (UBS Paper 034).

Weir, D. R. (1989). 'Tontines, Public Finance, and Revolution in France and England, 1688–1789', *Journal of Economic History*, 49(1): 95–124.

Wilhelm, M. (1996). 'Bequest Behavior and the Effect of Heirs' Earnings: Testing the Altruistic Model of Bequests', *American Economic Review*, 86: 874–92.

Willets, R. (1999). 'Mortality in the Next Millennium', Paper presented to the Staple Inn Actuarial Society.

Wilmoth, J. R. and Horiuchi, S. (1999). 'Rectangularization Revisited: Variability of Age at Death within Human Populations', *Demography*, 36(4): 475–95.

Wilson, A. and Levy, H. (1937). *Industrial Assurance: An Historical and Critical Study.* Oxford: Oxford University Press.

——and McKay, G. S. (1941). *Old Age Pensions: An Historical and Critical Study.* Oxford: Oxford University Press.

Wong-Fupuy, C. and Haberman, S. (2004). 'Projecting Mortality Trends: Recent Developments in the United Kingdom and the United States', *North American Actuarial Journal*, 8: 56–83.

Wood, M. (2006). 'An Introduction to the Buy out Market', Lecture at CASS Business School, September 13.

World Bank (1994). *Averting the Old Age Crisis: Policies to Protect the Old and Promote Growth.* Washington, DC: World Bank and Oxford University Press.

Yaari, M. (1965). 'Uncertain Lifetime, Life Assurance, and the Theory of the Consumer', *Review of Economic Studies*, 32(2): 137–50.

Young, J. (2004). *A Practitioner's Guide to the FSA Regulation of Insurance*, 2nd edn. Surrey: City & Financial Publishing.

Zeldes, S. P. (1989). 'Optimal Consumption with Stochastic Income: Deviations from Certainty Equivalence', *Quarterly Journal of Economics*, 104(2): 274–98.

Index

Figures and tables are indexed in bold e.g. **f**, **t**—more than one figure or table on the page is indexed in small letters e.g. 104**f(a)**.

Abel, A. B. 32, 196, 197, 197**f**, 198, 198**f**
accounting regulations 27
accumulation phase 2, 14, 35, 64, 98
   Chile 101
   Germany 106
   USA 115
actuarial life tables 47
actuarial methodology 77, 150–1, 236
actuarial notation 70–6, 212
actuarial profession 17, 67
A-Day 60–1, 64
Adda, J. 87
Administradoras de Fondos de Pensiones
   (AFPs) 101, 103, 104**f(a)**, 105
adverse selection 191
   annuity markets 192–4, 194**f**, 195–8,
     198**f**, 199–200, 207, 210, 214–17,
     219
   and welfare payments 199**f**
AEW, *see* Annuity Equivalent Wealth
age 28–9, 36, 48, 50
   cohorts 80, 82, 85–6, 88, 92
   pension 60, 100
ageing populations 1, 9, 14, 58–9
   Singapore 109
agents:
   of consumption 165
   preferences (model) 152, 154
     change in 189–90
   prudence 156
   irrationality 163
   rationality 161–2
   risk aversion 156, 159–60, 173
   utility, and life expectancy 157
Ainslie, R. 25
Akerlof, G. A. 181
allocated pensions (Australia) 98, 99
Alter, G. 50
Alternatively Secured Income (ASI) 61

Ameriks, J. 187
Amicable Society 48, 49, 50
Amounts (IMA) 119, 127**t(a)**, 129
Anderson, N. 75
Angeletos, G.-M. 161, 162, 163
annual bonuses 25, 66
annuitants 134, 207, 210, 246
   compulsory 212, 219
   demand curve 150
   life expectancy 32, 122, 155, 200, 216
   life tables 133, 211
   money's worth 117, 121, 214–15
   mortality 49, 51, 79, 80, 81**t**, 120, 121,
     198, 218–19, 249, 255, 257, 263
   payments made to 47, 76, 105, 253
   UK 77, 137, 228, 234, 260
   voluntary 54, 79, 212, 219
annuities 17, 24, 25, 43, 131, 226
   Australia 135, 136**t(a)**, 136
   Chile 102, 134, 134**f**
   costs of running 17, 95, 133
   Italy 108
   options 206**f**
   payments 23, 142, 186, 206**t**, 216, 220,
     229, 233, 246, 248, 251, 253, 257
   pricing 21**t**–3**t**, 32–6, 49, 74, 129, 191,
     192, 196, 219, 228
     Church 45–6; Roman 43–4, 44**t**
   products 19–27, 46, 95, 98, 102, 135,
     144, 148, 150, 166, 207–8, 216,
     234
   quotes 39, 39**f**
   risks 4, 129, 249–50
   Singapore 110, 110**t**, 136, 136**t(b)**, 137
   Switzerland 135, 135**f**
   UK 16–17, 20, 43, 54, 64, 65, 78–9,
     118–22, 229
     increased demand for 14–15, 15**t**, 16,
      16**f**; prices 27

USA 133**t**
valuation 76, 91
see also individual types of annuities
annuitization 2, 4, 5, 14, 15, 17, 35, 62, 79,
140, 142**f**, 145, 145**f**, 146**f**, 147, 150,
160, 169, 180, 182, 190–1, 195, 203,
204, 207, 221, 222
age 186–7
at 75 187
Chile 103
decision models 188**t**
deferring 184–9
Germany 106
with habitual preferences 175**t**
Italy 108
mandatory 218
pre-existing pension 183**f**
purchasing annuities 148–50
risk neutrality 159**f**
Sweden 112
Switzerland 114
UK 26, 58, 61, 221–2
Middle Ages 45; age 75 61
USA 223
see also wealth
annuity contracts 194, 217, 246
Abel–Walliser model 197**f**
funding of 248
UK 218, 228
annuity demands 152, 203**t**, 219, 222,
223–4
UK 226, 245
Annuity Equivalent Wealth (AEW) 146,
168, 172, 172**t**, 222, 223
annuity liabilities 241, 250
annuity markets 145**f**
annuity models 157
annuity providers 95, 130, 194, 195, 197,
226, 228, 233, 235, 250**f**, 251, 252–4,
256
Chile 104**f(a)**, 104**f(b)**
longevity risks 253
net cash flows 254**f(b)**
regulations 234–41
UK 228–34, 246, 247**f**
annuity purchases 140–1, 180, 182, 184,
198, 199, 200, 210, 214
deferral of 185
USA 205
annuity puzzle 140, 163, 180, 223
annuity rates 31–6, 39–40, 40**f(a)**, 46, 62,
66, 91, 95–6, 103, 104, 105, 105**f**,
130–1, 141–2, 195, 197, 215, 220
by age and gender 28, 28**f**

equilibrium 197–8
for men 37**f**, 92
aged 65 29**f**, 33**f**
Roman 44**t**
for women 38**f**
annuity regulations (UK) 235–41
Ansic, D. 187
Apfel, K. 115
arbitrage 257
ASI, *see* Alternatively Secured Income
asset-liability management 246
assets:
alternative 184–9
and liabilities 241
under management 8**t**
portfolio 184–5
risky 76, 187–8
value of 31–2
Assheton, W. 48, 49
Association of British Insurers 137
asymmetric information 192, 217, 234
Attanasio, O. P. 87, 182, 210
Australia 95–6, 96**f**, 98–9, 99**t**, 100**t**, 135–6,
136**t(a)**, 219, 233–4
Automatic Balancing Mechanism (ABM) 111
Aviva 229
AXA 20, 23, 24

back-loaded annuities 216, 217
B & CE Insurance 36
Backus, D. 161, 162
balance sheets 27, 239, 246
removal of debt 252
Balevich, I. 90
Ballotta, L. 66
Bank of Amsterdam 47
Bank of England 47, 75
banking industry 235
Banks, J. 182
Barro, R. J. 160
Barsky, R. B. 187
Basel 2 235, 236
Basic State Pension (BSP) 57
Bateman, H. 98, 99
behaviour 200–8
Benartzi, S. 205
benefits, reduction in 13–14
Benjamin, B. 87
bequests 46, 113, 141, 187, 217, 218, 222,
224, 264
Bernasek, A. 187
Bernheim, D. D. 224
Blake, D. 89, 90, 91, 186, 187, 188, 218–19,
222, 224, 248, 249, 252, 256

BNP Paribas 249
Board of Trade returns (UK) 53
Boardman, T. 52
Bodie, Z. 4
bonds 18, 141, 143, 147, 169, 186, 246
  annuities 183, 184, 204
  assets 119, 242
    durations 242–3, 243**f**
  index-linked 245–6
  markets, perfect 148, 166
  products 17–18, 189, 226
  rates of return 40**f(b)**, 207
  wealth in 143–4, 174–5
  yields 39–40, 40**f(a)**, 243, 244**f(a)**,
    244**f(b)**
  see also conventional bonds; corporate
    bonds; government bonds
Booth, P. 228, 235
Borella, M. 107
Borsch, K. 250, 251
Brachinger, H. W. 187
Britain, *see* UK
British Retirement Society 87
Brown, J. R. 17, 27, 117, 119, 133, 163, 175,
  190, 203, 214, 222, 223, 224
Brown, M. 187
Brugiavini, A. 107, 192
budget constraints 174, 182, 183–4, 184**f**,
  199, 200
  equations 142–7, 166–7, 203
bulk buy out 15, 16, 27, 233, 261
Bütler, M. 112, 114, 135
Burrows, W. 248
Byrne, A. 187

Cairns, A. J. G. 89, 90, 91, 186, 187, 188,
  249, 252, 256
CALCE reserves 106
Callund, J. 219
Canada 77, 219
Canada Life 229
Cannon, E. 28, 28**f**, 29**f**, 31, 35, 65, 75, 118,
  119, 120, 121, 211, 214, 215, 228, 233
capital:
  adequacy assessments (ICA) 14, 100,
    235–6, 238, 239
  coverage of risk components 235
  raising 45
  repayment 26
  sum 204
  notional 111
capital resources requirements (CRR) 236–7,
  237**f**, 238, 238**f**, 239–40, 240**f**
Cardinale, M. 97, 98, 233, 234

Carroll, C. D. 156
Cater, L. R. 84, 95, 91
cash flow 255, 256
catastrophe bonds 252
Central Provident Fund (CPF) 109–10, 110**t**
Chadburn, R. 228, 235
Chen, Y.-P. 204
Chiappori, P. A. 217
Chile 101, 101**f**, 102, 102**f**, 103–5, 105**f**,
  106, 134, 134**t**
Chow, K. V. 187
church accounts (UK) 44–5
Church of Scotland, reversionary
  annuities 49, 50–1
Clark, G. 47, 48, 49, 50, 51
Clark, G. L. 27
closed-end funds, *see* investment trusts
COB, *see* Conduct of Business rules
coinage 47
company pensions (UK) 79, 80
compulsory purchase annuities (CPA) 202,
  216, 217, 229
  with bond rates 40**f(b)**
  with bond yields 40**f(a)**
  and claim ratios 138**f**
  men 37**f**, 126t, 127**t(a)**, 127**t(b)**
  non-linear pricing 33, 34**f(a)**, 34**f(b)**
  payments 232**f**
  sales 230**f**, 231**f**
  UK 15, 20, 26, 27, 35–41, 61, 79, 211–12,
    217, 219–20, 220**t**, 221, 229, 230**t**
  women 126**t**
Conduct of Business rules (COB)
  [FSA] 240–1
Consolidated Life Directive (2202/83/EC) 234
consols 48
  rates 29, 31, 31**t**
Constant Absolute Risk Aversion
  (CARA) 157
Constant Relative Risk Aversion
  (CRRA) 157, 166–8, 187
Consumer Price Index (CPI) [UK] 24
consumption 45, 164, 200
  annuities 143–6, 154
    with 171**f(b)**; without perfect 171**f(a)**
  equations 145–6, 148, 152, 154–6, 161,
    163, 203
  expenditure 1, 24, 163–4, 174, 180,
    182
  paths 145, 148–50, 159, 162–3, 167–71,
    174–5, 176, 176**f**, 178
  puzzles 180
  retirement 163, 189
  risky 157–8

transfer of 175–6
of wealth 171, 176
Continuous Mortality Investigation Bureau
    (CMI) 32, 77–8, 78**t**, 79, 80, 81**t**, 89,
    119, 123, 130, 137, 227–8
contributions, increases in 14
conventional annuities 19–20, 142, 142**f**,
    143, 148–9, 161, 163, 175
  equations 141, 144, 166, 170
    plus deferred annuities 144, 144**f**, 145
  equivalent wealth (CEW) 160, 173, 173**t**,
    174–5
  and mortality drag 188
conventional bonds 182, 185, 190, 195
conventional models 203**t**
Cornaglia, F. 87
corporate bonds 39, 40–1, 76, 131, 241,
    248
  Australia 136
  UK 227, 245
  see also bonds; government bonds
corrodies 45–6
Coughlan, G. D. 90
coupon payments 248–9, 251
  equations 255
Cox, S. 251, 252
Cox, S. H. 252, 255, 256
credit risks 4, 76, 237–8, 249, 250,
    252
CARA, *see* Constant Absolute Risk Aversion
CRR, *see* capital resources requirements
CRRA, *see* Constant Relative Risk Aversion
cumulative prospect theory 201
Currie, I. D. 85

da Silva, L. C. 8
Datastream 39
Daunton, M. J. 52
Davidoff, T. 163, 175, 190, 203
Davis, E. P. 5, 8, 234
Daykin, C. D. 236
de Witt, J. 49
death 71, 77, 80, 81**t**, 82, 84, 95, 101, 155,
    218
  of annuitant 24–5, 35, 48, 61
  payments 1, 2, 19, 23, 61, 95, 118, 214,
    220
  see also mortality
debt instruments (UK) 243, 245
Debt Management Office (DMO) 227, 243,
    245
decision-making 154, 161, 187, 205
decumulation phase 2, 60, 64, 186
default risk 46, 48, 52, 53

deferred annuities 145, 145**f**, 149, 159, 183
  Italy 108
  temporary 149
  UK 20
  USA 115
defined benefit (DB) 1, 4
  Australia 98
  closure of schemes 27
  group scheme 4–5
  occupational scheme 27
  PAYG (Sweden) 111
  pension plans 252
  transfers to bulk buyouts 15
  UK 205, 222, 227
  USA 205, 222–3
defined contribution (DC) 1, 2, 4
  Chile 101
  group scheme 4–5
  Premium Pension Plan (Sweden) 112
  UK 14, 20, 205, 222, 227
  USA 205
demographics 1, 9, 12, 13, 58, 106, 111, 265
Department of Work and Pensions (UK) 14,
    60, 61, 62, 236
Diamond, P. A. 163, 175, 190, 203
Dickey–Fuller tests 31
Dickson, P. G. M. 46
Dilnot, A. 5
Dimson, E. 185
disability insurance 101
DMO (UK):
  2005: 11 243
  2005: 22 249
double dipping 100
Dowd, K. 89, 90, 91, 186, 187, 188, 248,
    249, 252, 256
Drinkwater, M. 205
Dyson, E. J. W. 53

early retirement, restriction of 13
earnings 3, 4, 16, 53, 57–9, 60, 75, 98, 106,
    107, 109, 111–12
earnings-related contributions:
  Italy 107
  UK (SERPS) 3, 53
Eckstein, Z. 193, 194, 195, 196
Eckstein–Eichenbaum–Peled model 193,
    199
economic psychology 200, 204
economic rationality 152, 206
economic theories 140, 152
ECR, *see* Enhanced Capital Requirement
Eichenbaum, M. S. 193, 194, 195, 196
Einav, L. 217, 218

Eisenhauer, J. G. 187
ELA, *see* equity-linked annuities
elderly:
  and bonds 188–9
  consumption 189
  health insurance 191–2
  and risk aversion 187
ELID, *see* income drawdown, equity-linked
embedded options 239
Emmerson, C. 87, 182, 210
endowment mortgages, mis-selling of 64–5
endowment policies, *see* investment policies
England:
  tontines 47
    internal rates of return 48
  see also UK
English Life Tables 211
English Longitudinal Study of Ageing
    (ELSA) 223
Enhanced Capital Requirement (ECR) 238,
    238**f**
Epstein, D. 90
Epstein–Zin models 164, 170, 175, 176**f**,
    177**f**, 177**t**, 178, 201
Equitable Assurance Society 50, 51
Equitable Life 64, 65–7, 228, 233, 235, 241
equity premium 204
equity premium puzzle 163, 164, 185,
    188–9
equity products 25, 181, 185–6, 188, 207
  investment in 185–6
  rate of return 185, 187, 207
  risk-free rate and 133
  wealth and 205
equity-linked annuities (ELA) 186
escalating annuities 24, 24**t**, 75, 199,
    214–16
EU Economics Directorate 12
Europe:
  bancassurance groups 233
  mortality rates (men) 97
  pension provision (Middle Ages) 44
European Investment Bank 249
European Union (EU):
  Life Directives for insurance
    industry 234–5
  public pensions 12, 13**f**
  solvency regulations 228
  Solvency 2 234–41
ex ante calculations 119
ex post calculations 119
Exley, C. J. 76
exotic utility functions 161–5
expected utility models 165–70, 187, 202

expected-utility maximization
    (equations) 150–60, 168, 189
  subjective discounting 162**f**

Fairchild, J. R. 252
fan charts (mortality) 89–90, 90**f**
  survival 91**f**
felicity function, *see* utility, maximization
female, *see* women
final salary earnings 4, 58
Finance Act 1947 (UK) 56
Finance Act 1956 (UK) 54, 192
Finance Act 2004 (UK) 60
financial assets 75–6
financial educations 205–8
financial markets 181
  transformation of 46–7
  UK 64–7
Financial Services and Markets Act 2000
    (UK) 236
Financial Services Authority (FSA) 26, 53,
    61, 65, 207, 228, 229, 234, 235–40,
    246
Findlater, A. 52, 97, 98, 233, 234
Finkelstein, A. 27, 33, 35, 39, 54, 79, 118,
    119, 120, 121, 123, 129, 199, 210,
    211, 212, 214, 215, 216, 217, 218,
    219, 220
Finlaison, J. 51
First Non-Life Directive
    (1973/239/EEC) 234–5
first pillar:
  Australia 99–100
  Germany 106
  Italy 108
  Sweden 111
  Switzerland 112
flat-rate pension 2, 53
Fong, W. F. 108, 110, 136
Forfar, D. O. 77
Fornero, E. 107, 108
401(k) scheme 204–5
fourth-root-rule 251
framing effects 181, 204–7
France 8, 9, 46–8, 50, 233–4
Franks, J. 8
Franzoni, F. 27
Friedman, B. M. 17
Friedman, J. W. 160
Friedman's permanent income 144
friendly societies 52
funds, under management 99, 112
FSA, *see* Financial Services Authority
FSA life insurance returns 39

FRS17 27, 60
FTSE100 firms 27
funded pensions 3, 5

GAD, *see* Government Actuaries Department
Galasso, V. 107
Gambling Act 1774 (UK) 51
Gardner, J. 221, 222
General Prudential Sourcebook (GENPRU
    2.1.8) 234, 236, 238, 239, 240
geometric discounting (GD) 153–5, 156–7,
    161, 163, 170, 172, 176, 177**f**, 178,
    189
Germany 8, 9, 12, 46, 106–7, 107**t**, 137,
    137**t**, 233–4
  Reister plans 106–7
gilts 245, 249
Gompertz–Makeham 218, 225
Gosden, M. 25
government (UK):
  insurance 52
  life annuities 51
    cessation 53; low demand for 52
government bonds 1, 41, 76, 241, 252
  long-term 226, 248
  tradable 46–7
  UK 226–7, 245, 249
  USA 133
  yields 76, 103–4, 105**f**, 131, 135, 226, 243
  see also bonds, corporate bonds
Government Actuaries Department
    (GAD) 77
Graetz, M. 115
Greenwood, M. 44
Gross Domestic Product 95
  growth in pension fund assets
      (Chile) 101, 102
G7 countries 8
G10 countries 9
guaranteed annuities 20, 23, 32, 36, 61, 66,
    117, 119, 120, 134, 137, 199, 204,
    214–17, 241
  Chile 134
  deferred 241
Guiso, L. 187
Gysler, M. 187

Haberman, S. 43, 44, 49, 50, 51, 66, 85, 87,
    228, 235
habit formation 201
Halek, M. 187
Hannah, L. 54, 56
HARA, *see* Hyperbolic Absolute Risk
    Aversion

health:
  expenditure 189, 191
  importance of 121
  insurance 71, 204
    annuities and 192, 207
  issues 13, 25, 26
  mortality projection 86–7
hedge funds 23, 191
Heywood, G. 49
Hill, C. 115
Hinz, R. 2, 57
historic expectations information 119
HM Revenue and Customs (UK) 20, 26,
    235
HM Treasury (UK) 15, 62
Holland, *see* Netherlands
Holmans, A. 246
Holmer, M. R. 203, 204
Holzmann, R. 2, 57
Horiuchi, S. 73
households 25, 223
  annuitization 223
  utilities 25
housing finance 109
housing wealth 9, 189, 260
Hopnes, H. W. 87
Howard, R. C. W. 77
Hoynes, H. W. 210
HRS, *see* US Health and Retirement Study
humped term structure 243
Hurd, M. 164
Hurd, M. D. 224
Hyperbolic Absolute Risk Aversion
    (HARA) 157
hyperbolic discounting 161, 170, 172

ICA, *see* capital adequacy assessments
Iceland 8
Immediate Annuities 79
immediate needs annuities 26
impaired-life annuities 25–6
income drawdown 4, 15, 16, 26, 61
  Chile 102
  equity-linked (ELID) 186
  rules 16
  secured (post-75 years) 27
  UK 64
  unsecured (pre-75 years) 26–7
  see also Unsecured Income
income payments 19, 25, 41, 44, 46, 62,
    142, 152, 182, 226
  as lump sum 54
    Australia 98, 99–100; Chile 102–3; on
        death 61; Switzerland 114; UK 56

income payments (*cont.*)
  monthly 20, 23–4, 24**t**, 76, 223
  temporary annuity 149
index-linked annuities 221
indifference curves 145–7, 149, 159,
    199–200, 203
individual accounts 112
individual annuities (USA) 115
individual pension schemes 4, 54
  Chile 101
inflation:
  and BSP 57
  Middle Ages 45
  protection against 35
  rates 24
inflation-linked annuities 23, 24, 130, 144,
    205, 214, 215
  formula 75–6
inflation-linked bonds 76
information 181, 206
  perfect 193, 193**f**, 194
  private 217
  UK 235–6
inheritance, *see* bequests
Inkmann, J. 223, 224
INSPRU, *see* Prudential Sourcebook for
    Insurers
Institute of Actuaries (UK) 77, 88–9, 192
insurance:
  agents and 159
  Chile 101–2, 102**f**
  companies 17, 20, 25, 39, 95, 133, 196,
    216, 226, 227, 229, 234, 246, 249
  debt instrument 241–2, 242**f**
  costs 215
  France 9
  Germany 9
  market premiums 137–8
  products 191, 235
  regulations 234
  salesmen 52–3
  UK 215
inter-generational transfer 61
interest rates 18, 24, 31, 104, 146, 149,
    169
  and annuities 36, 39, 71, 75–6, 91,
    148, 172, 173, 203
  expectations of 119, 122
  historic yield curves 119
  and mortality rates 97
  risks 161, 226, 241
  single riskless 184
  term structure 74
interest-only mortgages 65

International Accounting Standard (IAS) 19
    27
international bonds 227
investment funds, in Sweden 112
investment linked annuities 25, 186
investments 8
  of pensions 54
  products 25, 99, 138
  returns 66
  risks 4
  trusts 8
irrationality 163, 189, 201
Israel 219
Italy 8, 46, 107–9

James, D. 228, 235
James, E. 2, 95, 98, 131, 133, 213, 214, 248
James, K. R. 138
Japan 73, 97
Jianakoplos, N. A. 187
Johnson, P. 5, 52
Johnstone, S. 261
joint-life annuities 24, 203, 221
  Chile 134
Jordon, K. 235
Jullien, B. 217
Just Retirement 233
Juster, F. T. 187, 224

Kahneman, D. 201, 202, 202, 203, 204
Karley, N. K. 246
Katz, E. 158, 161
Khorasanee, Z. 228, 235
Kim, H. T. 219
Kimball, M. S. 156, 187
King, M. 227, 257
Kingston, G. 98
Knox, D. M. 99, 135, 136, 219
Kocherlakota, N. 163, 165, 176**f**
Kotlikoff, L. 222

labour markets 60
  Italy 108
labour supply 2, 187
Lagrangean method 167, 168
Laibson, D. 161, 162, 163
Laitner, J. 224
Latin America 219
Latvia 108
Lavery, J. 115
Lawson, N. 56
Lee, R. D. 84, 85, 91
Lee–Carter model 84, 85, 91
Legal and General 27, 35, 229

level annuities 24, 28, 35, 98, 186, 205,
    214
  men (65 yr) 130–1, 134, 137, 211
  single 20, 30**t**, 107
  UK 215
Levy, H. 52
Lewin, C. G. 44, 45, 46, 50, 51
life annuities 4, 19, 44, 70–1
  and age 50
  Chile 103
  combinations 151**t**
  France 47, 48
  Middle Ages 46
  Netherlands 47
  products 148
  UK 48, 51, 55**t**, 192
  USA 115
life expectancy 9, 17, 18, 25, 26, 29, 155,
    181, 211, 214, 217
  agents 157, 158, 160, 192–3
  annuities 128, 204
  Australia 99
  consumption 164
  equations 49–50, 73, 73**f**, 74, 119, 122,
    148, 155, 158, 164, 193, 202–3
  low 147, 222
  men 110–11
  modeling 80**f**, 89, 90, 90**f**
  pensioners 78, 141
  premiums based on 31
  projections 70, 72, 211
  Roman 44
  UK 9, 11**a(f)**, 89**f**, 212
  uncertainty 161, 180
  women 110–11
  see also death; mortality; wealth, and life
    expectancy
life insurance 17–18, 76, 80, 95
  and actuarial methods 50, 99–100
  based on mutual principle 48
  Chile 102, 104**f(a)**, 105
  companies 1, 20, 32, 33, 50, 51, 52, 119,
    233–4
  direct gross premiums 95
  industries (Australia) 95–6, 96**f**, 100, 100**t**
  liabilities 76
  Netherlands 53
  products 65, 70
  profits 79
  regulations 76
  UK 43, 48–9, 53, 77, 89, 95
    data 78; regulations 236–7, 237**f**;
    sales 51, 52
  USA 219

Life Insurance Actuarial Standards Board
    (Australia) 100
life insurers 49, 52, 104**f(a)**, 257
  and actuarial methods 50
  and annuities 99, 105, 128, 129, 214, 233,
    262–4
    contracts 193–4, 228
  and bonds 17–18, 226
    durations 242–3, 243**f**
  pricing 128
  private 52–3
  profits 129, 214
  reinsurance 257
  UK 53, 64, 65, 76–9
  USA 110
Life Office Pensioners 79, 80, 123
life-contingent products 182–3
lifestyle asset allocation 187
Lin, Y. 251, 252, 255, 256
Lives (IML) 119, 127**t(a)**, 127**f(b)**, 128**f(a)**,
    128**f(b)**, 138**f**
Lloyds TSB 229
log-mortality 218
Loh, M. 25
London Assurance 49
long-term care 191, 208, 261
longevity:
  Australia 99
  bonds 248–9, 251, 252, 257
  increases 121
  risks 1, 4, 17, 20, 23, 25, 31, 182, 222,
    226–8, 239, 246–9, 255, 257
    reinsurance 253–4, 257
  and wealth 78
Lopes, P. 4, 214, 223, 224
loss aversion 201
  and annuity markets 203–4
  and risk aversion 202**f**

McCarthy, D. 60, 97, 218
McCutcheon, J. J. 77
MacDonald, A. S. 77
Macer, A. 43, 44
McKay, G. S. 52
McKay, S. 224
Malaysia 8
mandatory state pensions 2
Marin, J. M. 27
maritime insurance 43
Marsh, P. 185
mathematical tools 47
Mayer, C. 8
Mays, W. J. 44
MCR, *see* Minimum Capital Requirement

Mehta, S. J. B. 76
men:
  annuity rates 37**f**, 92
    men aged 65 29, 29**f**, 30**t**, 33**f**, 34**f(a)**,
      34**f(b)**, 35–6, 96–7, 185–6, 212, 215,
      220–1; men aged 70+ 90
    compulsory annuities 37**f**, 123**t**, 124t**(a)**,
      124**t(b)**, 125**t**, 126**t(b)**, 127**f(a)**,
      127**t(b)**
    life expectancy 9, 20, 28, 29
    mortality 77, 78, 126
    and risk aversion 187
    UK 77
    USA 213**f(b)**
Mercers' Company of London 48, 49, 50
Merrill Lynch 39
Merton, R. C. 186
Michaelides, A. 223, 224
Michelides, A. 4
Milevsky, M. R. 185, 186, 187, 203
Millard Tucker Report (UK) 192
Minimum Capital Requirement (MCR) 238,
    238**f**, 240
minimum pension guarantee:
  Chile 101, 102–3
  Sweden 111
Minimum Sum (Singapore) 109–10
Mitchell, C. 51
Mitchell, O. S. 17, 27, 97, 117, 119, 133,
    200, 213, 214, 218
Moffet, D. 144, 182
monasteries 44–5
monetary policy 18, 46–7, 243
money's worth 150–1
  annuities 181, 200, 217
    amounts of 215; escalating 214;
      international 132**t**, 133, 138, 210,
      213, 233
  Australia 135, 136**t**
  Chile 134, 134**f**, 135
  compulsory annuities 117–18, 124,
      128–31
    men 124**t(a)**, 124**t(b)**, 125**t**, 126**t(b)**,
      127**f(a)**, 127**t(b)**, 128**f(b)**, 129–30;
      women 126, 126**t(a)**, 128**f(a)**
  conventional annuities 173–4
  ex ante 119, 120**t**, 122
  ex post 119, 121, 122**f**
  Germany 137, 137**t**
  level annuities 130–1
  life expectancy data 123, 210
  mortality 218
    men 126, 126**t(b)**; tables 129, 211
  older ages 129–30

Singapore 136, 136**t(b)**
Switzerland 135, 135**f**
UK 118–31, 138, 210, 215
USA 133, 133**t**, 214
voluntary annuities 118–21, 121**f**
Money Facts 35, 36, 39**f**
Monk, A. H. 27
monopoly power 17, 226
moral hazard 186, 217
morbidity 71
Morley, J. 52
Morris, D. 67
Morris Review 67
mortality 18, 71, 76, 252
  and annuities, purchase of 79, 81**t**, 82,
    185
  bonds 251–3, 254–5, 256–7
  data 49, 51, 73
    Canada 77; UK 76–82, 77–8, 88, 91–2;
      USA 77
  index 252, 256
  and interest rates 48, 97
  low 169, 185, 260
  men 126, 170
  modelling 91, 92, 97
  patterns 49, 82–6, 216
  pensioners 77, 78–9, 228
  population 77
  projections 77, 83, 87, 89, 211
  rates 97, 123, 212, 218–19, 248–9
  risks 45, 185, 252, 256–7
  swaps 256, 256**f**, 257
  tables 77, 79, 80, 87, 97, 100, 108, 128–9,
    133, 218, 241
    and money's worth 171, 211
  tontines 50
  uncertainty 164–5
  UK 89**f**, 90–2, 119, 121, 129–30
  USA 175, 192
mortality drag 20, 31, 187, 188
mortgages 227
  securitization (UK) 246
mortuary tontines 47, 48
Muir, M. 235
Murtaugh, C. M. 191, 192, 204
Murthi, M. 118, 119, 120
mutual funds 8, 48
  USA 9
mutual society 66
Myners, P. 67

national debt 1
  financed by tontines (France) 47
  UK 48, 226

National Insurance Act 1946 53
National Insurance contributions (UK) 57, 58
national pension savings scheme 16
net cash flows (NCF) 253–4, 254**f(b)**
Netherlands 8, 46–7, 49, 50, 53
Neuberger, A. 60
nominal annuities 216
non-geometric discounting 162–3, 201
non-guaranteed annuities 36, 215
non-OECD countries 7**f**, 8
non-profit funds, and annuities 239
Northampton Life Table 51
Norwich Union 52, 241, 246
  insurance business (2004) 247**t**
notation, *see* actuarial notation
notional capital 107–8
Notional Defined Contribution
      (NDC) 107–8
  Sweden 111–12, 112**t**

objective functions (equations) 152–6, 162, 164–5
occupational pensions 2
  defined benefit (DB) 4, 57–8
    decrease in 60–1
  defined contribution (DC) 2, 58, 60
  Germany 106
  Italy 109
  for private sector workers 58
  for public sector workers 58–9
  schemes 1, 4, 53, 241
  Sweden 112
  UK 54, 56, 58, 60–1
    for self-employed 54
  USA 115
OECD countries 6**f**, 8
Office of National Statistics (UK) 249
old-age dependency 10**f**
Oldfield, Z. 182
Oliver, Wyman, and Company 64
Ong, A. 90
Orszag, J. M. 97, 98, 118, 119, 120, 233, 234
Orszag, P. R. 118, 119, 120
overseas bonds, *see* bonds, overseas

Paiella, M. 187
Palacios, R. 5
Pallares-Miralles, M. 5
Palmon, O. 192
paper currency 47
parameter error, *see* survival probabilities
Pareto 251
PartnerRE 249

Partnership Assurance 233
passive selection 210, 214–15, 217, 219
pay-as-you go (PAYG) 2, 13, 14
  Germany 106
  Italy 107
  public (Chile) 100–1
  Sweden 111
  Switzerland 112
  unfunded 5–6
Pedersen, H. W. 252
Peled, D. 193, 194, 195, 196
Pelzman, J. 158, 197
Penrose, L. 66, 67, 241
pension annuities (UK) 55**t**
  by size of fund 62**t**, 63**f**
Pension Credit 57
Pension Research Forum 205
pensioners 56, 264
  Chile 102–3
  demand for annuities 62, 152, 226
  expenditure 13
  Germany 107
  guarantee in case of default 66, 101
  life expectancy 78, 123, 228
  mortality 77, 78–9, 228
  Singapore 110
  UK 72, 77–80
pensions 181
  Australia 98
  Chile 100, 100**f**, 103, 103**f**, 104**f(a)**, 104**f(b)**
  funds 8, 35, 192
    assets 5, 9, 6**f**, 7**f**, 27
    Germany 106
    Italy 107
    liabilities 27, 92
  life-cycle model 2
  means-tested (first pillar) 99–100
  policies 2, 13
  products 66
  provision 2–3, 3**f**, 4, 9, 14, 43, 44, 46, 227
  savings 1–3, 8
  Sweden 111, 112**t**
  systems 2, 95, 98
  tax-free lump sum 54–5
  UK 14, 53–4, 64
  see also individual types of pensions
Pensions Commission (Sweden) 111
Pensions Commission (UK) 9, 14, 16, 57, 59–60, 64, 163–4, 180, 182, 204, 205, 226, 227
  Second Report 15
pensions crisis 12–13

perfect annuitization 148, 150, 167, 168, 169
Permberton, H. 61
Perry, C. R. 52
personal pensions (PP) 15, 51–2, 79
  life expectancy 123
  mis-selling of 64
  portable 60
  for self-employed 54
  tax-advantaged 61–2
  UK 15, 54, 55**t**, 56–8, 59**f**, 61–2, 65, 79, 207, 212, 220, 225, 240
phased withdrawals, *see* income drawdown
Piatti, L. 108
Piggott, J. 98, 99
Pillar 1 (UK) 235, 237, 238
Pillar 2 (UK) 239
Pillar 3 (UK) 239
PLA, *see* voluntary annuity
Plott, C. R. 201, 204
Plumb, R. H. 228, 235
Poitras, G. 46, 50
Poland 108
Ponzetto, G. 107
pooling equilibrium 135, 195–6, 196**f**, 198, 198**f**, 199
population:
  mortality 120
  life expectancy 78
  life tables 47, 51, 80, 80**f**, 97, 112, 129, 133–6, 137, 210, 211, 215, 217
  mortality 77
  UK 88**t**
  USA 185
Portugal 12
Post Office (UK), annuity purchase 52
Poterba, J. M. 17, 27, 33, 35, 39, 43, 44, 46, 49, 54, 79, 115, 117, 118, 119, 120, 121, 123, 129, 133, 175, 180, 199, 210, 211, 212, 214, 215, 216, 217, 219, 220
Powell, M. 187
Powers, M. R. 251
pre-annuitized wealth 181–4, 184**f**
Premium Pensions Agency (PPM) 112
private annuities 17
  Germany 107**f**
  USA 219
private life insurance, Netherlands regulations 53
private pensions
  Australia 99–100
  funding 5**t**, 14

Germany 106
Italy 108–9
UK 14, 54, 57, 58, 59, 59**f**, 60, 221
tax-privileged 15
probability theory 47
prospect theory 203**t**
  cumulative 204
Prudential 27, 35, 229, 233
prudential management 236, 241, 248
Prudential Sourcebook for Insurers (INSPRU) 236, 237, 238
public pensions:
  EU 12, 13**f**
  Germany 106, 107**f**
  spending on pensions 9, 14
    age-related 9, 10**f**, 11**f(b)**
purchasing annuities 148–50
  life annuities (PLA) 186
  voluntary 28, 28**f**, 31, 31**t**

quasi-hyperbolic discounting 161, 170, 172

Rabin, M. 152, 195, 200
RAC, *see* Retirement Annuity Contracts
Radley Commission on the Civil Service 56
real annuities, *see* inflated-linked annuities
rectangularization 72–3, 73**f**
reference point 201, 202, 204
reforms (pensions) 1
  Chile 100–1
  Germany 106
  Italy 108
regulations:
  accounting 27
  annuities 95, 98, 105
  capital 105
  Chile 105–6
  EU 234–5
  life insurance 76
  UK 235–41
reinsurance 249–52, 257
  payment equations 253, 254**f(a)**
Reinsurance Directive (2005/68/EC) 234
reinsurers 250–1, 251**t**
Reister plans (Germany) 106–7
Reno, V. 115
Renshaw, A. E. 85
Repetto, A. 151, 162, 163
Report of the Equitable Life Inquiry, The (Penrose Report) 65–7
Resolution Group 233
retail investment (UK) 138
Retail Price Index (RPI) 23–4, 35, 36

Retirement Annuity Contracts (RAC) 79, 80, 123
retirement:
  age:
    extension of 13–14, 16: Singapore 110
  annuitization at point of 184–5
  Australia 98
  Chile 101, 103
  consumption 178
  dis-save/savings 180
  expenditures 190
  income 1, 4, 23, 172
  population 3
  provision 2
reversionary annuities 25, 48
  Church of Scotland 49
  policyholders 50
  price tables 50
  provision of income for wives 48–9
Rickayzen, B. 228, 235
Riley, J. C. 50
Riley, W. B. 187
risk management, alternative 250**f**
risk-free rate puzzle 163, 164
risks 237
  agents 156, 159–60, 172, 173, 175, 201
  and annuitization 186–7
  aversion 175, 185
  consumption 157–65
  individuals 17, 191, 201, 222
  and loss aversion 202**t**
  models 204
  neutrality 159**f**
  pooling 228, 251
  relative 164, 186, 187
  solvency requirements 235
  see also accumulation phase;
    decumulation phase
Rocha, R. 4, 100, 103, 104, 134
Rogers, T. 45
Rohwedder, S. 164
Roman annuity rates 43–4, 44**t**
Roussiang, D. 158, 197
Routledge, B. 161, 162
Rowlingson, K. 224
Royal Exchange 49
RPI, *see* Retail Price Index
Rubinstein, A. 152, 161
Ruesch, M. 112, 114, 135

safety net 3
Salanie, F. 217
Samuelson, P. A. 187
Sandler, R. 67

Sargent, T. J. 47
savings 1, 9
  banks 52, 141
  behaviour 180, 223
  choice 184
  decisions 140
  gap 64
  products 66
  schemes 162–3
  UK 14, 67, 235
  USA 223
Schnabel, R. 106
Schrimpf, P. 217, 218
Schubert, R. 187
Schwartz, B. 205
second pillar:
  Australia 98
  Singapore 109, 137
  Sweden 111, 112
  Switzerland 112, 114
Secured Income 61
securitization 249–52
  of mortality risk 253**f**
selection effects 17, 35, 50, 109, 121, 130,
    131, 133, 136, 137, 192, 212,
    210–19
Self-Administered Pensions (SAP) 80
self-employed 192
  personal pensions for 54, 79
Self-Invested Personal Pension plans
    (SIPPs) 78
self-investment 222
SERPS, *see* State Earnings Related Pension
    Scheme
severance pay 108
sex 28–9, 36
Shapiro, M. D. 187
Sharp, K. P. 219
Sheshinski, E. 140, 180, 192
Shubik, M. 251
Sibbett, T. A. 43, 44, 49, 50, 51
Singapore 2, 8, 108, 108**t**, 110, 136,
    136**t(b)**, 137, 219
  see also annuities, Singapore
single-crossing property 216
single level annuities 20
  Chile 134
  Germany 107
  men, voluntary (aged 65) 30**t**
SIPPs, *see* Self-Invested Personal Pension
    plans
Sleath, J. 75
Smith, A. D. 76
Smith, J. P. 182

social security:
  Italy 108
  risks 4
  Singapore 109
Social Security Pensions Act 1975
social welfare, payments 181–4
Soliman, A. 87
solvency requirements:
  Chile 100, 105
  UK 228
Solvency 2 (EU) 234–41
Sondergeld, E. T. 205
Song, X. 95, 98, 131, 133, 213, 214,
  248
South Sea Bubble 48, 49
Southall, P. 27
Spain 8
Special Purpose Vehicle (SPV) 250, 251–2,
  253, 254–5, 256
Spillman, B. C. 191, 192, 204
Spivak, A. 192, 219, 222
staggered-vesting, see phased-retirement
Stamhuis, I. H. 53
Stark, J. 28, 32, 35, 64, 192, 219, 221, 226,
  257
state pensions 2, 43, 181–2, 199–200
  UK 53–62, 182, 221
State Earnings Related Pension Scheme
  (SERPS) 57, 65
State Second Pension (S2P) 57
Statute of Westminster (1285) 45
Staunton, M. 185
Steil, B. 8
Sundén, A. 111, 112
Superannuation Guarantee (Australia) 98,
  99
Superintendencia de Administradoras de Fondos
  de Pensiones (SAFP) [Chile] 105
Superintendenciade Valores y Seguros (SVS)
  [Chile] 105
survival probabilities 71, 72f, 91, 119, 122,
  193, 211, 212, 215, 229
  cohort 257
  men (65 yr) 212f
  UK 212, 217–18, 223–4
  USA 213f(a)
survivorship insurance 101
swap agreements 256, 256f, 257
Sweden 73, 111–12, 112t
Swiss Re 252
Switzerland 8, 112–14, 114f, 114t, 135,
  135f, 219
Synthesis 26

TAS, see Time Additive Separability
tax 2, 26
  avoidance 61
  breaks 35, 61–2
  on pensions 61–2
tax-efficiency 2
Tax-exempt Act 1921 56
temporary annuities 20, 149, 150, 183
Tetlow, G. 182
Thaler, R. H. 205
Thornburn, C. 4, 100, 103, 104f(a), 134
three pillar system:
  Australia 98
  Sweden 111
  Switzerland 112–14
  World Bank 2, 3, 3f
Time Additive Separability (TAS) 153, 155,
  156–7, 161, 163, 175, 176, 177f, 178,
  189, 201
Tobacman, J. 161, 162, 163
Tonks, I. 8, 28, 28f, 29f, 31, 35, 65, 75, 118,
  119, 120, 121, 211, 214, 215, 228,
  233
tontines 47, 257
  England 47–8
  France 47–8, 50
  rates of return 48
transparency 27
Trattamento di Fine Rapporto (TFR) 108
Treasury Bills 243
Treasury Gilt 2055 (UK) 227
Tversky, A. 201, 202, 203, 204

UCITS (Undertaking for Collective
  Investment in Transferable
  Securities) 9
UK 11f(a), 15t, 16f, 55t, 59f, 62t, 63f, 89f,
  120t, 124t(a), 124t(b), 125t, 220t,
  237f, 238f, 240f, 244f(a), 244f(b),
  245f, 247t, 247f
UK Office of National Statistics 24
UK Pension Green Papers (1998/2002) 58
Ulpianus, D. 43, 44
underwriting 249–50, 257
unit-linked investment product 25
United Utilities Water plc 245–6
unity 75, 105, 111, 118–20, 134, 135, 137,
  141–2, 161, 204, 211, 241
Unsecured Income 61
  see also income drawdown
US Congressional Budget Office 11
US Health and Retirement Study
  (HRS) 222–4

US Projected Social security Benefits Expenditure 12
US Social Security Administration (Office of the Actuary) 133
USA 8, 9, 73, 77, 115, 115**t**, 117–18, 133, 133**t**, 175, 192, 204–5, 213, 213**f(b)**, 214, 218–19, 222–3
USA Treasury 246
usury 46
utility:
  agents' 150, 201
  functions 146, 153, 161, 165–6, 175, 182, 190, 201, 202, 217, 222
  maximization 146**f**, 170
    equations 153–8, 160, 161, 166–7, 203, 217
  models 165
    expected 165–70
  value 147, 150, 154
Utkus, S. P. 200

value functions (equation) 164, 168
value-protected annuities 23, 61
variable annuities 25
  USA 115
Velde, F. R. 47
Visco, I. 9, 11
Vittas, D. 2, 95, 98, 214
voluntary annuities (PLA) 202, 216, 217
  international markets 219, 233
  single cohorts 224
  UK 15, 54, 56–7, 211–12, 219–20, 220**t**, 223
voluntary private pensions 3–4
Von Gaudecker, H. 107, 137

Wadsworth, M. 15, 52, 221, 222, 226, 241, 245, 257
Walker, E. 103, 104
Waller, R. 235
Walliser, J. 32, 196, 197, 197**f**, 217
Warshawsky, M. J. 17, 27, 117, 119, 133, 175, 191, 192, 204, 210, 214
Watson-Wyatt 15, 219
wealth:
  actual 168–9
  annuities 189, 197, 203, 222
    equivalent 147**f**, 168–9, 175
  annuitization 141, 159, 159**f**, 175, 199–200
  deferring 185–6
  in bonds 143–4, 166

in equity 205
equivalent 186
importance of 121, 218
and life expectancy 78–9, 87, 129, 210
spreading effects 158
unconsumed 174**t**
Webb, D. C. 191
Weber, C. 107, 137
weighted utility metrics 202–3
Weinberg, S. 161, 162, 163
Weir, D. R. 47, 48
welfare 208, 218
  men (at 65) 186
  payments 182, 186
    and adverse selection 199**f**
  pensions 182
    concerns on 62; perfect annuity markets 168; provision 60
Westminster and Pelican 51
Whitehead, C. 246
Wilhelm, M. 224
Wilkie, A. D. 77
Willets, R. 87
Wilmoth, J. R. 73
Wilson, A. 52
with-profits annuities 25, 239
with-profits funds 25
with-profits insurance capital (WPICC) 238
women:
  compulsory annuity markets 38**f**
    money's worth 126, 126**t(a)**, 128**f(a)**
  life expectancy 29
  mortality 77, 78, 213
    after age 60 227, 227**t**
  and risk aversion 187
  voluntary annuity markets 220
  see also money's worth, compulsory annuities
Wong-Fupuy, C. 87
working lives, extension of 228
working population 3
World Bank 2

Yaari, M. 18, 140, 145, 148, 159, 161, 166, 184, 190
yield curves 119, 122, 133
Young, R. 185, 186, 203

Zeiler, K. 201, 204
Zeldes, S. P. 180, 187
Zin, S. 161, 162